T0246411

Modern Database
Management

Modern Database Management

Edited by
Mitchell Penn

Larsen & Keller
www.larsen-keller.com

Modern Database Management
Edited by Mitchell Penn
ISBN: 978-1-63549-084-8 (Hardback)

© 2017 Larsen & Keller

 Larsen & Keller

Published by Larsen and Keller Education,
5 Penn Plaza,
19th Floor,
New York, NY 10001, USA

Cataloging-in-Publication Data

Modern database management / edited by Mitchell Penn.
    p. cm.
Includes bibliographical references and index.
ISBN 978-1-63549-084-8
1. Database management. 2. Electronic data processing. I. Penn, Mitchell.
QA76.9.D3 M64 2017
005.756 5--dc23

This book contains information obtained from authentic and highly regarded sources. All chapters are published with permission under the Creative Commons Attribution Share Alike License or equivalent. A wide variety of references are listed. Permissions and sources are indicated; for detailed attributions, please refer to the permissions page. Reasonable efforts have been made to publish reliable data and information, but the authors, editors and publisher cannot assume any responsibility for the vailidity of all materials or the consequences of their use.

Trademark Notice: All trademarks used herein are the property of their respective owners. The use of any trademark in this text does not vest in the author or publisher any trademark ownership rights in such trademarks, nor does the use of such trademarks imply any affiliation with or endorsement of this book by such owners.

The publisher's policy is to use permanent paper from mills that operate a sustainable forestry policy. Furthermore, the publisher ensures that the text paper and cover boards used have met acceptable environmental accreditation standards.

Printed and bound in the United States of America.

For more information regarding Larsen and Keller Education and its products, please visit the publisher's website www.larsen-keller.com

Table of Contents

Preface   **VII**

Chapter 1   **Introduction to Database**   **1**

Chapter 2   **Various Types of Database**   **21**
    a. Cloud Database   21
    b. Data Warehouse   24
    c. Distributed Database   32
    d. Mobile Database   37
    e. Parallel Database   39
    f. Graph Database   40

Chapter 3   **Database Systems and Models**   **48**
    a. Relational Database Management System   48
    b. Object-relational Database   79
    c. Document-oriented Database   119
    d. Object Database   129
    e. In-memory Database   134
    f. Embedded Database   136
    g. Network Model   142
    h. Hierarchical Database Model   143
    i. Relational Model   145
    j. Entity–relationship Origins   164
    k. Entity–attribute–value Model   166

Chapter 4   **Database Design: An Integrated Study**   **184**
    a. Database Design   184
    b. Database Refactoring   187
    c. Database Normalization   188
    d. Data Structure   192
    e. Database Engine   194
    f. Database Server   197
    g. Database Schema   198

Chapter 5   **Tools and Techniques of Database Management**   **208**
    a. ACID   208
    b. Create, Read, Update and Delete   211
    c. Null (SQL)   213
    d. Candidate Key   230
    e. Foreign Key   233
    f. Unique Key   238
    g. Surrogate Key   243
    h. NoSQL   248

Chapter 6   **Computer Languages used in Database Management**   **257**
             a. Data Definition Language   257
             b. Data Manipulation Language   260
             c. Query Language   261

Chapter 7   **Database Security: A Comprehensive Study**   **264**
             a. Database Security   264
             b. Database Activity Monitoring   268
             c. HP Atalla   272
             d. Data Breach   272

Chapter 8   **Database Application: An Overview**   **281**
             a. Database Application   281
             b. Inventory Management Software   282
             c. Content Management System   288
             d. Airline Reservations System   289
             e. Enterprise Software   293

             Permissions

             Index

Preface

This book explores all the important aspects of database management in the present day scenario. Database is the collection of data which can comprise of tables, sheets, reports, schemas, etc. This data is crucial for any functioning organization. To manage data, a database management system (DBMS) is used. The topics covered in this extensive book deal with the core subjects of modern database management. The various sub-fields of the subject along with technological progress that have future implications are glanced at in this text. Most of the topics introduced in this book cover fundamental technique and application of modern database management. Coherent flow of topics, student-friendly language and extensive use of examples make this textbook an invaluable source of knowledge.

To facilitate a deeper understanding of the contents of this book a short introduction of every chapter is written below:

Chapter 1- Database is the collection of tables, reports and other information. Data is organized in a manner that supports process such as modeling the availability of a room in a hospital. This chapter is an overview of the topic incorporating all the major aspects of database.

Chapter 2- Cloud database usually runs on cloud computing platforms. The two methods used in cloud database are virtual machine image and database-as-a-service. Alternative types of database are data warehouse, distributed database, mobile database, parallel database, graph database etc. The topics discussed in the section are of great importance to broaden the existing knowledge on databases.

Chapter 3- A relational database management system is a database system. This system is based on the rational model system. The aspects of database systems that have been explained are MySQL, Microsoft SQL server, SAP HANA, Entity–relationship model, PostgreSQL etc. This chapter on database systems and models offers an insightful focus, keeping in mind the subject matter.

Chapter 4- Database design is a method that is particularly used in producing data models. The model usually contains the logical and physical designs that are needed to generate a design that helps in creating a database. Some of the aspects of database design database refactoring, data structure, database engine, database server and database schema. This section will provide an integrated understanding of database design.

Chapter 5- The tools and techniques of database management are ACID, null, candidate key, unique key, surrogate key and NoSQL. ACID is a collection of properties of database transactions whereas null is particularly used to indicate the existence of a data value in a database. The topics discussed in the chapter are of great importance to broaden the existing knowledge on database management.

Chapter 6- The computer languages used in database management are data definition language, data manipulation language and query language. Database definition language is a syntax that is very similar to programming languages and helps in defining data structures. The major components of database management are discussed in the following section.

Chapter 7- Database security is a process that is used to protect a database. The types of information security control are access control, auditing, authentication, encryption, backups and application security. The topics discussed in the chapter are of great importance the existing knowledge on database security.

Chapter 8- Database application is a program that is used in computers; the basic purpose of this program is to retrieve information from computerized database. Inventory management software, content management system, airline reservations system and enterprise software are other aspects elucidated in this section. This chapter discusses the application of database in a critical manner providing key analysis on the subject matter.

Finally, I would like to thank the entire team involved in the inception of this book for their valuable time and contribution. This book would not have been possible without their efforts. I would also like to thank my friends and family for their constant support.

Editor

Introduction to Database

Database is the collection of tables, reports and other information. Data is organized in a manner that supports process such as modeling the availability of a room in a hospital. This chapter is an overview of the topic incorporating all the major aspects of database.

A database is an organized collection of data. It is the collection of schemas, tables, queries, reports, views, and other objects. The data are typically organized to model aspects of reality in a way that supports processes requiring information, such as modelling the availability of rooms in hotels in a way that supports finding a hotel with vacancies.

A database management system (DBMS) is a computer software application that interacts with the user, other applications, and the database itself to capture and analyze data. A general-purpose DBMS is designed to allow the definition, creation, querying, update, and administration of databases. Well-known DBMSs include MySQL, PostgreSQL, MongoDB, Microsoft SQL Server, Oracle, Sybase, SAP HANA, and IBM DB2. A database is not generally portable across different DBMSs, but different DBMS can interoperate by using standards such as SQL and ODBC or JDBC to allow a single application to work with more than one DBMS. Database management systems are often classified according to the database model that they support; the most popular database systems since the 1980s have all supported the relational model as represented by the SQL language. Sometimes a DBMS is loosely referred to as a 'database'.

Terminology and Overview

Formally, a "database" refers to a set of related data and the way it is organized. Access to this data is usually provided by a "database management system" (DBMS) consisting of an integrated set of computer software that allows users to interact with one or more databases and provides access to all of the data contained in the database (although restrictions may exist that limit access to particular data). The DBMS provides various functions that allow entry, storage and retrieval of large quantities of information and provides ways to manage how that information is organized.

Because of the close relationship between them, the term "database" is often used casually to refer to both a database and the DBMS used to manipulate it.

Outside the world of professional information technology, the term *database* is often used to refer to any collection of related data (such as a spreadsheet or a card index). This article is concerned only with databases where the size and usage requirements necessitate use of a database management system.

Existing DBMSs provide various functions that allow management of a database and its data which can be classified into four main functional groups:

- Data definition – Creation, modification and removal of definitions that define the organization of the data.

- Update – Insertion, modification, and deletion of the actual data.

- Retrieval – Providing information in a form directly usable or for further processing by other applications. The retrieved data may be made available in a form basically the same as it is stored in the database or in a new form obtained by altering or combining existing data from the database.

- Administration – Registering and monitoring users, enforcing data security, monitoring performance, maintaining data integrity, dealing with concurrency control, and recovering information that has been corrupted by some event such as an unexpected system failure.

Both a database and its DBMS conform to the principles of a particular database model. "Database system" refers collectively to the database model, database management system, and database.

Physically, database servers are dedicated computers that hold the actual databases and run only the DBMS and related software. Database servers are usually multiprocessor computers, with generous memory and RAID disk arrays used for stable storage. RAID is used for recovery of data if any of the disks fail. Hardware database accelerators, connected to one or more servers via a high-speed channel, are also used in large volume transaction processing environments. DBMSs are found at the heart of most database applications. DBMSs may be built around a custom multitasking kernel with built-in networking support, but modern DBMSs typically rely on a standard operating system to provide these functions from databases before the inception of Structured Query Language (SQL). The data recovered was disparate, redundant and disorderly, since there was no proper method to fetch it and arrange it in a concrete structure.

Since DBMSs comprise a significant economical market, computer and storage vendors often take into account DBMS requirements in their own development plans.

Databases and DBMSs can be categorized according to the database model(s) that they support (such as relational or XML), the type(s) of computer they run on (from a server cluster to a mobile phone), the query language(s) used to access the database (such as SQL or XQuery), and their internal engineering, which affects performance, scalability, resilience, and security.

Applications

Databases are used to support internal operations of organizations and to underpin online interactions with customers and suppliers.

Databases are used to hold administrative information and more specialized data, such as engineering data or economic models. Examples of database applications include computerized library systems, flight reservation systems, computerized parts inventory systems, and many content management systems that store websites as collections of webpages in a database.

General-purpose and Special-purpose DBMSs

A DBMS has evolved into a complex software system and its development typically requires thousands of human years of development effort.[a] Some general-purpose DBMSs such as Adabas, Oracle and DB2 have been undergoing upgrades since the 1970s. General-purpose DBMSs aim to meet the needs of as many applications as possible, which adds to the complexity. However, the fact that their development cost can be spread over a large number of users means that they are often the most cost-effective approach. However, a general-purpose DBMS is not always the optimal solution: in some cases a general-purpose DBMS may introduce unnecessary overhead. Therefore, there are many examples of systems that use special-purpose databases. A common example is an email system that performs many of the functions of a general-purpose DBMS such as the insertion and deletion of messages composed of various items of data or associating messages with a particular email address; but these functions are limited to what is required to handle email and don't provide the user with all of the functionality that would be available using a general-purpose DBMS.

Many other databases have application software that accesses the database on behalf of end-users, without exposing the DBMS interface directly. Application programmers may use a wire protocol directly, or more likely through an application programming interface. Database designers and database administrators interact with the DBMS through dedicated interfaces to build and maintain the applications' databases, and thus need some more knowledge and understanding about how DBMSs operate and the DBMSs' external interfaces and tuning parameters.

History

Following the technology progress in the areas of processors, computer memory, computer storage, and computer networks, the sizes, capabilities, and performance of databases and their respective DBMSs have grown in orders of magnitude. The development of database technology can be divided into three eras based on data model or structure: navigational, SQL/relational, and post-relational.

The two main early navigational data models were the hierarchical model, epitomized by IBM's IMS system, and the CODASYL model (network model), implemented in a number of products such as IDMS.

The relational model, first proposed in 1970 by Edgar F. Codd, departed from this tradition by insisting that applications should search for data by content, rather than by following links. The relational model employs sets of ledger-style tables, each used for a different type of entity. Only in the mid-1980s did computing hardware become powerful enough to allow the wide deployment of relational systems (DBMSs plus applications). By the early 1990s, however, relational systems dominated in all large-scale data processing applications, and as of 2015 they remain dominant : IBM DB2, Oracle, MySQL, and Microsoft SQL Server are the top DBMS. The dominant database language, standardised SQL for the relational model, has influenced database languages for other data models.

Object databases were developed in the 1980s to overcome the inconvenience of object-relational impedance mismatch, which led to the coining of the term "post-relational" and also the development of hybrid object-relational databases.

The next generation of post-relational databases in the late 2000s became known as NoSQL databases, introducing fast key-value stores and document-oriented databases. A competing "next generation" known as NewSQL databases attempted new implementations that retained the relational/SQL model while aiming to match the high performance of NoSQL compared to commercially available relational DBMSs.

1960s, Navigational DBMS

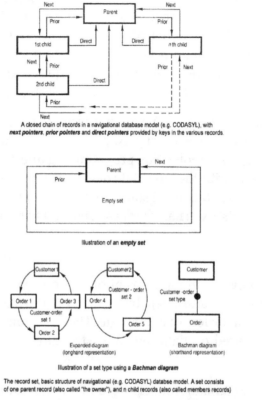

A closed chain of records in a navigational database model (e.g. CODASYL), with **next pointers**, **prior pointers** and **direct pointers** provided by keys in the various records.

Illustration of an **empty set**

Illustration of a set type using a **Bachman diagram**

The record set, basic structure of navigational (e.g. CODASYL) databse model. A set consists of one parent record (also called "the owner"), and n child records (also called members records)

Basic structure of navigational CODASYL database model

The introduction of the term *database* coincided with the availability of direct-access storage (disks and drums) from the mid-1960s onwards. The term represented a contrast with the tape-based systems of the past, allowing shared interactive use rather than daily batch processing. The Oxford English Dictionary cites a 1962 report by the System Development Corporation of California as the first to use the term "data-base" in a specific technical sense.

As computers grew in speed and capability, a number of general-purpose database systems emerged; by the mid-1960s a number of such systems had come into commercial use. Interest in a standard began to grow, and Charles Bachman, author of one such product, the Integrated Data Store (IDS), founded the "Database Task Group" within CODASYL, the group responsible for the creation and standardization of COBOL. In 1971, the Database Task Group delivered their standard, which generally became known as the "CODASYL approach", and soon a number of commercial products based on this approach entered the market.

The CODASYL approach relied on the "manual" navigation of a linked data set which was formed into a large network. Applications could find records by one of three methods:

1. Use of a primary key (known as a CALC key, typically implemented by hashing)

2. Navigating relationships (called sets) from one record to another

3. Scanning all the records in a sequential order

Later systems added B-trees to provide alternate access paths. Many CODASYL databases also added a very straightforward query language. However, in the final tally, CODASYL was very complex and required significant training and effort to produce useful applications.

IBM also had their own DBMS in 1966, known as Information Management System (IMS). IMS was a development of software written for the Apollo program on the System/360. IMS was generally similar in concept to CODASYL, but used a strict hierarchy for its model of data navigation instead of CODASYL's network model. Both concepts later became known as navigational databases due to the way data was accessed, and Bachman's 1973 Turing Award presentation was *The Programmer as Navigator*. IMS is classified as a hierarchical database. IDMS and Cincom Systems' TOTAL database are classified as network databases. IMS remains in use as of 2014.

1970s, Relational DBMS

Edgar Codd worked at IBM in San Jose, California, in one of their offshoot offices that was primarily involved in the development of hard disk systems. He was unhappy with the navigational model of the CODASYL approach, notably the lack of a "search" facility. In 1970, he wrote a number of papers that outlined a new approach to database construction that eventually culminated in the groundbreaking *A Relational Model of Data for Large Shared Data Banks*.

In this paper, he described a new system for storing and working with large databases. Instead of records being stored in some sort of linked list of free-form records as in CODASYL, Codd's idea was to use a "table" of fixed-length records, with each table used for a different type of entity. A linked-list system would be very inefficient when storing "sparse" databases where some of the data for any one record could be left empty. The relational model solved this by splitting the data into a series of normalized tables (or *relations*), with optional elements being moved out of the main table to where they would take up room only if needed. Data may be freely inserted, deleted and edited in these tables, with the DBMS doing whatever maintenance needed to present a table view to the application/user.

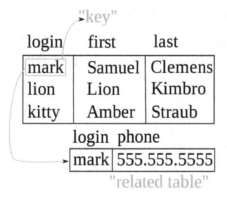

In the relational model, records are "linked" using virtual keys not stored in the database but defined as needed between the data contained in the records.

The relational model also allowed the content of the database to evolve without constant rewriting of links and pointers. The relational part comes from entities referencing other entities in what is known as one-to-many relationship, like a traditional hierarchical model, and many-to-many relationship, like a navigational (network) model. Thus, a relational model can express both hierarchical and navigational models, as well as its native tabular model, allowing for pure or combined modeling in terms of these three models, as the application requires.

For instance, a common use of a database system is to track information about users, their name, login information, various addresses and phone numbers. In the navigational approach, all of this data would be placed in a single record, and unused items would simply not be placed in the database. In the relational approach, the data would be *normalized* into a user table, an address table and a phone number table (for instance). Records would be created in these optional tables only if the address or phone numbers were actually provided.

Linking the information back together is the key to this system. In the relational model, some bit of information was used as a "key", uniquely defining a particular record. When information was being collected about a user, information stored in the optional tables would be found by searching for this key. For instance, if the login name of a user is unique, addresses and phone numbers for that user would be recorded with the login name as its key. This simple "re-linking" of related data back into a single collection is something that traditional computer languages are not designed for.

Just as the navigational approach would require programs to loop in order to collect records, the relational approach would require loops to collect information about any *one* record. Codd's solution to the necessary looping was a set-oriented language, a suggestion that would later spawn the ubiquitous SQL. Using a branch of mathematics known as tuple calculus, he demonstrated that such a system could support all the operations of normal databases (inserting, updating etc.) as well as providing a simple system for finding and returning *sets* of data in a single operation.

Codd's paper was picked up by two people at Berkeley, Eugene Wong and Michael Stonebraker. They started a project known as INGRES using funding that had already been allocated for a geographical database project and student programmers to produce code. Beginning in 1973, INGRES delivered its first test products which were generally ready for widespread use in 1979. INGRES was similar to System R in a number of ways, including the use of a "language" for data access, known as QUEL. Over time, INGRES moved to the emerging SQL standard.

IBM itself did one test implementation of the relational model, PRTV, and a production one, Business System 12, both now discontinued. Honeywell wrote MRDS for Multics, and now there are two new implementations: Alphora Dataphor and Rel. Most other DBMS implementations usually called *relational* are actually SQL DBMSs.

In 1970, the University of Michigan began development of the MICRO Information Management System based on D.L. Childs' Set-Theoretic Data model. MICRO was used to manage very large data sets by the US Department of Labor, the U.S. Environmental Protection Agency, and researchers from the University of Alberta, the University of Michigan, and Wayne State University. It ran on IBM mainframe computers using the Michigan Terminal System. The system remained in production until 1998.

Integrated Approach

In the 1970s and 1980s, attempts were made to build database systems with integrated hardware and software. The underlying philosophy was that such integration would provide higher performance at lower cost. Examples were IBM System/38, the early offering of Teradata, and the Britton Lee, Inc. database machine.

Another approach to hardware support for database management was ICL's CAFS accelerator, a hardware disk controller with programmable search capabilities. In the long term, these efforts were generally unsuccessful because specialized database machines could not keep pace with the rapid development and progress of general-purpose computers. Thus most database systems nowadays are software systems running on general-purpose hardware, using general-purpose computer data storage. However this idea is still pursued for certain applications by some companies like Netezza and Oracle (Exadata).

Late 1970s, SQL DBMS

IBM started working on a prototype system loosely based on Codd's concepts as *System R* in the early 1970s. The first version was ready in 1974/5, and work then started on multi-table systems in which the data could be split so that all of the data for a record (some of which is optional) did not have to be stored in a single large "chunk". Subsequent multi-user versions were tested by customers in 1978 and 1979, by which time a standardized query language – SQL – had been added. Codd's ideas were establishing themselves as both workable and superior to CODASYL, pushing IBM to develop a true production version of System R, known as *SQL/DS*, and, later, *Database 2* (DB2).

Larry Ellison's Oracle started from a different chain, based on IBM's papers on System R, and beat IBM to market when the first version was released in 1978.

Stonebraker went on to apply the lessons from INGRES to develop a new database, Postgres, which is now known as PostgreSQL. PostgreSQL is often used for global mission critical applications (the .org and .info domain name registries use it as their primary data store, as do many large companies and financial institutions).

In Sweden, Codd's paper was also read and Mimer SQL was developed from the mid-1970s at Uppsala University. In 1984, this project was consolidated into an independent enterprise. In the early 1980s, Mimer introduced transaction handling for high robustness in applications, an idea that was subsequently implemented on most other DBMSs.

Another data model, the entity–relationship model, emerged in 1976 and gained popularity for database design as it emphasized a more familiar description than the earlier relational model. Later on, entity–relationship constructs were retrofitted as a data modeling construct for the relational model, and the difference between the two have become irrelevant.

1980s, on the Desktop

The 1980s ushered in the age of desktop computing. The new computers empowered their users with spreadsheets like Lotus 1-2-3 and database software like dBASE. The dBASE product was lightweight and easy for any computer user to understand out of the box. C. Wayne Ratliff the creator of dBASE stated: "dBASE was different from programs like BASIC, C, FORTRAN, and COBOL in that a lot of the dirty work had already been done. The data manipulation is done by dBASE instead of by the user, so the user can concentrate on what he is doing, rather than having to mess with the dirty details of opening, reading, and closing files, and managing space allocation." dBASE was one of the top selling software titles in the 1980s and early 1990s.

1990s, Object-oriented

The 1990s, along with a rise in object-oriented programming, saw a growth in how data in various databases were handled. Programmers and designers began to treat the data in their databases as objects. That is to say that if a person's data were in a database, that person's attributes, such as their address, phone number, and age, were now considered to belong to that person instead of being extraneous data. This allows for relations between data to be relations to objects and their attributes and not to individual fields. The term "object-relational impedance mismatch" described the inconvenience of translating between programmed objects and database tables. Object databases and object-relational databases attempt to solve this problem by providing an object-oriented language (sometimes as extensions to SQL) that programmers can use as alternative to purely relational SQL. On the programming side, libraries known as object-relational mappings (ORMs) attempt to solve the same problem.

2000s, NoSQL and NewSQL

XML databases are a type of structured document-oriented database that allows querying based on XML document attributes. XML databases are mostly used in enterprise database management, where XML is being used as the machine-to-machine data interoperability standard. XML database management systems include commercial software MarkLogic and Oracle Berkeley DB XML, and a free use software Clusterpoint Distributed XML/JSON Database. All are enterprise software database platforms and support industry standard ACID-compliant transaction processing with strong database consistency characteristics and high level of database security.

NoSQL databases are often very fast, do not require fixed table schemas, avoid join operations by storing denormalized data, and are designed to scale horizontally. The most popular NoSQL systems include MongoDB, Couchbase, Riak, Memcached, Redis, CouchDB, Hazelcast, Apache Cassandra, and HBase, which are all open-source software products.

In recent years, there was a high demand for massively distributed databases with high partition tolerance but according to the CAP theorem it is impossible for a distributed system to simultaneously provide consistency, availability, and partition tolerance guarantees. A distributed system can satisfy any two of these guarantees at the same time, but not all three. For that reason, many NoSQL databases are using what is called eventual consistency to provide both availability and partition tolerance guarantees with a reduced level of data consistency.

NewSQL is a class of modern relational databases that aims to provide the same scalable performance of NoSQL systems for online transaction processing (read-write) workloads while still using SQL and maintaining the ACID guarantees of a traditional database system. Such databases include ScaleBase, Clustrix, EnterpriseDB, MemSQL, NuoDB, and VoltDB.

Research

Database technology has been an active research topic since the 1960s, both in academia and in the research and development groups of companies (for example IBM Research). Research activity includes theory and development of prototypes. Notable research topics have included models, the atomic transaction concept, and related concurrency control techniques, query languages and query optimization methods, RAID, and more.

The database research area has several dedicated academic journals (for example, *ACM Transactions on Database Systems*-TODS, *Data and Knowledge Engineering*-DKE) and annual conferences (e.g., ACM SIGMOD, ACM PODS, VLDB, IEEE ICDE).

Examples

One way to classify databases involves the type of their contents, for example: bibliographic, document-text, statistical, or multimedia objects. Another way is by their application area, for example: accounting, music compositions, movies, banking, manufacturing, or insurance. A third way is by some technical aspect, such as the database structure or interface type. This section lists a few of the adjectives used to characterize different kinds of databases.

- An in-memory database is a database that primarily resides in main memory, but is typically backed-up by non-volatile computer data storage. Main memory databases are faster than disk databases, and so are often used where response time is critical, such as in telecommunications network equipment. SAP HANA platform is a very hot topic for in-memory database. By May 2012, HANA was able to run on servers with 100TB main memory powered by IBM. The co founder of the company claimed that the system was big enough to run the 8 largest SAP customers.

- An active database includes an event-driven architecture which can respond to conditions both inside and outside the database. Possible uses include security monitoring, alerting, statistics gathering and authorization. Many databases provide active database features in the form of database triggers.

- A cloud database relies on cloud technology. Both the database and most of its DBMS reside remotely, "in the cloud", while its applications are both developed by programmers and later maintained and utilized by (application's) end-users through a web browser and Open APIs.

- Data warehouses archive data from operational databases and often from external sources such as market research firms. The warehouse becomes the central source of data for use by managers and other end-users who may not have access to operational data. For example, sales data might be aggregated to weekly totals and converted from internal product codes to use UPCs so that they can be compared with ACNielsen data. Some basic and essential components of data warehousing include extracting, analyzing, and mining data, transforming, loading, and managing data so as to make them available for further use.

- A deductive database combines logic programming with a relational database, for example by using the Datalog language.

- A distributed database is one in which both the data and the DBMS span multiple computers.

- A document-oriented database is designed for storing, retrieving, and managing document-oriented, or semi structured data, information. Document-oriented databases are one of the main categories of NoSQL databases.

- An embedded database system is a DBMS which is tightly integrated with an application software that requires access to stored data in such a way that the DBMS is hidden from the application's end-users and requires little or no ongoing maintenance.

- End-user databases consist of data developed by individual end-users. Examples of these are collections of documents, spreadsheets, presentations, multimedia, and other files. Several products exist to support such databases. Some of them are much simpler than full-fledged DBMSs, with more elementary DBMS functionality.

- A federated database system comprises several distinct databases, each with its own DBMS. It is handled as a single database by a federated database management system (FDBMS), which transparently integrates multiple autonomous DBMSs, possibly of different types (in which case it would also be a heterogeneous database system), and provides them with an integrated conceptual view.

- Sometimes the term *multi-database* is used as a synonym to federated database, though it may refer to a less integrated (e.g., without an FDBMS and a managed integrated schema) group of databases that cooperate in a single application. In this case, typically middleware is used for distribution, which typically includes an atomic commit protocol (ACP), e.g., the two-phase commit protocol, to allow distributed (global) transactions across the participating databases.

- A graph database is a kind of NoSQL database that uses graph structures with nodes, edges, and properties to represent and store information. General graph databases that can store any graph are distinct from specialized graph databases such as triplestores and network databases.

- An array DBMS is a kind of NoSQL DBMS that allows to model, store, and retrieve (usually large) multi-dimensional arrays such as satellite images and climate simulation output.

- In a hypertext or hypermedia database, any word or a piece of text representing an object, e.g., another piece of text, an article, a picture, or a film, can be hyperlinked to that object. Hypertext databases are particularly useful for organizing large amounts of disparate information. For example, they are useful for organizing online encyclopedias, where users can conveniently jump around the text. The World Wide Web is thus a large distributed hypertext database.

- A knowledge base (abbreviated KB, kb or Δ) is a special kind of database for knowledge management, providing the means for the computerized collection, organization, and retrieval of knowledge. Also a collection of data representing problems with their solutions and related experiences.

- A mobile database can be carried on or synchronized from a mobile computing device.

- Operational databases store detailed data about the operations of an organization. They typically process relatively high volumes of updates using transactions. Examples include customer databases that record contact, credit, and demographic information about a business' customers, personnel databases that hold information such as salary, benefits, skills data about employees, enterprise resource planning systems that record details about product components, parts inventory, and financial databases that keep track of the organization's money, accounting and financial dealings.

- A parallel database seeks to improve performance through parallelization for tasks such as loading data, building indexes and evaluating queries.

  The major parallel DBMS architectures which are induced by the underlying hardware architecture are:

  - Shared memory architecture, where multiple processors share the main memory space, as well as other data storage.

  - Shared disk architecture, where each processing unit (typically consisting of multiple processors) has its own main memory, but all units share the other storage.

  - Shared nothing architecture, where each processing unit has its own main memory and other storage.

- Probabilistic databases employ fuzzy logic to draw inferences from imprecise data.

- Real-time databases process transactions fast enough for the result to come back and be acted on right away.

- A spatial database can store the data with multidimensional features. The queries on such data include location-based queries, like "Where is the closest hotel in my area?".

- A temporal database has built-in time aspects, for example a temporal data model and a temporal version of SQL. More specifically the temporal aspects usually include valid-time and transaction-time.

- A terminology-oriented database builds upon an object-oriented database, often customized for a specific field.

- An unstructured data database is intended to store in a manageable and protected way diverse objects that do not fit naturally and conveniently in common databases. It may include email messages, documents, journals, multimedia objects, etc. The name may be misleading since some objects can be highly structured. However, the entire possible object collection does not fit into a predefined structured framework. Most established DBMSs now support unstructured data in various ways, and new dedicated DBMSs are emerging.

Design and Modeling

The first task of a database designer is to produce a conceptual data model that reflects the structure of the information to be held in the database. A common approach to this is to develop an entity-relationship model, often with the aid of drawing tools. Another popular approach is the Unified Modeling Language. A successful data model will accurately reflect the possible state of the external world being modeled: for example, if people can have more than one phone number, it will allow this information to be captured. Designing a good conceptual data model requires a good understanding of the application domain; it typically involves asking deep questions about the things of interest to an organisation, like "can a customer also be a supplier?", or "if a product is sold with two different forms of packaging, are those the same product or different products?", or "if a plane flies from New York to Dubai via Frankfurt, is that one flight or two (or maybe even three)?". The answers to these questions establish definitions of the terminology used for entities (customers, products, flights, flight segments) and their relationships and attributes.

Producing the conceptual data model sometimes involves input from business processes, or the analysis of workflow in the organization. This can help to establish what information is needed in the database, and what can be left out. For example, it can help when deciding whether the database needs to hold historic data as well as current data.

Having produced a conceptual data model that users are happy with, the next stage is to translate this into a schema that implements the relevant data structures within the database. This process is often called logical database design, and the output is a logical data model expressed in the form of a schema. Whereas the conceptual data model is (in theory at least) independent of the choice of database technology, the logical data model will be expressed in terms of a particular database model supported by the chosen DBMS. (The terms *data model* and *database model* are often used interchangeably, but in this article we use *data model* for the design of a specific database, and *database model* for the modelling notation used to express that design.)

The most popular database model for general-purpose databases is the relational model, or more precisely, the relational model as represented by the SQL language. The process of creating a logical database design using this model uses a methodical approach known as normalization. The goal of normalization is to ensure that each elementary "fact" is only recorded in one place, so that insertions, updates, and deletions automatically maintain consistency.

The final stage of database design is to make the decisions that affect performance, scalability, recovery, security, and the like. This is often called *physical database design*. A key goal during this stage is data independence, meaning that the decisions made for performance optimization purposes should be invisible to end-users and applications. Physical design is driven mainly by performance requirements, and requires a good knowledge of the expected workload and access patterns, and a deep understanding of the features offered by the chosen DBMS.

Another aspect of physical database design is security. It involves both defining access control to database objects as well as defining security levels and methods for the data itself.

Models

A database model is a type of data model that determines the logical structure of a database and fundamentally determines in which manner data can be stored, organized, and manipulated. The most popular example of a database model is the relational model (or the SQL approximation of relational), which uses a table-based format.

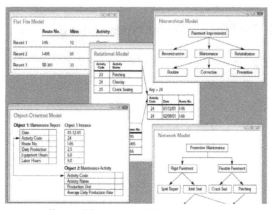

Collage of five types of database models

Common logical data models for databases include:

- Navigational databases

    o Hierarchical database model

    o Network model

    o Graph database

- Relational model

- Entity–relationship model

    o Enhanced entity–relationship model

- Object model

- Document model

- Entity–attribute–value model

- Star schema

An object-relational database combines the two related structures.

Physical data models include:

- Inverted index

- Flat file

Other models include:

- Associative model

- Multidimensional model

- Array model

- Multivalue model

Specialized models are optimized for particular types of data:

- XML database

- Semantic model

- Content store

- Event store

- Time series model

External, Conceptual, and Internal Views

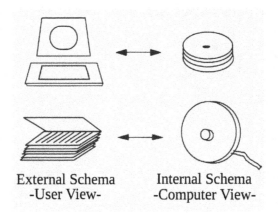

External Schema   Internal Schema
-User View-   -Computer View-

Traditional view of data

A database management system provides three views of the database data:

- The external level defines how each group of end-users sees the organization of data in the database. A single database can have any number of views at the external level.

- The conceptual level unifies the various external views into a compatible global view. It provides the synthesis of all the external views. It is out of the scope of the various database end-users, and is rather of interest to database application developers and database administrators.

- The internal level (or *physical level*) is the internal organization of data inside a DBMS. It is concerned with cost, performance, scalability and other operational matters. It deals with storage layout of the data, using storage structures such as indexes to enhance performance. Occasionally it stores data of individual views (materialized views), computed from generic data, if performance justification exists for such redundancy. It balances all the external views' performance requirements, possibly conflicting, in an attempt to optimize overall performance across all activities.

While there is typically only one conceptual (or logical) and physical (or internal) view of the data, there can be any number of different external views. This allows users to see database information in a more business-related way rather than from a technical, processing viewpoint. For example, a financial department of a company needs the payment details of all employees as part of the company's expenses, but does not need details about employees that are the interest of the human resources department. Thus different departments need different *views* of the company's database.

The three-level database architecture relates to the concept of *data independence* which was one of the major initial driving forces of the relational model. The idea is that changes made at a certain level do not affect the view at a higher level. For example, changes in the internal level do not affect application programs written using conceptual level interfaces, which reduces the impact of making physical changes to improve performance.

The conceptual view provides a level of indirection between internal and external. On one hand it provides a common view of the database, independent of different external view structures, and on the other hand it abstracts away details of how the data are stored or managed (internal level). In principle every level, and even every external view, can be presented by a different data model. In practice usually a given DBMS uses the same data model for both the external and the conceptual levels (e.g., relational model). The internal level, which is hidden inside the DBMS and depends on its implementation, requires a different level of detail and uses its own types of data structure types.

Separating the *external*, *conceptual* and *internal* levels was a major feature of the relational database model implementations that dominate 21st century databases.

Languages

Database languages are special-purpose languages, which do one or more of the following:

- Data definition language – defines data types and the relationships among them

- Data manipulation language – performs tasks such as inserting, updating, or deleting data occurrences

- Query language – allows searching for information and computing derived information

Database languages are specific to a particular data model. Notable examples include:

- SQL combines the roles of data definition, data manipulation, and query in a single language. It was one of the first commercial languages for the relational model, although it departs in some respects from the relational model as described by Codd (for example, the rows and columns of a table can be ordered). SQL became a standard of the American National Standards Institute (ANSI) in 1986, and of the International Organization for Standardization (ISO) in 1987. The standards have been regularly enhanced since and is supported (with varying degrees of conformance) by all mainstream commercial relational DBMSs.

- OQL is an object model language standard (from the Object Data Management Group). It has influenced the design of some of the newer query languages like JDOQL and EJB QL.

- XQuery is a standard XML query language implemented by XML database systems such as MarkLogic and eXist, by relational databases with XML capability such as Oracle and DB2, and also by in-memory XML processors such as Saxon.

- SQL/XML combines XQuery with SQL.

A database language may also incorporate features like:

- DBMS-specific Configuration and storage engine management

- Computations to modify query results, like counting, summing, averaging, sorting, grouping, and cross-referencing

- Constraint enforcement (e.g. in an automotive database, only allowing one engine type per car)

- Application programming interface version of the query language, for programmer convenience

Performance, Security, and Availability

Because of the critical importance of database technology to the smooth running of an enterprise, database systems include complex mechanisms to deliver the required performance, security, and availability, and allow database administrators to control the use of these features.

Storage

Database storage is the container of the physical materialization of a database. It comprises the *internal* (physical) *level* in the database architecture. It also contains all the information needed (e.g., metadata, "data about the data", and internal data structures) to reconstruct the *conceptual level* and *external level* from the internal level when needed. Putting data into permanent storage is generally the responsibility of the database engine a.k.a. "storage engine". Though typically accessed by a DBMS through the underlying operating system (and often utilizing the operating systems' file systems as intermediates for storage layout), storage properties and configuration setting are extremely important for the efficient operation of the DBMS, and thus are closely maintained by database administrators. A DBMS, while in operation, always has its database residing in several types of storage (e.g., memory and external storage). The database data and the additional needed information, possibly in very large amounts, are coded into bits. Data typically reside in the storage in structures that look completely different from the way the data look in the conceptual and external levels, but in ways that attempt to optimize (the best possible) these levels' reconstruction when needed by users and programs, as well as for computing additional types of needed information from the data (e.g., when querying the database).

Some DBMSs support specifying which character encoding was used to store data, so multiple encodings can be used in the same database.

Various low-level database storage structures are used by the storage engine to serialize the data model so it can be written to the medium of choice. Techniques such as indexing may be used to improve performance. Conventional storage is row-oriented, but there are also column-oriented and correlation databases.

Materialized Views

Often storage redundancy is employed to increase performance. A common example is storing *materialized views*, which consist of frequently needed *external views* or query results. Storing such views saves the expensive computing of them each time they are needed. The downsides of materialized views are the overhead incurred when updating them to keep them synchronized with their original updated database data, and the cost of storage redundancy.

Replication

Occasionally a database employs storage redundancy by database objects replication (with one or more copies) to increase data availability (both to improve performance of simultaneous multiple end-user accesses to a same database object, and to provide resiliency in a case of partial failure of a distributed database). Updates of a replicated object need to be synchronized across the object copies. In many cases, the entire database is replicated.

Security

Database security deals with all various aspects of protecting the database content, its owners, and its users. It ranges from protection from intentional unauthorized database uses to unintentional database accesses by unauthorized entities (e.g., a person or a computer program).

Database access control deals with controlling who (a person or a certain computer program) is allowed to access what information in the database. The information may comprise specific database objects (e.g., record types, specific records, data structures), certain computations over certain objects (e.g., query types, or specific queries), or utilizing specific access paths to the former (e.g., using specific indexes or other data structures to access information). Database access controls are set by special authorized (by the database owner) personnel that uses dedicated protected security DBMS interfaces.

This may be managed directly on an individual basis, or by the assignment of individuals and privileges to groups, or (in the most elaborate models) through the assignment of individuals and groups to roles which are then granted entitlements. Data security prevents unauthorized users from viewing or updating the database. Using passwords, users are allowed access to the entire database or subsets of it called "subschemas". For example, an employee database can contain all the data about an individual employee, but one group of users may be authorized to view only payroll data, while others are allowed access to only work history and medical data. If the DBMS provides a way to interactively enter and update the database, as well as interrogate it, this capability allows for managing personal databases.

Data security in general deals with protecting specific chunks of data, both physically (i.e., from corruption, or destruction, or removal), or the interpretation of them, or parts of them to meaningful information (e.g., by looking at the strings of bits that they comprise, concluding specific valid credit-card numbers.

Change and access logging records who accessed which attributes, what was changed, and when it was changed. Logging services allow for a forensic database audit later by keeping a record of access occurrences and changes. Sometimes application-level code is used to record changes rather than leaving this to the database. Monitoring can be set up to attempt to detect security breaches.

Transactions and Concurrency

Database transactions can be used to introduce some level of fault tolerance and data integrity after recovery from a crash. A database transaction is a unit of work, typically encapsulating a number of operations over a database (e.g., reading a database object, writing, acquiring lock, etc.), an abstraction supported in database and also other systems. Each transaction has well defined boundaries in terms of which program/code executions are included in that transaction (determined by the transaction's programmer via special transaction commands).

The acronym ACID describes some ideal properties of a database transaction: Atomicity, Consistency, Isolation, and Durability.

Migration

A database built with one DBMS is not portable to another DBMS (i.e., the other DBMS cannot run it). However, in some situations, it is desirable to move, migrate a database from one DBMS to another. The reasons are primarily economical (different DBMSs may have different total costs of ownership or TCOs), functional, and operational (different DBMSs may have different capabilities). The migration involves the database's transformation from one DBMS type to another. The transformation should maintain (if possible) the database related application (i.e., all related application programs) intact. Thus, the database's conceptual and external architectural levels should be maintained in the transformation. It may be desired that also some aspects of the architecture internal level are maintained. A complex or large database migration may be a complicated and costly (one-time) project by itself, which should be factored into the decision to migrate. This in spite of the fact that tools may exist to help migration between specific DBMSs. Typically, a DBMS vendor provides tools to help importing databases from other popular DBMSs.

Building, Maintaining, and Tuning

After designing a database for an application, the next stage is building the database. Typically, an appropriate general-purpose DBMS can be selected to be utilized for this purpose. A DBMS provides the needed user interfaces to be utilized by database administrators to define the needed application's data structures within the DBMS's respective data model. Other user interfaces are used to select needed DBMS parameters (like security related, storage allocation parameters, etc.).

When the database is ready (all its data structures and other needed components are defined), it is typically populated with initial application's data (database initialization, which is typically a distinct project; in many cases using specialized DBMS interfaces that support bulk insertion) before making it operational. In some cases, the database becomes operational while empty of application data, and data are accumulated during its operation.

After the database is created, initialised and populated it needs to be maintained. Various database parameters may need changing and the database may need to be tuned (tuning) for better performance; application's data structures may be changed or added, new related application programs may be written to add to the application's functionality, etc.

Backup and Restore

Sometimes it is desired to bring a database back to a previous state (for many reasons, e.g., cases when the database is found corrupted due to a software error, or if it has been updated with erroneous data). To achieve this, a backup operation is done occasionally or continuously, where each desired database state (i.e., the values of its data and their embedding in database's data structures) is kept within dedicated backup files (many techniques exist to do this effectively). When this state is needed, i.e., when it is decided by a database administrator to bring the database back to this state (e.g., by specifying this state by a desired point in time when the database was in this state), these files are utilized to restore that state.

Static Analysis

Static analysis techniques for software verification can be applied also in the scenario of query languages. In particular, the *Abstract interpretation framework has been extended to the field of query languages for relational databases as a way to support sound approximation techniques. The semantics of query languages can be tuned according to suitable abstractions of the concrete domain of data. The abstraction of relational database system has many interesting applications, in particular, for security purposes, such as fine grained access control, watermarking, etc.

Other

Other DBMS features might include:

- Database logs

- Graphics component for producing graphs and charts, especially in a data warehouse system

- Query optimizer – Performs query optimization on every query to choose for it the most efficient *query plan* (a partial order (tree) of operations) to be executed to compute the query result. May be specific to a particular storage engine.

- Tools or hooks for database design, application programming, application program maintenance, database performance analysis and monitoring, database configuration monitoring, DBMS hardware configuration (a DBMS and related database may span computers, networks, and storage units) and related database mapping (especially for a distributed DBMS), storage allocation and database layout monitoring, storage migration, etc.

- Increasingly, there are calls for a single systems and methodology that incorporates all of these core functionalities into the same build, test, and deployment framework for database management and source control. Borrowing from other developments in the software industry, some are labeling such offerings "DevOps for Database". Packaged thusly, these database management solutions are supposed to be stable, secure, backed up, compliant, testable, and consistent between environments.

References

- Development of an object-oriented DBMS; Portland, Oregon, United States; Pages: 472–482; 1986; ISBN 0-89791-204-7

- IBM Corporation. "IBM Information Management System (IMS) 13 Transaction and Database Servers delivers high performance and low total cost of ownership". Retrieved Feb 20, 2014.

Various Types of Database

Cloud database usually runs on cloud computing platforms. The two methods used in cloud database are virtual machine image and database-as-a-service. Alternative types of database are data warehouse, distributed database, mobile database, parallel database, graph database etc. The topics discussed in the section are of great importance to broaden the existing knowledge on databases.

Cloud Database

A cloud database is a database that typically runs on a cloud computing platform, access to it is provided as a service.

Database services take care of scalability and high availability of the database. Database services make the underlying software-stack transparent to the user.

Deployment Models

There are two primary methods to run a database in a cloud:

Virtual machine Image

> Cloud platforms allow users to purchase virtual-machine instances for a limited time, and one can run a database on such virtual machines. Users can either upload their own machine image with a database installed on it, or use ready-made machine images that already include an optimized installation of a database. For example, Oracle provides a ready-made machine image with an installation of Oracle Database 11g Enterprise Edition on Amazon EC2 and on Microsoft Azure.

Database-as-a-service (DBaaS)

> With a database as a service model, application owners do not have to install and maintain the database themselves. Instead, the database service provider takes responsibility for installing and maintaining the database, and application owners are charged according to their usage of the service. For example, Amazon Web Services provides three database as a service offerings as part of its cloud portfolio: SimpleDB, a NoSQL key-value store; Amazon RDS, a relational database service that includes support for MySQL, Oracle, and more ; and DynamoDB. Microsoft offers its SQL Database servicethird-party source needed on its Azure cloud service platform. Cloud computing platform Rackspace offers database as a service for MySQL and MongoDB. Database as a service providers are not limited to cloud computing platforms. For example, Mon-

goDB as a service provider mLab allows their customers to host their databases on AWS, Azure, or Google Cloud Platform. Database vendors have also launched their own services under this model. Oracle provides its own database as a service, allowing users to access Oracle Database 11g and 12c as cloud services. MongoDB recently launched its own hosted MongoDB as a service, MongoDB Atlas.

Architecture and Common Characteristics

- Most database services offer web-based consoles, which the end user can use to provision and configure database instances. For example, the Amazon Web Services web-console enables users to launch database instances, create snapshots (similar to backups) of databases, and monitor database statistics.

- Database services consist of a database-manager component, which controls the underlying database instances using a service API. The service API is exposed to the end user, and permits users to perform maintenance and scaling operations on their database instances. For example, the Amazon Relational Database Service's service API enables creating a database instance, modifying the resources available to a database instance, deleting a database instance, creating a snapshot (similar to a backup) of a database, and restoring a database from a snapshot.

- Underlying software-stack stack typically includes the operating system, the database and third-party software used to manage the database. The service provider (e.g. MongoLab or ObjectRocket) is responsible for installing, patching and updating the underlying software stack and ensuring the overall health and performance of the database.

- Scalability features differ between vendors - some offer auto-scaling, others enable the user to scale up using an API, but do not scale automatically. There is typically a commitment for a certain level of high availability (e.g. 99.9% or 99.99%).

Data Model

The design and development of typical systems utilize data management and relational databases as their key building blocks. Advanced queries expressed in SQL work well with the strict relationships that are imposed on information by relational databases. However, relational database technology was not initially designed or developed for use over distributed systems. This issue has been addressed with the addition of clustering enhancements to the relational databases, although some basic tasks require complex and expensive protocols, such as with data synchronization.

Modern relational databases have shown poor performance on data-intensive systems, therefore, the idea of NoSQL has been utilized within database management systems for cloud based systems. Within NoSQL implemented storage, there are no requirements for fixed table schemas, and the use of join operations is avoided. "The NoSQL databases have proven to provide efficient horizontal scalability, good performance, and ease of assembly into cloud applications."

It is also important to differentiate between cloud databases which are relational as opposed to non-relational or NoSQL:

SQL databases

> Such as PostgreSQL, EDB Postgres Advanced Server, NuoDB, Oracle Database, Microsoft SQL Server, MariaDB and MySQL, are one type of database which can run in the cloud, either in a virtual machine or as a service, depending on the vendor. While SQL databases are easily vertically scalable, horizontal scalability poses a challenge, that cloud database services based on SQL have started to address.

NoSQL databases

> Such as Apache Cassandra, CouchDB and MongoDB, are another type of database which can run in the cloud. NoSQL databases are built to service heavy read/write loads and can scale up and down easily, and therefore they are more natively suited to running in the cloud.: However, most contemporary applications are built around an SQL data model, so working with NoSQL databases often requires a complete rewrite of application code.

> Some SQL databases have developed NoSQL capabilities including JSON, binary JSON, and key-value store data types. These multi-model databases includePostgreSQL and EDB Postgres Advanced Server.

> A multi-model database with relational and non-relational capabilities provides a standard SQL interface to users and applications and thus facilitates the usage of such databases for contemporary applications built around an SQL data model.

Vendors

The following table lists notable database vendors with a cloud database offering, classified by their deployment model – machine image vs. database as a service – and data model, SQL vs. NoSQL.

Cloud database vendors by deployment and data model		
	Virtual Machine Deployment	**Database as a Service**
SQL Data Model	<ul><li>EDB Postgres Advanced Server</li><li>IBM DB2</li><li>Ingres (database)</li><li>MariaDB</li><li>MySQL</li><li>NuoDB</li><li>Oracle Database</li><li>PostgreSQL</li><li>SAP HANA</li></ul>	<ul><li>Amazon Relational Database Service</li><li>Clustrix Database as a Service</li><li>EnterpriseDB Postgres Plus Cloud Database</li><li>Google Cloud SQL</li><li>Heroku PostgreSQL as a Service (shared and dedicated database options)</li><li>Microsoft Azure SQL Database (MS SQL)</li><li>Xeround Cloud Database* - MySQL front-end (*service no longer available)</li></ul>

NoSQL Data Model	• Apache Cassandra on Amazon EC2 or Google Compute Engine • Clusterpoint Database Virtual Box VM • CouchDB on Amazon EC2 or Google Cloud Platform • EDB Postgres Advanced Server • Hadoop on Amazon EC2, Google Cloud Platform, or Rackspace • MarkLogic on Amazon EC2 or Google Cloud Platform • MongoDB on Amazon EC2, Google Compute Engine, Microsoft Azure, or Rackspace • Neo4J on Amazon EC2 or Microsoft Azure	• Amazon DynamoDB • Amazon SimpleDB • Azure DocumentDB • Cloudant Data Layer (CouchDB) • EnterpriseDB Postgres Plus Cloud Database • Google Cloud Bigtable • Google Cloud Datastore • MongoDB Database as a Service (several options)

Data Warehouse

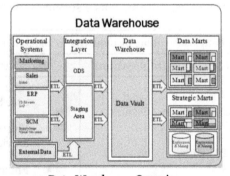

Data Warehouse Overview

In computing, a data warehouse (DW or DWH), also known as an enterprise data warehouse (EDW), is a system used for reporting and data analysis, and is considered a core component of business intelligence. DWs are central repositories of integrated data from one or more disparate sources. They store current and historical data and are used for creating analytical reports for knowledge workers throughout the enterprise. Examples of reports could range from annual and quarterly comparisons and trends to detailed daily sales analysis.

The data stored in the warehouse is uploaded from the operational systems (such as marketing or sales). The data may pass through an operational data store for additional operations before it is used in the DW for reporting.

Types of Systems

Data mart

A data mart is a simple form of a data warehouse that is focused on a single subject (or functional area), hence they draw data from a limited number of sources such as sales, finance or marketing. Data marts are often built and controlled by a single department within an organization. The sources could be internal operational systems, a central data warehouse, or external data. Denormalization is the norm for data modeling techniques in this system. Given that data marts generally cover only a subset of the data contained in a data warehouse, they are often easier and faster to implement.

Difference between data warehouse and data mart	
Data warehouse	**Data mart**
enterprise-wide data	department-wide data
multiple subject areas	single subject area
difficult to build	easy to build
takes more time to build	less time to build
larger memory	limited memory

Types of Data Marts

- Dependent data mart

- Independent data mart

- Hybrid data mart

Online analytical processing (OLAP)

OLAP is characterized by a relatively low volume of transactions. Queries are often very complex and involve aggregations. For OLAP systems, response time is an effectiveness measure. OLAP applications are widely used by Data Mining techniques. OLAP databases store aggregated, historical data in multi-dimensional schemas (usually star schemas). OLAP systems typically have data latency of a few hours, as opposed to data marts, where latency is expected to be closer to one day. The OLAP approach is used to analyze multi-dimensional data from multiple sources and perspectives. The three basic operations in OLAP are : Roll-up (Consolidation), Drill-down and Slicing & Dicing.

Online transaction processing (OLTP)

OLTP is characterized by a large number of short on-line transactions (INSERT, UPDATE, DELETE). OLTP systems emphasize very fast query processing and maintaining data integrity in multi-access environments. For OLTP systems, effectiveness is measured by the number of transactions per second. OLTP databases contain detailed and current data. The schema used to store transactional databases is the entity model (usually 3NF). Normalization is the norm for data modeling techniques in this system.

Predictive analysis

> Predictive analysis is about finding and quantifying hidden patterns in the data using complex mathematical models that can be used to predict future outcomes. Predictive analysis is different from OLAP in that OLAP focuses on historical data analysis and is reactive in nature, while predictive analysis focuses on the future. These systems are also used for CRM (customer relationship management).

Software Tools

The typical extract-transform-load (ETL)-based data warehouse uses staging, data integration, and access layers to house its key functions. The staging layer or staging database stores raw data extracted from each of the disparate source data systems. The integration layer integrates the disparate data sets by transforming the data from the staging layer often storing this transformed data in an operational data store (ODS) database. The integrated data are then moved to yet another database, often called the data warehouse database, where the data is arranged into hierarchical groups often called dimensions and into facts and aggregate facts. The combination of facts and dimensions is sometimes called a star schema. The access layer helps users retrieve data.

This definition of the data warehouse focuses on data storage. The main source of the data is cleaned, transformed, catalogued and made available for use by managers and other business professionals for data mining, online analytical processing, market research and decision support. However, the means to retrieve and analyze data, to extract, transform and load data, and to manage the data dictionary are also considered essential components of a data warehousing system. Many references to data warehousing use this broader context. Thus, an expanded definition for data warehousing includes business intelligence tools, tools to extract, transform and load data into the repository, and tools to manage and retrieve metadata.

Benefits

A data warehouse maintains a copy of information from the source transaction systems. This architectural complexity provides the opportunity to:

- Integrate data from multiple sources into a single database and data model. Mere congregation of data to single database so a single query engine can be used to present data is an ODS.

- Mitigate the problem of database isolation level lock contention in transaction processing systems caused by attempts to run large, long running, analysis queries in transaction processing databases.

- Maintain data history, even if the source transaction systems do not.

- Integrate data from multiple source systems, enabling a central view across the enterprise. This benefit is always valuable, but particularly so when the organization has grown by merger.

- Improve data quality, by providing consistent codes and descriptions, flagging or even fixing bad data.

- Present the organization's information consistently.

- Provide a single common data model for all data of interest regardless of the data's source.

- Restructure the data so that it makes sense to the business users.

- Restructure the data so that it delivers excellent query performance, even for complex analytic queries, without impacting the operational systems.

- Add value to operational business applications, notably customer relationship management (CRM) systems.

- Make decision–support queries easier to write.

- Optimized data warehouse architectures allow data scientists to organize and disambiguate repetitive data.

Generic Environment

The environment for data warehouses and marts includes the following:

- Source systems that provide data to the warehouse or mart;

- Data integration technology and processes that are needed to prepare the data for use;

- Different architectures for storing data in an organization's data warehouse or data marts;

- Different tools and applications for the variety of users;

- Metadata, data quality, and governance processes must be in place to ensure that the warehouse or mart meets its purposes.

In regards to source systems listed above, Rainer states, "A common source for the data in data warehouses is the company's operational databases, which can be relational databases".

Regarding data integration, Rainer states, "It is necessary to extract data from source systems, transform them, and load them into a data mart or warehouse".

Rainer discusses storing data in an organization's data warehouse or data marts.

Metadata are data about data. "IT personnel need information about data sources; database, table, and column names; refresh schedules; and data usage measures".

Today, the most successful companies are those that can respond quickly and flexibly to market changes and opportunities. A key to this response is the effective and efficient use of data and information by analysts and managers. A "data warehouse" is a repository of historical data that are organized by subject to support decision makers in the organization. Once data are stored in a data mart or warehouse, they can be accessed.

History

The concept of data warehousing dates back to the late 1980s when IBM researchers Barry Devlin and Paul Murphy developed the "business data warehouse". In essence, the data warehousing concept was intended to provide an architectural model for the flow of data from operational systems to decision support environments. The concept attempted to address the various problems associated with this flow, mainly the high costs associated with it. In the absence of a data warehousing architecture, an enormous amount of redundancy was required to support multiple decision support environments. In larger corporations it was typical for multiple decision support environments to operate independently. Though each environment served different users, they often required much of the same stored data. The process of gathering, cleaning and integrating data from various sources, usually from long-term existing operational systems (usually referred to as legacy systems), was typically in part replicated for each environment. Moreover, the operational systems were frequently reexamined as new decision support requirements emerged. Often new requirements necessitated gathering, cleaning and integrating new data from "data marts" that were tailored for ready access by users.

Key developments in early years of data warehousing were:

- 1960s – General Mills and Dartmouth College, in a joint research project, develop the terms *dimensions* and *facts*.

- 1970s – ACNielsen and IRI provide dimensional data marts for retail sales.

- 1970s – Bill Inmon begins to define and discuss the term: Data Warehouse.

- 1975 – Sperry Univac introduces MAPPER (MAintain, Prepare, and Produce Executive Reports) is a database management and reporting system that includes the world's first 4GL. First platform designed for building Information Centers (a forerunner of contemporary Enterprise Data Warehousing platforms)

- 1983 – Teradata introduces a database management system specifically designed for decision support.

- 1984 – Metaphor Computer Systems, founded by David Liddle and Don Massaro, releases Data Interpretation System (DIS). DIS was a hardware/software package and GUI for business users to create a database management and analytic system.

- 1988 – Barry Devlin and Paul Murphy publish the article *An architecture for a business and information system* where they introduce the term "business data warehouse".

- 1990 – Red Brick Systems, founded by Ralph Kimball, introduces Red Brick Warehouse, a database management system specifically for data warehousing.

- 1991 – Prism Solutions, founded by Bill Inmon, introduces Prism Warehouse Manager, software for developing a data warehouse.

- 1992 – Bill Inmon publishes the book *Building the Data Warehouse*.

- 1995 – The Data Warehousing Institute, a for-profit organization that promotes data warehousing, is founded.

- 1996 – Ralph Kimball publishes the book *The Data Warehouse Toolkit*.

- 2012 – Bill Inmon developed and made public technology known as "textual disambiguation". Textual disambiguation applies context to raw text and reformats the raw text and context into a standard data base format. Once raw text is passed through textual disambiguation, it can easily and efficiently be accessed and analyzed by standard business intelligence technology. Textual disambiguation is accomplished through the execution of textual ETL. Textual disambiguation is useful wherever raw text is found, such as in documents, Hadoop, email, and so forth.

Information Storage

Facts

A fact is a value or measurement, which represents a fact about the managed entity or system.

Facts as reported by the reporting entity are said to be at raw level. E.g. in a mobile telephone system, if a BTS (base transceiver station) received 1,000 requests for traffic channel allocation, it allocates for 820 and rejects the remaining then it would report 3 facts or measurements to a management system:

- tch_req_total = 1000

- tch_req_success = 820

- tch_req_fail = 180

Facts at the raw level are further aggregated to higher levels in various dimensions to extract more service or business-relevant information from it. These are called aggregates or summaries or aggregated facts.

For instance, if there are 3 BTSs in a city, then the facts above can be aggregated from the BTS to the city level in the network dimension. For example:

- $$tch\_req\_success\_city = tch\_req\_success\_bts1 + tch\_req\_success\_bts2 + tch\_req\_success\_bts3$$

- $$avg\_tch\_req\_success\_city = (tch\_req\_success\_bts1 + tch\_req\_success\_bts2 + tch\_req\_success\_bts3)/3$$

Dimensional Versus Normalized Approach for Storage of Data

There are three or more leading approaches to storing data in a data warehouse — the most important approaches are the dimensional approach and the normalized approach.

The dimensional approach refers to Ralph Kimball's approach in which it is stated that the data warehouse should be modeled using a Dimensional Model/star schema. The normalized approach, also called the 3NF model (Third Normal Form) refers to Bill Inmon's approach in which it is stated that the data warehouse should be modeled using an E-R model/normalized model.

In a dimensional approach, transaction data are partitioned into "facts", which are generally numeric transaction data, and "dimensions", which are the reference information that gives context to the facts. For example, a sales transaction can be broken up into facts such as the number of products ordered and the total price paid for the products, and into dimensions such as order date, customer name, product number, order ship-to and bill-to locations, and salesperson responsible for receiving the order.

A key advantage of a dimensional approach is that the data warehouse is easier for the user to understand and to use. Also, the retrieval of data from the data warehouse tends to operate very quickly. Dimensional structures are easy to understand for business users, because the structure is divided into measurements/facts and context/dimensions. Facts are related to the organization's business processes and operational system whereas the dimensions surrounding them contain context about the measurement (Kimball, Ralph 2008). Another advantage offered by dimensional model is that it does not involve a relational database every time. Thus, this type of modeling technique is very useful for end-user queries in data warehouse.

The main disadvantages of the dimensional approach are the following:

1. In order to maintain the integrity of facts and dimensions, loading the data warehouse with data from different operational systems is complicated.

2. It is difficult to modify the data warehouse structure if the organization adopting the dimensional approach changes the way in which it does business.

In the normalized approach, the data in the data warehouse are stored following, to a degree, database normalization rules. Tables are grouped together by *subject areas* that reflect general data categories (e.g., data on customers, products, finance, etc.). The normalized structure divides data into entities, which creates several tables in a relational database. When applied in large enterprises the result is dozens of tables that are linked together by a web of joins. Furthermore, each of the created entities is converted into separate physical tables when the database is implemented (Kimball, Ralph 2008). The main advantage of this approach is that it is straightforward to add information into the database. Some disadvantages of this approach are that, because of the number of tables involved, it can be difficult for users to join data from different sources into meaningful information and to access the information without a precise understanding of the sources of data and of the data structure of the data warehouse.

Both normalized and dimensional models can be represented in entity-relationship diagrams as both contain joined relational tables. The difference between the two models is the degree of normalization (also known as Normal Forms). These approaches are not mutually exclusive, and there are other approaches. Dimensional approaches can involve normalizing data to a degree (Kimball, Ralph 2008).

In *Information-Driven Business*, Robert Hillard proposes an approach to comparing the two approaches based on the information needs of the business problem. The technique shows that normalized models hold far more information than their dimensional equivalents (even when the same fields are used in both models) but this extra information comes at the cost of usability. The technique measures information quantity in terms of information entropy and usability in terms of the Small Worlds data transformation measure.

Design Methods

Bottom-up Design

In the *bottom-up* approach, data marts are first created to provide reporting and analytical capabilities for specific business processes. These data marts can then be integrated to create a comprehensive data warehouse. The data warehouse bus architecture is primarily an implementation of "the bus", a collection of conformed dimensions and conformed facts, which are dimensions that are shared (in a specific way) between facts in two or more data marts.

Top-down Design

The *top-down* approach is designed using a normalized enterprise data model. "Atomic" data, that is, data at the greatest level of detail, are stored in the data warehouse. Dimensional data marts containing data needed for specific business processes or specific departments are created from the data warehouse.

Hybrid Design

Data warehouses (DW) often resemble the hub and spokes architecture. Legacy systems feeding the warehouse often include customer relationship management and enterprise resource planning, generating large amounts of data. To consolidate these various data models, and facilitate the extract transform load process, data warehouses often make use of an operational data store, the information from which is parsed into the actual DW. To reduce data redundancy, larger systems often store the data in a normalized way. Data marts for specific reports can then be built on top of the DW.

The DW database in a hybrid solution is kept on third normal form to eliminate data redundancy. A normal relational database, however, is not efficient for business intelligence reports where dimensional modelling is prevalent. Small data marts can shop for data from the consolidated warehouse and use the filtered, specific data for the fact tables and dimensions required. The DW provides a single source of information from which the data marts can read, providing a wide range of business information. The hybrid architecture allows a DW to be replaced with a master data management solution where operational, not static information could reside.

The Data Vault Modeling components follow hub and spokes architecture. This modeling style is a hybrid design, consisting of the best practices from both third normal form and star schema. The Data Vault model is not a true third normal form, and breaks some of its rules, but it is a top-down architecture with a bottom up design. The Data Vault model is geared to be strictly a data warehouse. It is not geared to be end-user accessible, which when built, still requires the use of a data mart or star schema based release area for business purposes.

Versus Operational System

Operational systems are optimized for preservation of data integrity and speed of recording of business transactions through use of database normalization and an entity-relationship model. Operational system designers generally follow the Codd rules of database normalization in order to ensure data integrity. Codd defined five increasingly stringent rules of normalization. Fully normalized database designs (that is, those satisfying all five Codd rules) often result in information from a business transaction being stored in dozens to hundreds of tables. Relational databases are efficient at managing the relationships between these tables. The databases have very fast insert/update performance because only a small amount of data in those tables is affected each time a transaction is processed. Finally, in order to improve performance, older data are usually periodically purged from operational systems.

Data warehouses are optimized for analytic access patterns. Analytic access patterns generally involve selecting specific fields and rarely if ever 'select *' as is more common in operational databases. Because of these differences in access patterns, operational databases (loosely, OLTP) benefit from the use of a row-oriented DBMS whereas analytics databases (loosely, OLAP) benefit from the use of a column-oriented DBMS. Unlike operational systems which maintain a snapshot of the business, data warehouses generally maintain an infinite history which is implemented through ETL processes that periodically migrate data from the operational systems over to the data warehouse.

Evolution in Organization Use

These terms refer to the level of sophistication of a data warehouse:

Offline operational data warehouse

> Data warehouses in this stage of evolution are updated on a regular time cycle (usually daily, weekly or monthly) from the operational systems and the data is stored in an integrated reporting-oriented data

Offline data warehouse

> Data warehouses at this stage are updated from data in the operational systems on a regular basis and the data warehouse data are stored in a data structure designed to facilitate reporting.

On time data warehouse

> Online Integrated Data Warehousing represent the real time Data warehouses stage data in the warehouse is updated for every transaction performed on the source data

Integrated data warehouse

> These data warehouses assemble data from different areas of business, so users can look up the information they need across other systems.

Distributed Database

A distributed database is a database in which storage devices are not all attached to a common processor. It may be stored in multiple computers, located in the same physical location; or may be dispersed over a network of interconnected computers. Unlike parallel systems, in which the processors are tightly coupled and constitute a single database system, a distributed database system consists of loosely coupled sites that share no physical components.

System administrators can distribute collections of data (e.g. in a database) across multiple physical locations. A distributed database can reside on organized network servers or decentralized independent computers on the Internet, on corporate intranets or extranets, or on other organization networks. Because they store data across multiple computers, distributed databases may improve performance at end-user worksites by allowing transactions to be processed on many machines, instead of being limited to one.

Two processes ensure that the distributed databases remain up-to-date and current: replication and duplication.

1. Replication involves using specialized software that looks for changes in the distributive database. Once the changes have been identified, the replication process makes all the databases look the same. The replication process can be complex and time-consuming depending on the size and number of the distributed databases. This process can also require a lot of time and computer resources.

2. Duplication, on the other hand, has less complexity. It basically identifies one database as a master and then duplicates that database. The duplication process is normally done at a set time after hours. This is to ensure that each distributed location has the same data. In the duplication process, users may change only the master database. This ensures that local data will not be overwritten.

Both replication and duplication can keep the data current in all distributive locations.

Besides distributed database replication and fragmentation, there are many other distributed database design technologies. For example, local autonomy, synchronous and asynchronous distributed database technologies. These technologies' implementations can and do depend on the needs of the business and the sensitivity/confidentiality of the data stored in the database, and the price the business is willing to spend on ensuring data security, consistency and integrity.

When discussing access to distributed databases, Microsoft favors the term distributed query, which it defines in protocol-specific manner as "[a]ny SELECT, INSERT, UPDATE, or DELETE statement that references tables and rowsets from one or more external OLE DB data sources". Oracle provides a more language-centric view in which distributed queries and distributed transactions form part of distributed SQL.

Today the distributed DBMS market is evolving dramatically, with new, innovative entrants and incumbents supporting the growing use of unstructured data and NoSQL DBMS engines, as well as XML databases and NewSQL databases. These databases are increasingly supporting distributed database architecture that provides high availability and fault tolerance through replication and scale out ability. Some examples are Aerospike, Cassandra, Clusterpoint, ClustrixDB, Couchbase, Druid (open-source data store), FoundationDB, NuoDB, Riak and OrientDB. The blockchain technology popularised by bitcoin is an implementation of a distributed database.

Architecture

A database user accesses the distributed database through:

Local applications

applications which do not require data from other sites.

Global applications

applications which do require data from other sites.

A homogeneous distributed database has identical software and hardware running all databases instances, and may appear through a single interface as if it were a single database. A heterogeneous distributed database may have different hardware, operating systems, database management systems, and even data models for different databases.

Homogeneous Distributed Databases Management System

In homogeneous distributed database all sites have identical software and are aware of each other and agree to cooperate in processing user requests. Each site surrenders part of its autonomy in terms of right to change schema or software. A homogeneous DBMS appears to the user as a single system. The homogeneous system is much easier to design and manage. The following conditions must be satisfied for homogeneous database:

- The operating system used at each location must be same or compatible.

- The data structures used at each location must be same or compatible.

- The database application (or DBMS) used at each location must be same or compatible.

Heterogeneous DDBMS

In a heterogeneous distributed database, different sites may use different schema and software. Difference in schema is a major problem for query processing and transaction processing. Sites may not be aware of each other and may provide only limited facilities for cooperation in transaction processing. In heterogeneous systems, different nodes may have different hardware & software and data structures at various nodes or locations are also incompatible. Different computers and operating systems, database applications or data models may be used at each of the locations. For example, one location may have the latest relational database management technology, while another location may store data using conventional files or old version of database management system. Similarly, one location may have the Windows 10 operating system, while another may have UNIX. Heterogeneous systems are usually used when individual sites use their own hardware and software. On heterogeneous system, translations are required to allow communication between different sites (or DBMS). In this system, the users must be able to make requests in a database language at their local sites. Usually the SQL database language is used for this purpose. If the hardware is different, then the translation is straightforward, in which computer codes and word-length is changed. The heterogeneous system is often not technically or economically feasible. In this system, a user at one location may be able to read but not update the data at another location.

Important Considerations

Care with a distributed database must be taken to ensure the following:

- The distribution is transparent — users must be able to interact with the system as if it were one logical system. This applies to the system's performance, and methods of access among other things.

- Transactions are transparent — each transaction must maintain database integrity across multiple databases. Transactions must also be divided into sub-transactions, each sub-transaction affecting one database system.

There are two principal approaches to store a relation r in a distributed database system:

A) Replication

B) Fragmentation/Partitioning

A) Replication: In replication, the system maintains several identical replicas of the same relation r in different sites.

- Data is more available in this scheme.

- Parallelism is increased when read request is served.

- Increases overhead on update operations as each site containing the replica needed to be updated in order to maintain consistency.

- Multi-datacenter replication provides geographical diversity, like in Clusterpoint or Riak.

B) Fragmentation: The relation r is fragmented into several relations $r_1, r_2, r_3....r_n$ in such a way that the actual relation could be reconstructed from the fragments and then the fragments are scattered to different locations. There are basically two schemes of fragmentation:

- Horizontal fragmentation - splits the relation by assigning each tuple of r to one or more fragments.

- Vertical fragmentation - splits the relation by decomposing the schema R of relation r.

A distributed database can be run by independent or even competing parties as, for example, in bitcoin or Hasq.

Advantages

- Management of distributed data with different levels of transparency like network transparency, fragmentation transparency, replication transparency, etc.

- Increase reliability and availability

- Easier expansion

- Reflects organizational structure — database fragments potentially stored within the departments they relate to

- Local autonomy or site autonomy — a department can control the data about them (as they are the ones familiar with it)

- Protection of valuable data — if there were ever a catastrophic event such as a fire, all of the data would not be in one place, but distributed in multiple locations

- Improved performance — data is located near the site of greatest demand, and the database systems themselves are parallelized, allowing load on the databases to be balanced among servers. (A high load on one module of the database won't affect other modules of the database in a distributed database)

- Economics — it may cost less to create a network of smaller computers with the power of a single large computer

- Modularity — systems can be modified, added and removed from the distributed database without affecting other modules (systems)

- Reliable transactions - due to replication of the database

- Hardware, operating-system, network, fragmentation, DBMS, replication and location independence

- Continuous operation, even if some nodes go offline (depending on design)

- Distributed query processing can improve performance

- Single-site failure does not affect performance of system.

- For those systems that support full distributed transactions, operations enjoy the ACID properties:

  o A-atomicity, the transaction takes place as a whole or not at all

  o C-consistency, maps one consistent DB state to another

  o I-isolation, each transaction sees a consistent DB

  o D-durability, the results of a transaction must survive system failures

The Merge Replication Method is popularly used to consolidate the data between databases.

Disadvantages

- Complexity — DBAs may have to do extra work to ensure that the distributed nature of the system is transparent. Extra work must also be done to maintain multiple disparate systems, instead of one big one. Extra database design work must also be done to account for the disconnected nature of the database — for example, joins become prohibitively expensive when performed across multiple systems.

- Economics — increased complexity and a more extensive infrastructure means extra labour costs

- Security — remote database fragments must be secured, and they are not centralized so the remote sites must be secured as well. The infrastructure must also be secured (for example, by encrypting the network links between remote sites).

- Difficult to maintain integrity — but in a distributed database, enforcing integrity over a network may require too much of the network's resources to be feasible

- Inexperience — distributed databases are difficult to work with, and in such a young field there is not much readily available experience in "proper" practice

- Lack of standards — there are no tools or methodologies yet to help users convert a centralized DBMS into a distributed DBMS

- Database design more complex — In addition to traditional database design challenges, the design of a distributed database has to consider fragmentation of data, allocation of fragments to specific sites and data replication

- Additional software is required

- Operating system should support distributed environment

- Concurrency control poses a major issue. It can be solved by locking and timestamping.

- Distributed access to data

- Analysis of distributed data

Mobile Database

Mobile computing devices (e.g., smartphones and PDAs) store and share data over a mobile network, or a database which is actually stored by the mobile device. This could be a list of contacts, price information, distance travelled, or any other information.

Many applications require the ability to download information from an information repository and operate on this information even when out of range or disconnected. An example of this is your contacts and calendar on the phone. In this scenario, a user would require access to update information from files in the home directories on a server or customer records from a database. This type of access and work load generated by such users is different from the traditional workloads seen in client–server systems of today.

Mobile databases are not used solely for the revision of company contacts and calendars, but used in a number of industries.

Considerations

- Mobile users must be able to work without a network connection due to poor or even non-existent connections. A cache could be maintained to hold recently accessed data and transactions so that they are not lost due to connection failure. Users might not require access to truly live data, only recently modified data, and uploading of changing might be deferred until reconnected.

- Bandwidth must be conserved (a common requirement on wireless networks that charge per megabyte or data transferred).

- Mobile computing devices tend to have slower CPUs and limited battery life.

- Users with multiple devices (e.g. smartphone and tablet) need to synchronize their devices to a centralized data store. This may require application-specific automation features.

This is in database theory known as "replication", and good mobile database system should provide tools for automatic replication that takes into account that others may have modified the same data as you while you were away, and not just the last update is kept, but also supports "merge" of variants.

- Users may change location geographically and on the network. Usually dealing with this is left to the operating system, which is responsible for maintaining the wireless network connection.

Products

Commercially available mobile databases include those shown on this comparison chart. *Peer To Peer (P2P) or Device To Device

Name	Developer	Type	Sync Central	Sync P2P	Description	License
Couchbase Lite	Couchbase	JSON Document	Yes	Yes	Embedded/portable database, can synchronize with multiple stationary database and/or mobile devices.	Apache 2.0 License
InterBase	Embarcadero Technologies	Relational	Dependent	Dependent	IoT Award winning embedded/portable database, can synchronize with multiple stationary database and/or mobile devices using patent pending Change Views	Proprietary
SQL Anywhere	Sybase iAnywhere	Relational	Dependent	No	Embedded/portable database, can synchronize with stationary database	Proprietary
DB2 Everyplace	IBM	Relational	Dependent	No	Portable, can synchronize with stationary database	Proprietary EULA
SQL Server Compact	Microsoft	Relational	No	No	Small-footprint embedded/portable database for Microsoft Windows mobile devices and desktops, supports synchronization with Microsoft SQL Server	Proprietary
SQL Server Express	Microsoft	Relational	No	No	Embedded database, free download	Proprietary
Oracle Database Lite	Oracle Corporation	Relational	No	No	Portable, can synchronize with stationary database	Proprietary
SQLite	D. Richard Hipp	Relational	No	No	C programming library	Public domain
SQLBase	Gupta Technologies LLC of Redwood Shores, California		No	No		Proprietary

Parallel Database

A parallel database system seeks to improve performance through parallelization of various operations, such as loading data, building indexes and evaluating queries. Although data may be stored in a distributed fashion, the distribution is governed solely by performance considerations. Parallel databases improve processing and input/output speeds by using multiple CPUs and disks in parallel. Centralized and client–server database systems are not powerful enough to handle such applications. In parallel processing, many operations are performed simultaneously, as opposed to serial processing, in which the computational steps are performed sequentially. Parallel databases can be roughly divided into two groups, the first group of architecture is the multiprocessor architecture, the alternatives of which are the following:

Shared memory architecture

> Where multiple processors share the main memory (RAM) space but each processor has its own disk (HDD). If many processes run simultaneously, the speed is reduced, the same as a computer when many parallel tasks run and the computer slows down.

Shared disk architecture

> Where each node has its own main memory, but all nodes share mass storage, usually a storage area network. In practice, each node usually also has multiple processors.

Shared nothing architecture

> Where each node has its own mass storage as well as main memory.

The other architecture group is called hybrid architecture, which includes:

- Non-Uniform Memory Architecture (NUMA), which involves the non-uniform memory access.

- Cluster (shared nothing + shared disk: SAN/NAS), which is formed by a group of connected computers.

in this switches hubs are used to connect different computers its most cheapest way and simplest way only simple topologies are used to connect different computers . much smarter if switches are implemented.

Types of parallelism :

• Interquery parallelism. Execution of multiple queries in parallel

• Interoperation parallelism - Execution of single queries that may consist of more than one operations to be performed. two forms of interoperation parallelism:

- Independent Parallelism - Execution of each operation individually in different processors only if they can be executed independent of each other. For example, if we need to join four tables, then two can be joined at one processor and the other two can be joined at another processor. Final join can be done later.

- Pipe-lined parallelism - Execution of different operations in pipe-lined fashion. For example, if we need to join three tables, one processor may join two tables and send the result set records as and when they are produced to the other processor. In the other processor the third table can be joined with the incoming records and the final result can be produced.

• Intraoperation parallelism Execution of single complex or large operations in parallel in multiple processors. For example, ORDER BY clause of a query that tries to execute on millions of records can be parallelized on multiple processors.

Graph Database

In computing, a graph database is a database that uses graph structures for semantic queries with nodes, edges and properties to represent and store data. A key concept of the system is the *graph* (or *edge* or *relationship*), which directly relates data items in the store. The relationships allow data in the store to be linked together directly, and in many cases retrieved with a single operation.

This contrasts with conventional relational databases, where links between data are stored in the data itself, and queries search for this data within the store and use the JOIN concept to collect the related data. Graph databases, by design, allow simple and rapid retrieval of complex hierarchical structures that are difficult to model in relational systems. Graph databases are similar to 1970s network-model databases in that both represent general graphs, but network-model databases operate at a lower level of abstraction and lack easy traversal over a chain of edges.

The underlying storage mechanism of graph database products varies. Some depend on a relational engine and store the graph data in a table while others use a key-value store or document-oriented database for storage, making them inherently NoSQL structures. Most graph databases based on non-relational storage engines also add the concept of *tags* or *properties*, which are essentially relationships lacking a pointer to another document. This allows data elements to be categorized for easy retrieval *en masse*.

Retrieving data from a graph database requires a query language other than SQL, which was designed for relational databases and does not elegantly handle traversing a graph. As of 2016, no single graph query language has been universally adopted in the same fashion as SQL was for relational databases, and there are a wide variety of systems - most often tightly tied to a particular product. Some standardization efforts have taken place, leading to multi-vendor query languages like Gremlin, SPARQL, and Cypher. In addition to having query language interfaces, some graph databases are accessed through APIs.

Description

Graph databases are based on graph theory. Graph databases employ nodes, edges and properties.

- Nodes represent entities such as people, businesses, accounts, or any other item you might want to keep track of. They are roughly the equivalent of the *record, relation* or *row* in a relational database, or the *document* in a document database.

- Edges, also known as *graphs* or *relationships*, are the lines that connect nodes to other nodes; they represent the relationship between them. Meaningful patterns emerge when examining the connections and interconnections of nodes, properties, and edges. Edges are the key concept in graph databases, representing an abstraction that is not directly implemented in other systems.

- Properties are pertinent information that relate to nodes. For instance, if *Wikipedia* were one of the nodes, one might have it tied to properties such as *website, reference material,* or *word that starts with the letter w*, depending on which aspects of *Wikipedia* are pertinent to the particular database.

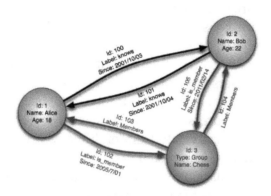

Graph databases employ nodes, properties, and edges.

The relational model gathers data together using information in the data itself. For instance, one might look for all the "users" whose phone number contains the area code "311". This would be accomplished by searching selected datastores, or tables, looking in the selected phone number fields for the string "311". This can be a time consuming process in large tables, so relational databases offer the concept of an index which allows data like this to be stored in a smaller sub-table, containing only the selected data and a unique key (or *primary key*) of the record it is part of. If the phone numbers are indexed, the same search would take place in the smaller index table, gathering the keys of matching records, and then looking in the main data table for the records with those keys. Generally, the tables are physically stored so that lookups on these keys are rapid.

Relational databases do not *inherently* contain the idea of fixed relationships between records. Instead, related data is linked to each other by storing one record's unique key in another record's data. For instance, a table containing email addresses for users might hold a data item called userpk, which contains the primary key of the user record it is associated with. In order to link users and their email addresses, the system first looks up the selected user records primary keys, looks for those keys in the userpk column in the email table (or more likely, an index of them), extracts the email data, and then links the user and email records to make composite records containing all the selected data. This operation, known as a join, can be computationally expensive. Depending on the complexity of the query, the number of joins, and the indexing of the various keys, the system may have to search through multiple tables and indexes, gather up lots of information, and then sort it all to match it together.

In contrast, graph databases directly store the relationships between records. Instead of an email address being found by looking up its user's key in the userpk column, the user record has a pointer directly to the email address record. That is, having selected a user, the pointer can be followed directly to the email records, there is no need to search the email table to find the matching records. This can eliminate the costly join operations. For instance, if one searches for all of the email addresses for users in area code "311", the engine would first perform a conventional search to find the users in "311", but then retrieve the email addresses by following the links found in those records. A relational database would first find all the users in "311", extract a list of the pk's, perform another search for any records in the email table with those pk's, and link the matching records together. For these types of common operations, a graph database (in theory at least) is significantly faster.

The true value of the graph approach becomes evident when one performs searches that are more than one level deep. For instance, consider a search for users who have "subscribers" (a table linking users to other users) in the "311" area code. In this case a relational database has to first look for all the users with an area code in "311", then look in the subscribers table for any of those users, and then finally look in the users table to retrieve the matching users. In comparison, a graph database would look for all the users in "311", then follow the back-links through the subscriber relationship to find the subscriber users. This avoids several searches, lookups and the memory involved in holding all of the temporary data from multiple records needed to construct the output. Technically, this sort of lookup is completed in $O(\log(n)) + O(1)$ time, that is, roughly relative to the logarithm of the size of the data. In comparison, the relational version would be multiple $O(\log(n))$ lookups plus additional time to join all the data.

The relative advantage of graph retrieval grows with the complexity of the query. For instance, one might want to know "that movie about submarines with the actor who was in that movie with that other actor that played the lead in Gone With the Wind". This first requires the system to find the actors in Gone With the Wind, find all the movies they were in, find all the actors in all of those movies who were not the lead in Gone With the Wind, and then find all of the movies they were in, finally filtering that list to those with descriptions containing "submarine". In a relational database this will require several separate searches through the movies and actors tables, doing another search on submarine movies, finding all the actors in those movies, and the comparing the (large) collected results. In comparison, the graph database would simply walk from Gone With the Wind to Clark Gable, gather the links to the movies he has been in, gather the links out of those movies to other actors, and then follow the links out of those actors back to the list of movies. The resulting list of movies can then be searched for "submarine". All of this can be accomplished using a single search.

Properties add another layer of abstraction to this structure that also improves many common queries. Properties are essentially labels that can be applied to any record, or in some cases, edges as well. For instance, one might label Clark Gable as "actor", which would then allow the system to quickly find all the records that are actors, as opposed to director or camera operator. If labels on edges are allowed, one could also label the relationship between Gone With the Wind and Clark Gable as "lead", and by performing a search on people that are "lead" "actor" in the movie Gone With the Wind, the database would produce Vivien Leigh, Olivia de Havilland and Clark Gable. The equivalent SQL query would have to rely on additional data in the table linking people and movies, adding more complexity to the query syntax. These sorts of labels may improve search performance under certain circumstances, but are generally more useful in providing additional semantic data for end users.

Relational databases are very well suited to flat data layouts, where relationships between data is one or two levels deep. For instance, an accounting database might need to look up all the line items for all the invoices for a given customer, a three-join query. Graph databases are aimed at datasets that contain many more links. They are especially well suited to social networking systems, where the "friends" relationship is essentially unbounded. These properties make graph databases naturally suited to types of searches that are increasingly common in online systems, and in big data environments. For this reason, graph databases are becoming very popular for large online systems like Facebook, Google, Twitter and similar systems with deep links between records.

Properties

Compared with relational databases, graph databases are often faster for associative data sets and map more directly to the structure of object-oriented applications. They can scale more naturally to large data sets as they do not typically require expensive join operations. As they depend less on a rigid schema, they are more suitable to manage ad hoc and changing data with evolving schemas. Conversely, relational databases are typically faster at performing the same operation on large numbers of data elements.

Graph databases are a powerful tool for graph-like queries, for example computing the shortest path between two nodes in the graph. Other graph-like queries can be performed over a graph database in a natural way (for example graph's diameter computations or community detection).

History

In the pre-history of graph databases, in the mid-1960s Navigational databases such as IBM's IMS supported tree-like structures in its hierarchical model, but the strict tree structure could be circumvented with virtual records.

Graph structures could be represented in network model databases from the late 1960s. CODASYL, which had defined COBOL in 1959, defined the Network Database Language in 1969.

Labeled graphs could be represented in graph databases from the mid-1980s, such as the Logical Data Model.

A number of improvements to graph databases appeared in the early 1990s, accelerating in the late 1990s with endeavors to index web pages.

In the mid-late 2000s, commercial ACID graph databases such as Neo4j and Oracle Spatial and Graph became available.

In the 2010s, commercial ACID graph databases that could be scaled horizontally became available. SAP HANA additionally brought in-memory and columnar technologies to graph databases. Also in the 2010s, Multi-model databases that supported graph models (in addition to other models such as relational database or Document-oriented database) became available, such as OrientDB, ArangoDB, and MarkLogic (starting with its 7.0 version). During this time, graph databases of various types have become particularly popular with social network analysis with the advent of social media companies.

List of Graph Databases

The following is a list of notable graph databases:

Name	Version	License	Language	Description
AllegroGraph	5.1 (May 2015)	Proprietary. Clients: Eclipse Public License v1.	C#, C, Common Lisp, Java, Python	An RDF and graph database.
ArangoDB	3.1.3 (December 2016)	Apache 2	C++, Javascript	The most popular NoSQL database available that has an open source license.
Blazegraph	2.1 (April 2016)	GPLv2, evaluation license, or commercial license.	Java	A RDF/graph database capable of clustered deployment and GPU (in the commercial version). Blazegraph supports high availability (HA) mode, embedded mode, single server mode. Supports the Blueprints and SPARQL.
Cayley	0.6.0 (September 2016)	Apache 2	Go	An open-source graph database.
DataStax Enterprise Graph	v5.0.2 (August 2016)	Proprietary	Java	A distributed, real-time, scalable graph database inspired by Titan. Supports Tinkerpop and integrates with Cassandra.
DEX/Sparksee	5.2.0 (2015)	Evaluation, research or development use is free; commercial use is not free	C++	A high-performance and scalable graph database management system from Sparsity Technologies. Its main characteristics is its query performance for the retrieval & exploration of large networks. Sparksee offers bindings for Java, C++, C#, Python and Objective-C. Sparksee 5 mobile is the first graph database for mobile devices.
InfiniteGraph	3.0 (January 2013)	Proprietary	Java	A distributed and cloud-enabled commercial product.
MarkLogic	8.0.4 (2015)	Proprietary, free developer version	Java, JavaScript, XQuery	Multi-model NoSQL database that stores documents (JSON and XML) and semantic graph data (RDF triples). MarkLogic also has a built-in search engine and a full-list of enterprise features such as ACID transactions, high availability and disaster recovery, certified security, and scalability and elasticity.

Neo4j	3.0.6 (September 2016)	GPLv3 Community Edition. Commercial & AGPLv3 options for enterprise and advanced editions	Java, .NET, JavaScript, Python	A highly scalable open source graph database that supports ACID, has high-availability clustering for enterprise deployments, and comes with a web-based administration tool that includes full transaction support and visual node-link graph explorer. Neo4j is accessible from most programming languages using its built-in REST web API interface, as well as a proprietary Bolt protocol with official drivers. Neo4j is the most popular graph database in use as of March 2016.
OpenCog		AGPL	C++, Scheme, Python	Includes a satisfiability modulo theories solver and a unified rule engine for performing both crisp (boolean) logic and probabilistic reasoning. Backed onto Postgres.
Ontotext GraphDB	7	GraphDB Free is free. GraphDB Standard and GraphDB Enterprise are commercially licensed.	Java	A graph database engine, based fully on Semantic Web standards from W3C: RDF, RDFS, OWL, SPARQL. GraphDB Free is a database engine for small projects. GraphDB Standard is robust standalone database engine. GraphDB Enterprise is a clustered version which offers horizontal scalability and failover support and other enterprise features.
OpenLink Virtuoso	7.2.4 (April 2016)	GPLv2 for Open Source Edition. Proprietary for Enterprise Edition.	C, C++	A hybrid database server handling RDF and other graph data, RDB/SQL data, XML data, filesystem documents/ objects, and free text. May be deployed as a local embedded instance (as used in the NEPOMUK Semantic Desktop), a single-instance network server, or a shared-nothing elastic-cluster multiple-instance networked server.
Oracle Spatial and Graph (part of Oracle Database)	12.1.0.2 (2014)	Proprietary	Java, PL/ SQL	1) RDF Semantic Graph: comprehensive W3C RDF graph management in Oracle Database with native reasoning and triple-level label security. 2) Network Data Model property graph: for physical/logical networks with persistent storage and a Java API for in-memory graph analytics.
Profium Sense	6.2 (November 2016)	Proprietary	Java	Profium Sense is a native in-memory graph database. Profium Sense contains a rule engine that is optimized for information streams that require continuous inferencing on-the-fly. Profium architecture is based on an in-memory database with ACID transaction support and supports distributed high-availability deployment. Profium Sense supports open standards such as RDF and SPARQL.

OrientDB	2.2.0 (May 2016)	Community Edition is Apache 2, Enterprise Edition is commercial	Java	OrientDB is an open source 2nd Generation Distributed Graph Database with the flexibility of Documents in one product (i.e., it is both a graph database and a document nosql database at the same time.) It has an open source commercial friendly (Apache 2) license. It is a highly scalable graph database with full ACID support. It has a multi-master replication and sharding. Supports schema-less, schema-full and schema-mixed modes. Has a strong security profiling system based on user and roles. Supports a query language that is so similar to SQL which is friendly to those coming from a SQL and relational database background decreasing the learning curve needed. It has HTTP REST + JSON API.
SAP HANA	SPS12 Revision 120	Proprietary	C, C++, Java, JavaScript & SQL like language	In-memory ACID transaction supported property graph
Sqrrl Enterprise	2.0 (February 2015)	Proprietary	Java	Distributed, real-time graph database featuring cell-level security and mass-scalability.
Stardog	3.1.5 (July 2015)	Proprietary	Java	Fast, scalable, pure Java semantic graph database.
Teradata Aster	v7 (2016)	Proprietary	Java, SQL, Python, C++, R	A high performance, multi-purpose, highly scalable and extensible MPP database incorporating patented engines supporting native SQL, MapReduce and Graph data storage and manipulation. An extensive set of analytical function libraries and data visualization capabilities are also provided.

APIs and Graph Query-programming Languages

- Cypher – a declarative graph query language for Neo4j that enables ad hoc and programmatic (SQL-like) access to the graph. Spec opened up as openCypher project.

- GraphQL – Facebook query language for any backend service

- Gremlin – an open-source graph programming language that works over various graph database systems. Part of the Apache TinkerPop project

- SPARQL – a query language for databases, able to retrieve and manipulate data stored in Resource Description Framework format.

References

- Silberschatz, Avi (28 January 2010). Database System Concepts, Sixth Edition (PDF). McGraw-Hill. p. D-29. ISBN 0-07-352332-1.

- Kuper, Gabriel M (1985). The Logical Data Model: A New Approach to Database Logic (PDF) (Ph.D.). Docket STAN-CS-85-1069. Retrieved 31 May 2016.

- Vaughan, Jack (25 January 2016). "Beyond gaming, GPU technology takes on graphs, machine learning". techtarget.com. TechTarget. Retrieved 30 August 2016.

- Yegulalp, Serdar (26 September 2016). "Faster with GPUs: 5 turbocharged databases". infoworld.com. InfoWorld. Retrieved 29 September 2016.

- Woodie, Alex (21 June 2016). "Beyond Titan: The Evolution of DataStax's New Graph Database". datanami.com. Datanami. Retrieved 29 August 2016.

- Vanian, Jonathan (18 February 2015). "NSA-linked Sqrrl eyes cyber security and lands $7M in funding". gigaom.com. Gigaom. Retrieved 29 August 2016.

- Woodie, Alex (23 October 2015). "The Art of Analytics, Or What the Green-Haired People Can Teach Us". datanami.com. Datanami. Retrieved 29 August 2016.

- Margaret, Alyson (23 June 2015). "How Bitcoin and the blockchain are a transformative technology". Retrieved 23 July 2015.

- "Information Theory & Business Intelligence Strategy - Small Worlds Data Transformation Measure - MIKE2.0, the open source methodology for Information Development". Mike2.openmethodology.org. Retrieved 2013-06-14.

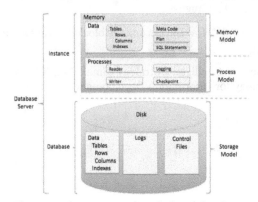

Database Systems and Models

A relational database management system is a database system. This system is based on the rational model system. The aspects of database systems that have been explained are MySQL, Microsoft SQL server, SAP HANA, Entity–relationship model, PostgreSQL etc. This chapter on database systems and models offers an insightful focus, keeping in mind the subject matter.

Relational Database Management System

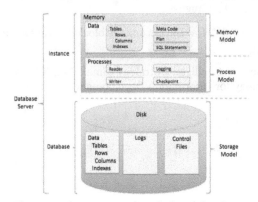

The general structure of a relational database.

A relational database management system (RDBMS) is a database management system (DBMS) that is based on the relational model as invented by E. F. Codd, of IBM's San Jose Research Laboratory. In 2016, many of the databases in widespread use are based on the relational database model.

RDBMSs have been a common choice for the storage of information in new databases used for financial records, manufacturing and logistical information, personnel data, and other applications since the 1980s. Relational databases have often replaced legacy hierarchical databases and network databases because they are easier to understand and use. However, relational databases have received unsuccessful challenge attempts by object database management systems in the 1980s and 1990s (which were introduced trying to address the so-called object-relational impedance mismatch between relational databases and object-oriented application programs) and also by XML database management systems in the 1990s. Despite such attempts, RDBMSs keep most of the market share, which has also grown over the years.

Market share

According to DB-Engines, in 2016, the most widely used systems are Oracle, MySQL (open source), Microsoft SQL Server, PostgreSQL (open source), IBM DB2, Microsoft Access, and SQLite (open source).

According to research company Gartner, in 2011, the five leading commercial relational database vendors by revenue were Oracle (48.8%), IBM (20.2%), Microsoft (17.0%), SAP including Sybase (4.6%), and Teradata (3.7%).

According to Gartner, in 2008, the percentage of database sites using any given technology were (a given site may deploy multiple technologies):

- Oracle Database – 70%

- Microsoft SQL Server – 68%

- MySQL (Oracle Corporation) – 50%

- IBM DB2 – 39%

- IBM Informix – 18%

- SAP Sybase Adaptive Server Enterprise – 15%

- SAP Sybase IQ – 14%

- Teradata – 11%

History

In 1974, IBM began developing System R, a research project to develop a prototype RDBMS. However, the first commercially available RDBMS was Oracle, released in 1979 by Relational Software, now Oracle Corporation. Other examples of an RDBMS include DB2, SAP Sybase ASE, and Informix. In 1984, the first RDBMS for Macintosh began being developed, code-named Silver Surfer, it was later released in 1987 as 4th Dimension and known today as 4D.

Historical Usage of the term

The term "relational database" was invented by E. F. Codd at IBM in 1970. Codd introduced the term in his seminal paper "A Relational Model of Data for Large Shared Data Banks". In this paper and later papers, he defined what he meant by "relational". One well-known definition of what constitutes a relational database system is composed of Codd's 12 rules. However, many of the early implementations of the relational model did not conform to all of Codd's rules, so the term gradually came to describe a broader class of database systems, which at a minimum:

- Present the data to the user as relations (a presentation in tabular form, i.e. as a *collection* of tables with each table consisting of a set of rows and columns);

- Provide relational operators to manipulate the data in tabular form.

The first systems that were relatively faithful implementations of the relational model were from the University of Michigan; Micro DBMS (1969), the Massachusetts Institute of Technology; (1971), and from IBM UK Scientific Centre at Peterlee; IS1 (1970–72) and its followon PRTV (1973–79). The first system sold as an RDBMS was Multics Relational Data Store, first sold in 1978. Others have been Ingres and IBM BS12.

The most common definition of an RDBMS is a product that presents a view of data as a collection of rows and columns, even if it is not based strictly upon relational theory. By this definition, RDBMS products typically implement some but not all of Codd's 12 rules.

A second school of thought argues that if a database does not implement all of Codd's rules (or the current understanding on the relational model, as expressed by Christopher J Date, Hugh Darwen and others), it is not relational. This view, shared by many theorists and other strict adherents to Codd's principles, would disqualify most DBMSs as not relational. For clarification, they often refer to some RDBMSs as *truly-relational database management systems* (TRDBMS), naming others *pseudo-relational database management systems* (PRDBMS).

As of 2009, most commercial relational DBMSes employ SQL as their query language.

Alternative query languages have been proposed and implemented, notably the pre-1996 implementation of Ingres QUEL.

MySQL

MySQL is an open-source relational database management system (RDBMS). Its name is a combination of "My", the name of co-founder Michael Widenius' daughter, and "SQL", the abbreviation for Structured Query Language. The MySQL development project has made its source code available under the terms of the GNU General Public License, as well as under a variety of proprietary agreements. MySQL was owned and sponsored by a single for-profit firm, the Swedish company MySQL AB, now owned by Oracle Corporation. For proprietary use, several paid editions are available, and offer additional functionality.

MySQL is a central component of the LAMP open-source web application software stack (and other "AMP" stacks). LAMP is an acronym for "Linux, Apache, MySQL, Perl/PHP/Python". Applications that use the MySQL database include: TYPO3, MODx, Joomla, WordPress, phpBB, MyBB, and Drupal. MySQL is also used in many high-profile, large-scale websites, including Google (though not for searches), Facebook, Twitter, Flickr, and YouTube.

Overview

MySQL is written in C and C++. Its SQL parser is written in yacc, but it uses a home-brewed lexical analyzer. MySQL works on many system platforms, including AIX, BSDi, FreeBSD, HP-UX, eComStation, i5/OS, IRIX, Linux, OS X, Microsoft Windows, NetBSD, Novell NetWare, OpenBSD, OpenSolaris, OS/2 Warp, QNX, Oracle Solaris, Symbian, SunOS, SCO OpenServer, SCO UnixWare, Sanos and Tru64. A port of MySQL to OpenVMS also exists.

The MySQL server software itself and the client libraries use dual-licensing distribution. They are offered under GPL version 2, beginning from 28 June 2000 (which in 2009 has been extended with a FLOSS License Exception) or to use a proprietary license.

Support can be obtained from the official manual. Free support additionally is available in different IRC channels and forums. Oracle offers paid support via its MySQL Enterprise products. They differ in the scope of services and in price. Additionally, a number of third party organisations exist to provide support and services, including MariaDB and Percona.

MySQL has received positive reviews, and reviewers noticed it "performs extremely well in the average case" and that the "developer interfaces are there, and the documentation (not to mention feedback in the real world via Web sites and the like) is very, very good". It has also been tested to be a "fast, stable and true multi-user, multi-threaded sql database server".

History

MySQL was created by a Swedish company, MySQL AB, founded by David Axmark, Allan Larsson and Michael "Monty" Widenius. Original development of MySQL by Widenius and Axmark began in 1994. The first version of MySQL appeared on 23 May 1995. It was initially created for personal usage from mSQL based on the low-level language ISAM, which the creators considered too slow and inflexible. They created a new SQL interface, while keeping the same API as mSQL. By keeping the API consistent with the mSQL system, many developers were able to use MySQL instead of the (proprietarily licensed) mSQL antecedent.

Milestones

Additional milestones in MySQL development included:

- First internal release on 23 May 1995

- Version 3.19: End of 1996, from www.tcx.se

- Version 3.20: January 1997

- Windows version was released on 8 January 1998 for Windows 95 and NT

- Version 3.21: production release 1998, from www.mysql.com

- Version 3.22: alpha, beta from 1998

- Version 3.23: beta from June 2000, production release 22 January 2001

- Version 4.0: beta from August 2002, production release March 2003 (unions)

- Version 4.01: beta from August 2003, Jyoti adopts MySQL for database tracking

- Version 4.1: beta from June 2004, production release October 2004 (R-trees and B-trees, subqueries, prepared statements)

- Version 5.0: beta from March 2005, production release October 2005 (cursors, stored procedures, triggers, views, XA transactions)

  The developer of the Federated Storage Engine states that "The Federated Storage Engine is a proof-of-concept storage engine", but the main distributions of MySQL version 5.0 included it and turned it on by default. Documentation of some of the short-comings appears in "MySQL Federated Tables: The Missing Manual".

- Sun Microsystems acquired MySQL AB in 2008.

- Version 5.1: production release 27 November 2008 (event scheduler, partitioning, plugin API, row-based replication, server log tables)

Version 5.1 contained 20 known crashing and wrong result bugs in addition to the 35 present in version 5.0 *(almost all fixed as of release 5.1.51)*.

MySQL 5.1 and 6.0-alpha showed poor performance when used for data warehousing – partly due to its inability to utilize multiple CPU cores for processing a single query.

- Oracle acquired Sun Microsystems on 27 January 2010.

- The day Oracle announced the purchase of Sun, Michael "Monty" Widenius forked MySQL, launching MariaDB, and took a swath of MySQL developers with him.

- MySQL Server 5.5 was generally available (as of December 2010). Enhancements and features include:

    o The default storage engine is InnoDB, which supports transactions and referential integrity constraints.

    o Improved InnoDB I/O subsystem

    o Improved SMP support

    o Semisynchronous replication.

    o SIGNAL and RESIGNAL statement in compliance with the SQL standard.

    o Support for supplementary Unicode character sets utf16, utf32, and utf8mb4.

    o New options for user-defined partitioning.

- MySQL Server 6.0.11-alpha was announced on 22 May 2009 as the last release of the 6.0 line. Future MySQL Server development uses a New Release Model. Features developed for 6.0 are being incorporated into future releases.

- The general availability of MySQL 5.6 was announced in February 2013. New features included performance improvements to the query optimizer, higher transactional throughput in InnoDB, new NoSQL-style memcached APIs, improvements to partitioning for querying and managing very large tables, TIMESTAMP column type that correctly stores milliseconds, improvements to replication, and better performance monitoring by expanding the data available through the PERFORMANCE_SCHEMA. The InnoDB storage engine also included support for full-text search and improved group commit performance.

- The general availability of MySQL 5.7 was announced in October 2015.

- MySQL Server 8.0.0-dmr (Milestone Release) was announced 12 September 2016.

Legal Disputes and Acquisitions

On 15 June 2001, NuSphere sued MySQL AB, TcX DataKonsult AB and its original authors Michael ("Monty") Widenius and David Axmark in U.S District Court in Boston for "breach of contract, tortious interference with third party contracts and relationships and unfair competition".

In 2002, MySQL AB sued Progress NuSphere for copyright and trademark infringement in United States district court. NuSphere had allegedly violated MySQL's copyright by linking MySQL's GPL'ed code with NuSphere Gemini table without being in compliance with the license. After a preliminary hearing before Judge Patti Saris on 27 February 2002, the parties entered settlement talks and eventually settled. After the hearing, FSF commented that "Judge Saris made clear that she sees the GNU GPL to be an enforceable and binding license."

In October 2005, Oracle Corporation acquired Innobase OY, the Finnish company that developed the third-party InnoDB storage engine that allows MySQL to provide such functionality as transactions and foreign keys. After the acquisition, an Oracle press release mentioned that the contracts that make the company's software available to MySQL AB would be due for renewal (and presumably renegotiation) some time in 2006. During the MySQL Users Conference in April 2006, MySQL issued a press release that confirmed that MySQL and Innobase OY agreed to a "multi-year" extension of their licensing agreement.

In February 2006, Oracle Corporation acquired Sleepycat Software, makers of the Berkeley DB, a database engine providing the basis for another MySQL storage engine. This had little effect, as Berkeley DB was not widely used, and was dropped (due to lack of use) in MySQL 5.1.12, a pre-GA release of MySQL 5.1 released in October 2006.

In January 2008, Sun Microsystems bought MySQL for $1 billion.

In April 2009, Oracle Corporation entered into an agreement to purchase Sun Microsystems, then owners of MySQL copyright and trademark. Sun's board of directors unanimously approved the deal. It was also approved by Sun's shareholders, and by the U.S. government on 20 August 2009. On 14 December 2009, Oracle pledged to continue to enhance MySQL as it had done for the previous four years.

A movement against Oracle's acquisition of MySQL, to "Save MySQL" from Oracle was started by one of the MySQL founders, Monty Widenius. The petition of 50,000+ developers and users called upon the European Commission to block approval of the acquisition. At the same time, several Free Software opinion leaders (including Eben Moglen, Pamela Jones of Groklaw, Jan Wildeboer and Carlo Piana, who also acted as co-counsel in the merger regulation procedure) advocated for the unconditional approval of the merger. As part of the negotiations with the European Commission, Oracle committed that MySQL server will continue until at least 2015 to use the dual-licensing strategy long used by MySQL AB, with proprietary and GPL versions available. The antitrust of the EU had been "pressuring it to divest MySQL as a condition for approval of the merger". But, as revealed by WikiLeaks, the US Department of Justice and Antitrust, at the request of Oracle, pressured the EU to approve the merger unconditionally. The European Commission eventually unconditionally approved Oracle's acquisition of MySQL on 21 January 2010.

In January 2009, prior to Oracle's acquisition of MySQL, Monty Widenius started a GPL-only fork, MariaDB. MariaDB is based on the same code base as MySQL server 5.5 and aims to maintain compatibility with Oracle-provided versions.

Features

MySQL is offered under two different editions: the open source MySQL Community Server and the proprietary Enterprise Server. MySQL Enterprise Server is differentiated by a series of proprietary extensions which install as server plugins, but otherwise shares the version numbering system and is built from the same code base.

Major features as available in MySQL 5.6:

- A broad subset of ANSI SQL 99, as well as extensions

- Cross-platform support

- Stored procedures, using a procedural language that closely adheres to SQL/PSM

- Triggers

- Cursors

- Updatable views

- Online DDL when using the InnoDB Storage Engine.

- Information schema

- Performance Schema that collects and aggregates statistics about server execution and query performance for monitoring purposes.

- A set of SQL Mode options to control runtime behavior, including a strict mode to better adhere to SQL standards.

- X/Open XA distributed transaction processing (DTP) support; two phase commit as part of this, using the default InnoDB storage engine

- Transactions with savepoints when using the default InnoDB Storage Engine. The NDB Cluster Storage Engine also supports transactions.

- ACID compliance when using InnoDB and NDB Cluster Storage Engines

- SSL support

- Query caching

- Sub-SELECTs (i.e. nested SELECTs)

- Built-in replication support (i.e., master-master replication and master-slave replication) with one master per slave, many slaves per master. Multi-master replication is provided in MySQL Cluster, and multi-master support can be added to unclustered configurations using Galera Cluster.

- Full-text indexing and searching

- Embedded database library

- Unicode support

- Partitioned tables with pruning of partitions in optimizer

- Shared-nothing clustering through MySQL Cluster

- Multiple storage engines, allowing one to choose the one that is most effective for each table in the application.

- Native storage engines InnoDB, MyISAM, Merge, Memory (heap), Federated, Archive, CSV, Blackhole, NDB Cluster.

- Commit grouping, gathering multiple transactions from multiple connections together to increase the number of commits per second.

The developers release minor updates of the MySQL Server approximately every two months. The sources can be obtained from MySQL's website or from MySQL's GitHub repository, both under the GPL license.

Limitations

When using some storage engines other than the default of InnoDB, MySQL does not comply with the full SQL standard for some of the implemented functionality, including foreign key references and check constraints.

Up until MySQL 5.7, triggers are limited to one per action / timing, meaning that at most one trigger can be defined to be executed after an INSERT operation, and one before INSERT on the same table. No triggers can be defined on views.

MySQL database's inbuilt functions like UNIX_TIMESTAMP() will return 0 after 03:14:07 UTC on 19 January 2038.

Deployment

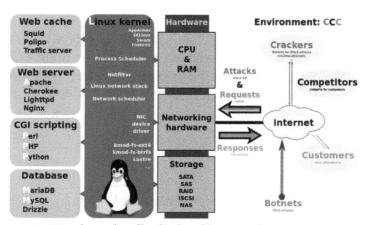

LAMP software bundle, displayed here together with Squid.

MySQL can be built and installed manually from source code, but it is more commonly installed from a binary package unless special customizations are required. On most Linux distributions, the package management system can download and install MySQL with minimal effort, though further configuration is often required to adjust security and optimization settings.

Though MySQL began as a low-end alternative to more powerful proprietary databases, it has gradually evolved to support higher-scale needs as well. It is still most commonly used in small to medium scale single-server deployments, either as a component in a LAMP-based web application or as a standalone database server. Much of MySQL's appeal originates in its relative simplicity and ease of use, which is enabled by an ecosystem of open source tools such as phpMyAdmin. In the medium range, MySQL can be scaled by deploying it on more powerful hardware, such as a multi-processor server with gigabytes of memory.

There are, however, limits to how far performance can scale on a single server ('scaling up'), so on larger scales, multi-server MySQL ('scaling out') deployments are required to provide improved performance and reliability. A typical high-end configuration can include a powerful master database which handles data write operations and is replicated to multiple slaves that handle all read operations. The master server continually pushes binlog events to connected slaves so in the event of failure a slave can be promoted to become the new master, minimizing downtime. Further improvements in performance can be achieved by caching the results from database queries in memory using memcached, or breaking down a database into smaller chunks called shards which can be spread across a number of distributed server clusters.

Backup Software

mysqldump is a logical backup tool included with both community and enterprise editions of MySQL. It supports backing up from all storage engines. MySQL Enterprise Backup is a hot backup utility included as part of the MySQL Enterprise subscription from Oracle, offering native InnoDB hot backup, as well as backup for other storage engines.

XtraBackupp is an open-source MySQL hot backup software program. Features include hot, non-locking backups for InnoDB storage, incremental backups, streaming, parallel-compressed backups, throttling based on the number of I/O operations per second, etc.

High Availability Software

MySQL Fabric is an integrated system for managing a collection of MySQL servers, and a framework on top of which high availability and database sharding is built. MySQL Fabric is opensource, and supports procedure execution in the presence of failure, providing an execution model usually called *resilient execution*. MySQL client libraries are extended so they are hiding the complexities of handling failover in the event of a server failure, as well as correctly dispatching transactions to the shards.

Cloud Deployment

MySQL can also be run on cloud computing platforms such as Amazon EC2. Some common deployment models for MySQL on the cloud are:

Virtual machine image

> In this implementation, cloud users can upload a machine image of their own with MySQL installed, or use a ready-made machine image with an optimized installation of MySQL on it, such as the one provided by Amazon EC2.

MySQL as a service

> Some cloud platforms offer MySQL "as a service". In this configuration, application owners do not have to install and maintain the MySQL database on their own. Instead, the database service provider takes responsibility for installing and maintaining the database, and application owners pay according to their usage. Notable cloud-based MySQL services are the Amazon Relational Database Service; Rackspace; HP Converged Cloud; Heroku and Jelastic.

User Interfaces

Graphical User Interfaces

A graphical user interface (GUI) is a type of interface that allows users to interact with electronic devices or programs through graphical icons and visual indicators such as secondary notation, as opposed to text-based interfaces, typed command labels or text navigation. GUIs are easier to learn than command-line interfaces (CLIs), which require commands to be typed on the keyboard.

Third-party proprietary and free graphical administration applications (or "front ends") are available that integrate with MySQL and enable users to work with database structure and data visually. Some well-known front ends are:

MySQL Workbench running on OS X

MySQL Workbench

> MySQL Workbench is the official integrated environment for MySQL. It was developed by MySQL AB, and enables users to graphically administer MySQL databases and visually design database structures. MySQL Workbench replaces the previous package of software, MySQL GUI Tools. Similar to other third-party packages, but still considered the authoritative MySQL front end, MySQL Workbench lets users manage database design & modeling, SQL development (replacing MySQL Query Browser) and Database administration (replacing MySQL Administrator).

> MySQL Workbench is available in two editions, the regular free and open source *Community Edition* which may be downloaded from the MySQL website, and the proprietary *Standard Edition* which extends and improves the feature set of the Community Edition.

Adminer

Adminer (formerly known as phpMinAdmin) is a free MySQL front end for managing content in MySQL databases (since version 2, it also works on PostgreSQL, MS SQL, SQLite and Oracle SQL databases). Adminer is distributed under the Apache license (or GPL v2) in the form of a single PHP file (around 300 KiB in size), and is capable of managing multiple databases, with many CSS skins available. Its author is Jakub Vrána who started to develop this tool as a light-weight alternative to phpMyAdmin, in July 2007.

Database Workbench

Database Workbench is a software application for development and administration of multiple relational databases using SQL, with interoperationality between different database systems, developed by Upscene Productions.

Because Databases Workbench supports multiple database systems, it can provide software developers with the same interface and development environment for these otherwise different database systems and also includes cross database tools.

Database Workbench supports the following relational databases: Oracle Database, Microsoft SQL Server, SQL Anywhere, Firebird, NexusDB, InterBase, MySQL and MariaDB. Database Workbench 5 runs on 32-bit or 64 bit Windows platforms. Under Linux, FreeBSD or Mac OS X Database Workbench can operate using Wine.

DBEdit

DBEdit is a database editor, which can connect to an Oracle, DB2, MySQL and any database that provides a JDBC driver. It runs on Windows, Linux and Solaris. DBEdit is free and open source software and distributed under the GNU General Public License. The source code is hosted on SourceForge.

HeidiSQL

HeidiSQL, previously known as MySQL-Front, is a free and open source client, or frontend for MySQL (and for its forks like MariaDB and Percona Server), Microsoft SQL Server and PostgreSQL. HeidiSQL is developed by German programmer Ansgar Becker and a few other contributors in Delphi. To manage databases with HeidiSQL, users must login to a local or remote MySQL server with acceptable credentials, creating a session. Within this session users may manage MySQL Databases within the connected MySQL server, disconnecting from the server when done. Its feature set is sufficient for most common and advanced database, table and data record operations but remains in active development to move towards the full functionality expected in a MySQL Frontend.

LibreOffice Base

LibreOffice Base allows the creation and management of databases, preparation of forms and reports that provide end users easy access to data. Like Microsoft Access, it can be used as a front-end for various database systems, including Access databases (JET), ODBC data sources, and MySQL or PostgreSQL

Navicat

Navicat is a series of graphical database management and development software produced by PremiumSoft CyberTech Ltd. for MySQL, MariaDB, Oracle, SQLite, PostgreSQL and Microsoft SQL Server. It has an Explorer-like graphical user interface and supports multiple database connections for local and remote databases. Its design is made to meet the needs of a variety of audiences, from database administrators and programmers to various businesses/companies that serve clients and share information with partners.

Navicat is a cross-platform tool and works on Microsoft Windows, OS X and Linux platforms. Upon purchase, users are able to select a language for the software from eight available languages: English, French, German, Spanish, Japanese, Polish, Simplified Chinese and Traditional Chinese.

OpenOffice.org

OpenOffice.org Base is freely available and can manage MySQL databases if the entire suite is installed.

phpMyAdmin

phpMyAdmin is a free and open source tool written in PHP intended to handle the administration of MySQL with the use of a web browser. It can perform various tasks such as creating, modifying or deleting databases, tables, fields or rows; executing SQL statements; or managing users and permissions. The software, which is available in 78 languages, is maintained by *The phpMyAdmin Project*.

It can import data from CSV and SQL, and transform stored data into any format using a set of predefined functions, like displaying BLOB-data as images or download-links.

SQLBuddy

SQLBuddy is an open-source web-based application written in PHP intended to handle the administration of MySQL and SQLite with the use of a Web browser. The project places an emphasis on ease of installation and a simple user interface.

SQLeo

SQLeo is a Visual query builder that helps users create or understand SQL queries. The source code is hosted on SourceForge.

SQLyog

SQLyog is a GUI tool available in free as well as paid versions. Data manipulations (e.g., insert, update, and delete) may be done from a spreadsheet-like interface. Its editor has syntax highlighting and various automatic formatting options. Both raw table data and a result set from a query can be manipulated. Its data search feature uses Google-like search syntax and translates to SQL transparently for the user. It has a backup tool for performing unattended backups. Backups may be compressed and optionally stored as a file-per-table as well as identified with a timestamp.

Toad for MySQL

Toad for MySQL is a software application from Dell Software that database developers, database administrators and data analysts use to manage both relational and non-relational databases using SQL. Toad supports many databases and environments. It runs on all 32-bit/64-bit Windows platforms, including Microsoft Windows Server, Windows XP, Windows Vista, Windows 7 and 8 (32-Bit or 64-Bit). Dell Software has also released a Toad Mac Edition. Dell provides Toad in commercial and trial/freeware versions. The freeware version is available from the ToadWorld.com community.

Webmin

Webmin is a web-based system configuration tool for Unix-like systems, although recent versions can also be installed and run on Windows. With it, it is possible to configure operating system internals, such as users, disk quotas, services or configuration files, as well as modify and control open source apps, such as the Apache HTTP Server, PHP or MySQL.

Webmin is largely based on Perl, running as its own process and web server. It defaults to TCP port 10000 for communicating, and can be configured to use SSL if OpenSSL is installed with additional required Perl Modules.

It is built around modules, which have an interface to the configuration files and the Webmin server. This makes it easy to add new functionality. Due to Webmin's modular design, it is possible for anyone who is interested to write plugins for desktop configuration.

Webmin also allows for controlling many machines through a single interface, or seamless login on other webmin hosts on the same subnet or LAN.

Command-line Interfaces

A command-line interface is a means of interacting with a computer program where the user issues commands to the program by typing in successive lines of text (command lines). MySQL ships with many command line tools, from which the main interface is the mysql client.

MySQL Utilities is a set of utilities designed to perform common maintenance and administrative tasks. Originally included as part of the MySQL Workbench, the utilities are a stand-alone download available from Oracle.

Percona Toolkit is a cross-platform toolkit for MySQL, developed in Perl. Percona Toolkit can be used to prove replication is working correctly, fix corrupted data, automate repetitive tasks, and speed up servers. Percona Toolkit is included with several Linux distributions such as CentOS and Debian, and packages are available for Fedora and Ubuntu as well. Percona Toolkit was originally developed as Maatkit, but as of late 2011, Maatkit is no longer developed.

Application Programming Interfaces

Many programming languages with language-specific APIs include libraries for accessing MySQL databases. These include MySQL Connector/Net for integration with Microsoft's Visual Studio (languages such as C# and VB are most commonly used) and the JDBC driver for Java. In addition, an ODBC interface called MySQL Connector/ODBC allows additional programming languages that support the ODBC interface to communicate with a MySQL database, such as ASP or ColdFusion. The HTSQL – URL-based query method also ships with a MySQL adapter, allowing direct interaction between a MySQL database and any web client via structured URLs.

Project Forks

In software engineering, a project fork happens when developers take a copy of source code from one software package and start independent development on it, creating a distinct and separate piece of software – a new (third-party) version. The term often implies not merely creating a development branch, but also a split in the developer community (a form of schism). MySQL forks include the following:

Drizzle

> Drizzle is a free software/open source relational database management system (DBMS) that was forked from the now-defunct 6.0 development branch of the MySQL DBMS. Like MySQL, Drizzle has a client/server architecture and uses SQL as its primary command language. Drizzle is distributed under version 2 and 3 of the GNU General Public License (GPL) with portions, including the protocol drivers and replication messaging under the BSD license.

MariaDB

> MariaDB is a community-developed fork of the MySQL relational database management system intended to remain free under the GNU GPL. Being a fork of a leading open source software system, it is notable for being led by the original developers of MySQL, who forked it due to concerns over its acquisition by Oracle. Contributors are required to share their copyright with the MariaDB Foundation. MariaDB intends to maintain high compatibility with MySQL, ensuring a "drop-in" replacement capability with library binary equivalency and exact matching with MySQL APIs and commands. There are some documented differences and incompatibilities between versions of MySQL and MariaDB, however, and some tools for interacting with MySQL, such as the MySQL Workbench, are not fully compatible with MariaDB. It includes the XtraDB storage engine for replacing InnoDB, as well as a new storage engine, Aria, that intends to be both a transactional and non-transactional engine perhaps even included in future versions of MySQL.

Percona Server

> Percona Server, forked by Percona, aims to retain close compatibility to the official MySQL releases, while focusing on performance and increased visibility into server operations. Also included in Percona Server is XtraDB, Percona's fork of the InnoDB Storage Engine. Percona freely includes a number of scalability, availability, security and backup features only available in MySQL's commercial Enterprise edition.

WebScaleSQL

> WebScaleSQL is a software branch of MySQL 5.6, and was announced on 27 March 2014 by Facebook, Google, LinkedIn and Twitter as a joint effort to provide a centralized development structure for extending MySQL with new features specific to its large-scale deployments, such as building large replicated databases running on server farms. Thus, WebScaleSQL opens a path toward deduplicating the efforts each company had been putting into maintaining its own branch of MySQL, and toward bringing together more developers. By combining the efforts of these companies and incorporating various changes and new features into MySQL, WebScaleSQL aims at supporting the deployment of MySQL in large-scale environments. The project's source code is licensed under version 2 of the GNU General Public License, and is hosted on GitHub.

Microsoft SQL Server

Microsoft SQL Server is a relational database management system developed by Microsoft. As a database server, it is a software product with the primary function of storing and retrieving data as requested by other software applications—which may run either on the same computer or on another computer across a network (including the Internet).

Microsoft markets at least a dozen different editions of Microsoft SQL Server, aimed at different audiences and for workloads ranging from small single-machine applications to large Internet-facing applications with many concurrent users.

History

The history of Microsoft SQL Server begins with the first Microsoft SQL Server product - SQL Server 1.0, a 16-bit server for the OS/2 operating system in 1989 - and extends to the current day.

As of December 2016 the following versions are supported by Microsoft:

- SQL Server 2008
- SQL Server 2008 R2
- SQL Server 2012
- SQL Server 2014
- SQL Server 2016

The current version is Microsoft SQL Server 2016, released June 1, 2016. The RTM version is 13.0.1601.5.

SQL Server 2016 is supported on x64 processors only.

Editions

Microsoft makes SQL Server available in multiple editions, with different feature sets and targeting different users. These editions are:

Mainstream Editions

Enterprise

SQL Server Enterprise Edition includes both the core database engine and add-on services, with a range of tools for creating and managing a SQL Server cluster. It can manage databases as large as 524 petabytes and address 12 terabytes of memory and supports 640 logical processors (cpu cores).

Standard

SQL Server Standard edition includes the core database engine, along with the stand-alone services. It differs from Enterprise edition in that it supports fewer active instances (number of nodes in a cluster) and does not include some high-availability functions such as hot-add memory (allowing memory to be added while the server is still running), and parallel indexes.

Web

SQL Server Web Edition is a low-TCO option for Web hosting.

Business Intelligence

Introduced in SQL Server 2012 and focusing on Self Service and Corporate Business Intelligence. It includes the Standard Edition capabilities and Business Intelligence tools: PowerPivot, Power View, the BI Semantic Model, Master Data Services, Data Quality Services and xVelocity in-memory analytics.

Workgroup

SQL Server Workgroup Edition includes the core database functionality but does not include the additional services. Note that this edition has been retired in SQL Server 2012.

Express

SQL Server Express Edition is a scaled down, free edition of SQL Server, which includes the core database engine. While there are no limitations on the number of databases or users supported, it is limited to using one processor, 1 GB memory and 10 GB database files (4 GB database files prior to SQL Server Express 2008 R2). It is intended as a replacement for MSDE. Two additional editions provide a superset of features not in the original Express Edition. The first is *SQL Server Express with Tools*, which includes SQL Server Management Studio Basic. *SQL Server Express with Advanced Services* adds full-text search capability and reporting services.

Specialized Editions

Azure

Azure SQL Database is the cloud-based version of Microsoft SQL Server, presented as a platform as a service offering on Microsoft Azure.

Compact (SQL CE)

The compact edition is an embedded database engine. Unlike the other editions of SQL Server, the SQL CE engine is based on SQL Mobile (initially designed for use with hand-held devices) and does not share the same binaries. Due to its small size (1 MB DLL foot-print), it has a markedly reduced feature set compared to the other editions. For example, it supports a subset of the standard data types, does not support stored procedures or Views or multiple-statement batches (among other limitations). It is limited to 4 GB maximum database size and cannot be run as a Windows service, Compact Edition must be hosted by the application using it. The 3.5 version includes support for ADO.NET Synchronization Services. SQL CE does not support ODBC connectivity, unlike SQL Server proper.

Developer

SQL Server Developer Edition includes the same features as SQL Server Enterprise Edition, but is limited by the license to be only used as a development and test system, and not as pro-duction server. Starting early 2016, Microsoft made this version free of charge to the public.

Embedded (SSEE)

SQL Server 2005 Embedded Edition is a specially configured named instance of the SQL Server Express database engine which can be accessed only by certain Windows Services.

Evaluation

SQL Server Evaluation Edition, also known as the *Trial Edition*, has all the features of the Enterprise Edition, but is limited to 180 days, after which the tools will continue to run, but the server services will stop.

Fast Track

SQL Server Fast Track is specifically for enterprise-scale data warehousing storage and business intelligence processing, and runs on reference-architecture hardware that is op-timized for Fast Track.

LocalDB

Introduced in SQL Server Express 2012, LocalDB is a minimal, on-demand, version of SQL Server that is designed for application developers. It can also be used as an embedded database.

Analytics Platform System (APS)

Formerly Parallel Data Warehouse (PDW) A massively parallel processing (MPP) SQL Server appliance optimized for large-scale data warehousing such as hundreds of terabytes.

Datawarehouse Appliance Edition

Pre-installed and configured as part of an appliance in partnership with Dell & HP base on the Fast Track architecture. This edition does not include SQL Server Integration Services, Analysis Services, or Reporting Services.

Discontinued Editions

MSDE

> Microsoft SQL Server Data Engine / Desktop Engine / Desktop Edition. SQL Server 7 and SQL Server 2000. Intended for use as an application component, it did not include GUI management tools. Later, Microsoft also made available a web admin tool. Included with some versions of Microsoft Access, Microsoft development tools, and other editions of SQL Server.

Personal Edition

> SQL Server 2000. Had workload or connection limits like MSDE, but no database size limit. Includes standard management tools. Intended for use as a mobile / disconnected proxy, licensed for use with SQL Server 2000 Standard edition.

Datacenter

> SQL Server 2008 R2 Datacenter is a full-featured edition of SQL Server and is designed for datacenters that need high levels of application support and scalability. It supports 256 logical processors and virtually unlimited memory and comes with StreamInsight Premium edition. The Datacenter edition has been retired in SQL Server 2012; all of its features are available in SQL Server 2012 Enterprise Edition.

Architecture

The protocol layer implements the external interface to SQL Server. All operations that can be invoked on SQL Server are communicated to it via a Microsoft-defined format, called Tabular Data Stream (TDS). TDS is an application layer protocol, used to transfer data between a database server and a client. Initially designed and developed by Sybase Inc. for their Sybase SQL Server relational database engine in 1984, and later by Microsoft in Microsoft SQL Server, TDS packets can be encased in other physical transport dependent protocols, including TCP/IP, named pipes, and shared memory. Consequently, access to SQL Server is available over these protocols. In addition, the SQL Server API is also exposed over web services.

Data Storage

Data storage is a database, which is a collection of tables with typed columns. SQL Server supports different data types, including primary types such as *Integer*, *Float*, *Decimal*, *Char* (including character strings), *Varchar* (variable length character strings), binary (for unstructured blobs of data), *Text* (for textual data) among others. The rounding of floats to integers uses either Symmetric Arithmetic Rounding or Symmetric Round Down (*fix*) depending on arguments: SELECT Round(2.5, 0) gives 3.

Microsoft SQL Server also allows user-defined composite types (UDTs) to be defined and used. It also makes server statistics available as virtual tables and views (called Dynamic Management Views or DMVs). In addition to tables, a database can also contain other objects including views, stored procedures, indexes and constraints, along with a transaction log. A SQL Server database can contain a maximum of 2^{31} objects, and can span multiple OS-level files with a maximum file size of 2^{60} bytes (1 exabyte). The data in the database are stored in primary data files with an extension .mdf. Secondary data files, identified with a .ndf extension, are used to allow the data of a single database to be spread across more than one file, and optionally across more than one file system. Log files are identified with the .ldf extension.

Storage space allocated to a database is divided into sequentially numbered *pages*, each 8 KB in size. A *page* is the basic unit of I/O for SQL Server operations. A page is marked with a 96-byte header which stores metadata about the page including the page number, page type, free space on the page and the ID of the object that owns it. Page type defines the data contained in the page: data stored in the database, index, allocation map which holds information about how pages are allocated to tables and indexes, change map which holds information about the changes made to other pages since last backup or logging, or contain large data types such as image or text. While page is the basic unit of an I/O operation, space is actually managed in terms of an *extent* which consists of 8 pages. A database object can either span all 8 pages in an extent ("uniform extent") or share an extent with up to 7 more objects ("mixed extent"). A row in a database table cannot span more than one page, so is limited to 8 KB in size. However, if the data exceeds 8 KB and the row contains *varchar* or *varbinary* data, the data in those columns are moved to a new page (or possibly a sequence of pages, called an *allocation unit*) and replaced with a pointer to the data.

For physical storage of a table, its rows are divided into a series of partitions (numbered 1 to n). The partition size is user defined; by default all rows are in a single partition. A table is split into multiple partitions in order to spread a database over a computer cluster. Rows in each partition are stored in either B-tree or heap structure. If the table has an associated, clustered index to allow fast retrieval of rows, the rows are stored in-order according to their index values, with a B-tree providing the index. The data is in the leaf node of the leaves, and other nodes storing the index values for the leaf data reachable from the respective nodes. If the index is non-clustered, the rows are not sorted according to the index keys. An indexed view has the same storage structure as an indexed table. A table without a clustered index is stored in an unordered heap structure. However, the table may have non-clustered indices to allow fast retrieval of rows. In some situations the heap structure has performance advantages over the clustered structure. Both heaps and B-trees can span multiple allocation units.

Buffer Management

SQL Server buffers pages in RAM to minimize disk I/O. Any 8 KB page can be buffered in-memory, and the set of all pages currently buffered is called the buffer cache. The amount of memory available to SQL Server decides how many pages will be cached in memory. The buffer cache is managed by the *Buffer Manager*. Either reading from or writing to any page copies it to the buffer cache. Subsequent reads or writes are redirected to the in-memory copy, rather than the on-disc version. The page is updated on the disc by the Buffer Manager only if the in-memory cache has not been referenced for some time. While writing pages back to disc, asynchronous I/O is used whereby the I/O operation is done in a background thread so that other operations do not have to wait for the I/O operation to complete. Each page is written along with its checksum when it is written. When reading the page back, its checksum is computed again and matched with the stored version to ensure the page has not been damaged or tampered with in the meantime.

Concurrency and Locking

SQL Server allows multiple clients to use the same database concurrently. As such, it needs to control concurrent access to shared data, to ensure data integrity—when multiple clients update the same data, or clients attempt to read data that is in the process of being changed by another client. SQL Server provides two modes of concurrency control: pessimistic concurrency and optimistic concurrency. When pessimistic concurrency control is being used, SQL Server controls concurrent access by using locks. Locks can be either shared or exclusive. Exclusive lock grants the user exclusive access to the data—no other user can access the data as long as the lock is held. Shared locks are used when some data is being read—multiple users can read from data locked with a shared lock, but not acquire an exclusive lock. The latter would have to wait for all shared locks to be released. Locks can be applied on different levels of granularity—on entire tables, pages, or even on a per-row basis on tables. For indexes, it can either be on the entire index or on index leaves. The level of granularity to be used is defined on a per-database basis by the database administrator. While a fine grained locking system allows more users to use the table or index simultaneously, it requires more resources. So it does not automatically turn into higher performing solution. SQL Server also includes two more lightweight mutual exclusion solutions—latches and spinlocks—which are less robust than locks but are less resource intensive. SQL Server uses them for DMVs and other resources that are usually not busy. SQL Server also monitors all worker threads that acquire locks to ensure that they do not end up in deadlocks—in case they do, SQL Server takes remedial measures, which in many cases is to kill one of the threads entangled in a deadlock and rollback the transaction it started. To implement locking, SQL Server contains the *Lock Manager*. The Lock Manager maintains an in-memory table that manages the database objects and locks, if any, on them along with other metadata about the lock. Access to any shared object is mediated by the lock manager, which either grants access to the resource or blocks it.

SQL Server also provides the optimistic concurrency control mechanism, which is similar to the multiversion concurrency control used in other databases. The mechanism allows a new version of a row to be created whenever the row is updated, as opposed to overwriting the row, i.e., a row is additionally identified by the ID of the transaction that created the version of the row. Both the old as well as the new versions of the row are stored and maintained, though the old versions are moved out of the database into a system database identified as Tempdb. When a row is in the process of being updated, any other requests are not blocked (unlike locking) but are executed on the older version of the row. If the other request is an update statement, it will result in two different versions of the rows—both of them will be stored by the database, identified by their respective transaction IDs.

Data Retrieval and Programmability

The main mode of retrieving data from a SQL Server database is querying for it. The query is expressed using a variant of SQL called T-SQL, a dialect Microsoft SQL Server shares with Sybase SQL Server due to its legacy. The query declaratively specifies what is to be retrieved. It is processed by the query processor, which figures out the sequence of steps that will be necessary to retrieve the requested data. The sequence of actions necessary to execute a query is called a query plan. There might be multiple ways to process the same query. For example, for a query that contains a join statement and a select statement, executing join on both the tables and then executing select on the results would give the same result as selecting from each table and then executing the join, but result in different execution plans. In such case, SQL Server chooses the plan that is expected to yield the results in the shortest possible time. This is called query optimization and is performed by the query processor itself.

SQL Server includes a cost-based query optimizer which tries to optimize on the cost, in terms of the resources it will take to execute the query. Given a query, then the query optimizer looks at the database schema, the database statistics and the system load at that time. It then decides which sequence to access the tables referred in the query, which sequence to execute the operations and what access method to be used to access the tables. For example, if the table has an associated index, whether the index should be used or not: if the index is on a column which is not unique for most of the columns (low "selectivity"), it might not be worthwhile to use the index to access the data. Finally, it decides whether to execute the query concurrently or not. While a concurrent execution is more costly in terms of total processor time, because the execution is actually split to different processors might mean it will execute faster. Once a query plan is generated for a query, it is temporarily cached. For further invocations of the same query, the cached plan is used. Unused plans are discarded after some time.

SQL Server also allows stored procedures to be defined. Stored procedures are parameterized T-SQL queries, that are stored in the server itself (and not issued by the client application as is the case with general queries). Stored procedures can accept values sent by the client as input parameters, and send back results as output parameters. They can call defined functions, and other stored procedures, including the same stored procedure (up to a set number of times). They can be selectively provided access to. Unlike other queries, stored procedures have an associated name, which is used at runtime to resolve into the actual queries. Also because the code need not be sent from the client every time (as it can be accessed by name), it reduces network traffic and somewhat improves performance. Execution plans for stored procedures are also cached as necessary.

T-SQL

T-SQL (Transact-SQL) is the secondary means of programming and managing SQL Server. It exposes keywords for the operations that can be performed on SQL Server, including creating and altering database schemas, entering and editing data in the database as well as monitoring and managing the server itself. Client applications that consume data or manage the server will leverage SQL Server functionality by sending T-SQL queries and statements which are then processed by the server and results (or errors) returned to the client application. SQL Server allows it to be managed using T-SQL. For this it exposes read-only tables from which server statistics can be read. Management functionality is exposed via system-defined stored procedures which can be invoked from T-SQL queries to perform the management operation. It is also possible to create linked Servers using T-SQL. Linked servers allow a single query to process operations performed on multiple servers.

SQL Native Client (aka SNAC)

SQL Native Client is the native client side data access library for Microsoft SQL Server, version 2005 onwards. It natively implements support for the SQL Server features including the Tabular Data Stream implementation, support for mirrored SQL Server databases, full support for all data types supported by SQL Server, asynchronous operations, query notifications, encryption support, as well as receiving multiple result sets in a single database session. SQL Native Client is used under the hood by SQL Server plug-ins for other data access technologies, including ADO or OLE DB. The SQL Native Client can also be directly used, bypassing the generic data access layers.

On November 28, 2011, a preview release of the SQL Server ODBC driver for Linux was released.

SQL CLR

Microsoft SQL Server 2005 includes a component named SQL CLR ("Common Language Runtime") via which it integrates with .NET Framework. Unlike most other applications that use .NET Framework, SQL Server itself hosts the .NET Framework runtime, i.e., memory, threading and resource management requirements of .NET Framework are satisfied by SQLOS itself, rather than the underlying Windows operating system. SQLOS provides deadlock detection and resolution services for .NET code as well. With SQL CLR, stored procedures and triggers can be written in any managed .NET language, including C# and VB.NET. Managed code can also be used to define UDT's (user defined types), which can persist in the database. Managed code is compiled to CLI assemblies and after being verified for type safety, registered at the database. After that, they can be invoked like any other procedure. However, only a subset of the Base Class Library is available, when running code under SQL CLR. Most APIs relating to user interface functionality are not available.

When writing code for SQL CLR, data stored in SQL Server databases can be accessed using the ADO.NET APIs like any other managed application that accesses SQL Server data. However, doing that creates a new database session, different from the one in which the code is executing. To avoid this, SQL Server provides some enhancements to the ADO.NET provider that allows the connection to be redirected to the same session which already hosts the running code. Such connections are called context connections and are set by setting context connection parameter to true in the connection string. SQL Server also provides several other enhancements to the ADO.NET API, including classes to work with tabular data or a single row of data as well as classes to work with internal metadata about the data stored in the database. It also provides access to the XML features in SQL Server, including XQuery support. These enhancements are also available in T-SQL Procedures in consequence of the introduction of the new XML Datatype (query,value,nodes functions).

Services

SQL Server also includes an assortment of add-on services. While these are not essential for the operation of the database system, they provide value added services on top of the core database management system. These services either run as a part of some SQL Server component or out-of-process as Windows Service and presents their own API to control and interact with them.

Service Broker

Used inside an instance, programming environment. For cross instance applications, Service Broker communicates over TCP/IP and allows the different components to be synchronized together, via exchange of messages. The Service Broker, which runs as a part of the database engine, provides a reliable messaging and message queuing platform for SQL Server applications.

Replication Services

SQL Server Replication Services are used by SQL Server to replicate and synchronize database objects, either in entirety or a subset of the objects present, across replication agents, which might be other database servers across the network, or database caches on the client side. Lulla follows a publisher/subscriber model, i.e., the changes are sent out by one database server ("publisher") and are received by others ("subscribers"). SQL Server supports three different types of replication:

Transaction replication

> Each transaction made to the publisher database (master database) is synced out to subscribers, who update their databases with the transaction. Transactional replication synchronizes databases in near real time.

Merge replication

> Changes made at both the publisher and subscriber databases are tracked, and periodically the changes are synchronized bi-directionally between the publisher and the subscribers. If the same data has been modified differently in both the publisher and the subscriber databases, synchronization will result in a conflict which has to be resolved, either manually or by using pre-defined policies. rowguid needs to be configured on a column if merge replication is configured.

Snapshot replication

> Snapshot replication publishes a copy of the entire database (the then-snapshot of the data) and replicates out to the subscribers. Further changes to the snapshot are not tracked.

Analysis Services

SQL Server Analysis Services adds OLAP and data mining capabilities for SQL Server databases. The OLAP engine supports MOLAP, ROLAP and HOLAP storage modes for data. Analysis Services supports the XML for Analysis standard as the underlying communication protocol. The cube data can be accessed using MDX and LINQ queries. Data mining specific functionality is exposed via the DMX query language. Analysis Services includes various algorithms—Decision trees, clustering algorithm, Naive Bayes algorithm, time series analysis, sequence clustering algorithm, linear and logistic regression analysis, and neural networks—for use in data mining.

Reporting Services

SQL Server Reporting Services is a report generation environment for data gathered from SQL Server databases. It is administered via a web interface. Reporting services features a web services interface to support the development of custom reporting applications. Reports are created as RDL files.

Reports can be designed using recent versions of Microsoft Visual Studio (Visual Studio.NET 2003, 2005, and 2008) with Business Intelligence Development Studio, installed or with the included Report Builder. Once created, RDL files can be rendered in a variety of formats, including Excel, PDF, CSV, XML, BMP, EMF, GIF, JPEG, PNG, and TIFF, and HTML Web Archive.

Notification Services

Originally introduced as a post-release add-on for SQL Server 2000, Notification Services was bundled as part of the Microsoft SQL Server platform for the first and only time with SQL Server 2005. SQL Server Notification Services is a mechanism for generating data-driven notifications, which are sent to Notification Services subscribers. A subscriber registers for a specific event or transaction (which is registered on the database server as a trigger); when the event occurs, Notification Services can use one of three methods to send a message to the subscriber informing about the occurrence of the event. These methods include SMTP, SOAP, or by writing to a file in the filesystem. Notification Services was discontinued by Microsoft with the release of SQL Server 2008 in August 2008, and is no longer an officially supported component of the SQL Server database platform.

Integration Services

SQL Server Integration Services (SSIS) provides ETL capabilities for SQL Server for data import, data integration and data warehousing needs. Integration Services includes GUI tools to build workflows such as extracting data from various sources, querying data, transforming data—including aggregation, de-duplication, de-/normalization and merging of data—and then exporting the transformed data into destination databases or files.

Full Text Search Service

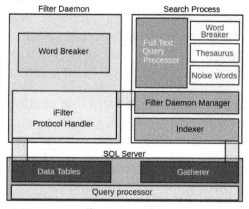

The SQL Server Full Text Search service architecture

SQL Server Full Text Search service is a specialized indexing and querying service for unstructured text stored in SQL Server databases. The full text search index can be created on any column with character based text data. It allows for words to be searched for in the text columns. While it can be performed with the SQL LIKE operator, using SQL Server Full Text Search service can be more efficient. Full allows for inexact matching of the source string, indicated by a *Rank* value which can range from 0 to 1000—a higher rank means a more accurate match. It also allows linguistic matching ("inflectional search"), i.e., linguistic variants of a word (such as a verb in a different tense) will also be a match for a given word (but with a lower rank than an exact match). Proximity searches are also supported, i.e., if the words searched for do not occur in the sequence they are specified in the query but are near each other, they are also considered a match. T-SQL exposes special operators that can be used to access the FTS capabilities.

The Full Text Search engine is divided into two processes: the *Filter Daemon* process (msftefd.exe) and the *Search* process (msftesql.exe). These processes interact with the SQL Server. The Search process includes the indexer (that creates the full text indexes) and the full text query processor. The indexer scans through text columns in the database. It can also index through binary columns, and use iFilters to extract meaningful text from the binary blob (for example, when a Microsoft Word document is stored as an unstructured binary file in a database). The iFilters are hosted by the Filter Daemon process. Once the text is extracted, the Filter Daemon process breaks it up into a sequence of words and hands it over to the indexer. The indexer filters out *noise words*, i.e., words like *A, And* etc., which occur frequently and are not useful for search. With the remaining words, an inverted index is created, associating each word with the columns they were found in. SQL Server itself includes a *Gatherer* component that monitors changes to tables and invokes the indexer in case of updates.

When a full text query is received by the SQL Server query processor, it is handed over to the FTS query processor in the Search process. The FTS query processor breaks up the query into the constituent words, filters out the noise words, and uses an inbuilt thesaurus to find out the linguistic variants for each word. The words are then queried against the inverted index and a rank of their accurateness is computed. The results are returned to the client via the SQL Server process.

SQLCMD

SQLCMD is a command line application that comes with Microsoft SQL Server, and exposes the management features of SQL Server. It allows SQL queries to be written and executed from the command prompt. It can also act as a scripting language to create and run a set of SQL statements as a script. Such scripts are stored as a .sql file, and are used either for management of databases or to create the database schema during the deployment of a database.

SQLCMD was introduced with SQL Server 2005 and this continues with SQL Server 2012 and 2014. Its predecessor for earlier versions was OSQL and ISQL, which is functionally equivalent as it pertains to TSQL execution, and many of the command line parameters are identical, although SQLCMD adds extra versatility.

Visual Studio

Microsoft Visual Studio includes native support for data programming with Microsoft SQL Server. It can be used to write and debug code to be executed by SQL CLR. It also includes a *data designer* that can be used to graphically create, view or edit database schemas. Queries can be created either visually or using code. SSMS 2008 onwards, provides intellisense for SQL queries as well.

SQL Server Management Studio

SQL Server Management Studio is a GUI tool included with SQL Server 2005 and later for configuring, managing, and administering all components within Microsoft SQL Server. The tool includes both script editors and graphical tools that work with objects and features of the server. SQL Server Management Studio replaces Enterprise Manager as the primary management interface for Microsoft SQL Server since SQL Server 2005. A version of SQL Server Management Studio is also available for SQL Server Express Edition, for which it is known as *SQL Server Management Studio Express* (SSMSE).

A central feature of SQL Server Management Studio is the Object Explorer, which allows the user to browse, select, and act upon any of the objects within the server. It can be used to visually observe and analyze query plans and optimize the database performance, among others. SQL Server Management Studio can also be used to create a new database, alter any existing database schema by adding or modifying tables and indexes, or analyze performance. It includes the query windows which provide a GUI based interface to write and execute queries.

Business Intelligence Development Studio

Business Intelligence Development Studio (BIDS) is the IDE from Microsoft used for developing data analysis and Business Intelligence solutions utilizing the Microsoft SQL Server Analysis Services, Reporting Services and Integration Services. It is based on the Microsoft Visual Studio development environment but is customized with the SQL Server services-specific extensions and project types, including tools, controls and projects for reports (using Reporting Services), Cubes and data mining structures (using Analysis Services). For SQL Server 2012 and later, this IDE has been renamed SQL Server Data Tools (SSDT).

SAP HANA

SAP HANA is an in-memory, column-oriented, relational database management system developed and marketed by SAP SE. Its primary function as database server is to store and retrieve data as requested by the applications. In addition, it performs advanced analytics (predictive analytics, spatial data processing, text analytics, text search, streaming analytics, graph data processing) and includes ETL capabilities and an application server.

History

To create SAP HANA, SAP SE developed or acquired technologies, including TREX search engine (in-memory column-oriented search engine), P*TIME (in-memory OLTP Platform acquired by SAP in 2005), and MaxDB with its in-memory liveCache engine. In 2008, teams from SAP SE, working with Hasso Plattner Institute and Stanford University, demonstrated an application architecture for real-time analytics and aggregation, mentioned as "Hasso's New Architecture" in former SAP executive Vishal Sikka's blog. Before the name "HANA" stabilized, people referred to this product as "New Database".

The software was previously called "SAP High-Performance Analytic Appliance".

The first product shipped in late November 2010. By mid-2011, the technology had attracted interest but the experienced business customers still considered it "in early days". HANA support for SAP NetWeaver Business Warehouse was announced in September 2011 for availability by November.

In 2012, SAP promoted aspects of cloud computing. In October 2012, SAP announced a platform as a service offering called the SAP HANA Cloud Platform and a variant called SAP HANA One that used a smaller amount of memory.

In January 2013, SAP enterprise resource planning software from its Business Suite was announced and became available by May.

In May 2013, a managed private cloud offering called the HANA Enterprise Cloud service was announced.

Rather than versioning, the software utilizes service packs for major releases. Service packs are released every 6 months.

Architecture

Overview

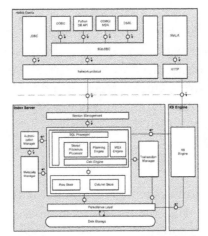

Indexer components

The index server performs session management, authorization, transaction management and command processing. The database has both a row store and a columnar store. Users can create tables using either store, but the columnar store has more capabilities and most frequently used. The index server also manages persistence between cached memory images of database objects, log files and permanent storage files. XS engine allows to build web applications.

MVCC

HANA manages concurrency through the use of multiversion concurrency control (MVCC), which gives every transaction a snapshot of the database at a point in time. When an MVCC database needs to update an item of data, it will not overwrite the old data with new data, but will instead mark the old data as obsolete and add the newer version.

Supported Platforms

- Linux on x86-64 (Red Hat Enterprise Linux, and SUSE distributions are supported)
- Linux on POWER Systems

Deployment

SAP HANA can be deployed on-premises as an appliance from a certified hardware vendor or on certified hardware with tailored data center integration (TDI). With tailored data center integration (TDI) approach, existing hardware components such as storage and network can be reused. Both horizontal and vertical scalability are supported. HANA is also available in the cloud as a Database as a Service on Amazon Web Services, Microsoft Azure, IBM Softlayer, Huawei Fusion-Sphere, HP Helion, or the SAP HANA Cloud Platform (PaaS) as well as SAP HANA Enterprise Could (MCaaS).

Editions

SAP HANA licensing is primarily divided into two categories.

Runtime License:

Used to run SAP applications such as SAP Business Warehouse powered by SAP HANA and SAP S/4HANA.

Full Use License:

Used to run both SAP and non-SAP applications. This licensing can be used to create custom applications.

As part of the full use license, features are grouped as editions targeting various use cases.

- Base Edition: Provides core database features and development tools but does not support SAP applications.

- Platform Edition: Base edition plus spatial, predictive, R server integration, search, text, analytics, graph engines and additional packaged business libraries.

- Enterprise Edition: Platform edition plus additional bundled components for some of the data loading capabilities and the rule framework.

In addition, capabilities such as streaming and ETL are licensed as an additional options.

IBM DB2

IBM DB2 contains database server products developed by IBM. These products all support the relational model, but in recent years some products have been extended to support object-relational features and non-relational structures like JSON and XML.

Historically and unlike other database vendors, IBM produced a platform-specific DB2 product for each of its major operating systems. However, in the 1990s IBM changed track and produced a DB2 "common server" product, designed with a common code base to run on different platforms.

Current Supported Platforms

DB2 for Linux, UNIX and Windows (informally known as DB2 LUW) DB2 for z/OS (mainframe) DB2 for i (formerly OS/400). DB2 for VM / VSE

History

DB2 traces its roots back to the beginning of the 1970s when Edgar F. Codd, a researcher working for IBM, described the theory of relational databases and in June 1970 published the model for data manipulation.

In 1974 the IBM San Jose Research center developed a relational DBMS, System R, to implement Codd's concepts. A key development of the System R project was SQL. To apply the relational model Codd needed a relational database language he named DSL/Alpha. At the time IBM didn't believe in the potential of Codd's ideas, leaving the implementation to a group of programmers not under Codd's supervision, who violated several fundamentals of Codd's relational model; the result was Structured English QUEry Language or SEQUEL. When IBM released its first relational database product, they wanted to have a commercial-quality sublanguage as well, so it overhauled SEQUEL and renamed the basically new language Structured Query Language (SQL) to differentiate it from SEQUEL. The acronym SEQUEL was changed to SQL because "SEQUEL" was a trademark of the UK-based Hawker Siddeley aircraft company.

IBM bought Metaphor Computer Systems to utilize their GUI interface and encapsulating SQL platform that had already been in use since the mid 80's. In parallel with the development of SQL IBM also developed Query by Example (QBE), the first graphical query language.

IBM's first commercial relational database product, SQL/DS, was released for the DOS/VSE and VM/CMS operating systems in 1981. In 1976 IBM released Query by Example for the VM platform where the table-oriented front-end produced a linear-syntax language that drove transactions to its relational database. Later the QMF feature of DB2 produced real SQL and brought the same "QBE" look and feel to DB2.

The name DB2, or IBM Database 2, was first given to the Database Management System or DBMS in 1983 when IBM released DB2 on its MVS mainframe platform.

When Informix Corporation acquired Illustra and made their database engine an object-SQL DBMS by introducing their Universal Server, both Oracle and IBM followed suit by changing their database engines to be capable of object-relational extensions. In 2001, IBM bought Informix Software and in the following years incorporated Informix technology into the DB2 product suite. DB2 can technically be considered to be an object-SQL DBMS.

For some years DB2, as a full-function DBMS, was exclusively available on IBM mainframes. Later IBM brought DB2 to other platforms, including OS/2, UNIX and MS Windows servers, then Linux (including Linux on z Systems) and PDAs. This process occurred through the 1990s. The inspiration for the mainframe version of DB2's architecture came in part from IBM IMS, a hierarchical database, and its dedicated database manipulation language, IBM DL/I. DB2 is also embedded in the i5/OS operating system for IBM System i (iSeries, formerly the AS/400), and versions are available for z/VSE and z/VM.An earlier version of the code that would become DB2 LUW (Linux, Unix, Windows) was part of an Extended Edition component of OS/2 called Database Manager.

IBM extended the functionality of Database Manager a number of times, including the addition of distributed database functionality by means of Distributed Relational Database Architecture

(DRDA) that allowed shared access to a database in a remote location on a LAN. (Note that DRDA is based on objects and protocols defined by Distributed Data Management Architecture (DDM).)

Eventually IBM took the decision to completely rewrite the software. The new version of Database Manager was called DB2/2 and DB2/6000 respectively. Other versions of DB2, with different code bases, followed the same '/' naming convention and became DB2/400 (for the AS/400), DB2/VSE (for the DOS/VSE environment) and DB2/VM (for the VM operating system). IBM lawyers stopped this handy naming convention from being used and decided that all products needed to be called "product FOR platform" (for example, DB2 for OS/390). The next iteration of the mainframe and the server-based products were named DB2 Universal Database (or DB2 UDB).

In the mid-1990s, IBM released a clustered DB2 implementation called DB2 Parallel Edition, which initially ran on AIX. This edition allowed scalability by providing a shared nothing architecture, in which a single large database is partitioned across multiple DB2 servers that communicate over a high-speed interconnect. This DB2 edition was eventually ported to all Linux, UNIX, and Windows (LUW) platforms and was renamed to DB2 Extended Enterprise Edition (EEE). IBM now refers to this product as the Database Partitioning Feature (DPF) and sells it as an add-on to their flagship DB2 Enterprise product.

In mid 2006, IBM announced "Viper," which is the codename for DB2 9 on both distributed platforms and z/OS. DB2 9 for z/OS was announced in early 2007. IBM claimed that the new DB2 was the first relational database to store XML "natively". Other enhancements include OLTP-related improvements for distributed platforms, business intelligence/data warehousing-related improvements for z/OS, more self-tuning and self-managing features, additional 64-bit exploitation (especially for virtual storage on z/OS), stored procedure performance enhancements for z/OS, and continued convergence of the SQL vocabularies between z/OS and distributed platforms.

In October 2007, IBM announced "Viper 2," which is the codename for DB2 9.5 on the distributed platforms. There were three key themes for the release, Simplified Management, Business Critical Reliability and Agile XML development.

In June 2009, IBM announced "Cobra" (the codename for DB2 9.7 for LUW). DB2 9.7 adds data compression for database indexes, temporary tables, and large objects. DB2 9.7 also supports native XML data in hash partitioning (database partitioning), range partitioning (table partitioning), and multi-dimensional clustering. These native XML features allows users to directly work with XML in data warehouse environments. DB2 9.7 also adds several features that make it easier for Oracle Database users to work with DB2. These include support for the most commonly used SQL syntax, PL/SQL syntax, scripting syntax, and data types from Oracle Database. DB2 9.7 also enhanced its concurrency model to exhibit behavior that is familiar to users of Oracle Database and Microsoft SQL Server.

In October 2009, IBM introduced its second major release of the year when it announced DB2 pureScale. DB2 pureScale is a database cluster solution for non-mainframe platforms, suitable for Online Transaction Processing (OLTP) workloads. IBM based the design of DB2 pureScale on the Parallel Sysplex implementation of DB2 data sharing on the mainframe. DB2 pureScale provides a fault-tolerant architecture and shared-disk storage. A DB2 pureScale system can grow to 128 database servers, and provides continuous availability and automatic load balancing.

In 2009, it was announced that DB2 can be an engine in MySQL. This allows users on the System i platform to natively access the DB2 under the IBM i operating system (formerly called OS/400), and for users on other platforms to access these files through the MySQL interface. On the System i and its predecessors the AS/400 and the System/38, DB2 is tightly integrated into the operating system, and comes as part of the operating system. It provides journaling, triggers and other features.

In early 2012, IBM announced the next version of DB2, DB2 10.1 (code name Galileo) for Linux, UNIX, and Windows.DB2 10.1 contained a number of new data management capabilities including row and column access control which enables 'fine-grained' control of the database and multi-temperature data management that moves data to cost effective storage based on how"hot" or "cold" (how frequently the data is accessed) the data is. IBM also introduced 'adaptive compression' capability in DB2 10.1, a new approach to compressing data tables.

In June 2013, IBM released DB2 10.5 (code name "Kepler").

On 12 April 2016, IBM announced DB2 LUW 11.1, and in June 2016 it was released.

Editions

IBM offers seven editions: Advanced Enterprise Server Edition Advanced Workgroup Server Edition Enterprise Server Edition Workgroup Server Edition Express Edition Developer Edition and Express-C.

DB2 Express-C is free of charge version of DB2 but limited to two CPU cores and 16GB of RAM and without Enterprise support and fixpacks. DB2 Express-C has no limit on number of users or on database size.

DB2 for z/OS (the mainframe) is available in its traditional product packaging, or in the Value Unit Edition, which allows customers to instead pay a one-time charge.

DB2 also powers IBM InfoSphere Warehouse, which offers data warehouse capabilities. InfoSphere Warehouse is available for z/OS. It includes several BI features such as ETL, data mining, OLAP acceleration, and in-line analytics.

DB2 10.5 for Linux, UNIX and Windows, contains all of the functionality and tools offered in the prior generation of DB2 and InfoSphere Warehouse on Linux, UNIX and Windows.

IBM provides 2 cloud services for DB2 on its Bluemix platform:

- DB2 on Cloud: An unmanaged, hosted version of DB2.

- IBM dashDB: A managed cloud database based on the DB2 engine, with additional capabilities from the Netezza engine. Inside the dashDB family, there are 3 editions: IBM dashDB for Transactions (general purpose, transactional or web workloads), dashDB for Analytics (data warehouse), and dashDB Local (a Docker container image allowing deployment on private clouds.)

Technical Information

DB2 can be administered from either the command-line or a GUI. The command-line interface requires more knowledge of the product but can be more easily scripted and automated. The GUI is a multi-platform Java client that contains a variety of wizards suitable for novice users. DB2 supports both SQL and XQuery. DB2 has native implementation of XML data storage, where XML data is stored as XML (not as relational data or CLOB data) for faster access using XQuery.

DB2 has APIs for REXX, PL/I, COBOL, RPG, FORTRAN, C++, C, Delphi, .NET CLI, Java, Python, Perl, PHP, Ruby, and many other programming languages. DB2 also supports integration into the Eclipse and Visual Studio integrated development environments.

pureQuery is IBM's data access platform focused on applications that access data. pureQuery supports both Java and .NET. pureQuery provides access to data in databases and in-memory Java objects via its tools, APIs, and runtime environment as delivered in *IBM Data Studio Developer* and *IBM Data Studio pureQuery Runtime*.

Error Processing

An important feature of DB2 computer programs is error handling. The SQL communications area (SQLCA) structure was once used exclusively within a DB2 program to return error information to the application program after every SQL statement was executed. The primary, but not singularly useful, error diagnostic is held in the field SQLCODE within the SQLCA block.

The SQL return code values are:

- 0 means successful execution.

- A positive number means successful execution with one or more warnings. An example is +100, which means no rows found.

- A negative number means unsuccessful with an error. An example is -911, which means a lock timeout (or deadlock) has occurred, triggering a rollback.

Later versions of DB2 added functionality and complexity to the execution of SQL. Multiple errors or warnings could be returned by the execution of an SQL statement; it may, for example, have initiated a Database Trigger and other SQL statements. Instead of the original SQLCA, error information should now be retrieved by successive executions of a GET DIAGNOSTICS statement.

Object-relational Database

An object-relational database (ORD), or object-relational database management system (ORDBMS), is a database management system (DBMS) similar to a relational database, but with an object-oriented database model: objects, classes and inheritance are directly supported in database schemas and in the query language. In addition, just as with pure relational systems, it supports extension of the data model with custom data-types and methods.

Object-Oriented Model

Object 1: Maintenance Report   Object 1 Instance

Date		01-12-01
Activity Code		24
Route No.		I-95
Daily Production		2.5
Equipment Hours		6.0
Labor Hours		6.0

Object 2: Maintenance Activity

Activity Code	
Activity Name	
Production Unit	
Average Daily Production Rate	

Example of an object-oriented database model

An object-relational database can be said to provide a middle ground between relational databases and *object-oriented databases* (object database). In object-relational databases, the approach is essentially that of relational databases: the data resides in the database and is manipulated collectively with queries in a query language; at the other extreme are OODBMSes in which the database is essentially a persistent object store for software written in an object-oriented programming language, with a programming API for storing and retrieving objects, and little or no specific support for querying.

Overview

The basic need of Object-relational database arises from the fact that both Relational and Object database have their individual advantages and drawbacks. The isomorphism of the relational database system with a mathematical relation allows it to exploit many useful techniques and theorems from set theory. But these types of databases are not useful when the matter comes to data complexity and mismatch between application and the DBMS. An object oriented database model allows containers like sets and lists, arbitrary user-defined datatypes as well as nested objects. This brings commonality between the application type systems and database type systems which removes any issue of impedance mismatch. But Object databases, unlike relational do not provide any mathematical base for their deep analysis.

The basic goal for the Object-relational database is to bridge the gap between relational databases and the object-oriented modeling techniques used in programming languages such as Java, C++, Visual Basic .NET or C#. However, a more popular alternative for achieving such a bridge is to use a standard relational database systems with some form of object-relational mapping (ORM) software. Whereas traditional RDBMS or SQL-DBMS products focused on the efficient management of data drawn from a limited set of data-types (defined by the relevant language standards), an object-relational DBMS allows software developers to integrate their own types and the methods that apply to them into the DBMS.

The ORDBMS (like ODBMS or OODBMS) is integrated with an object-oriented programming language. The characteristic properties of ORDBMS are 1) complex data, 2) type inheritance, and 3) object behavior. Complex data creation in most SQL ORDBMSs is based on preliminary schema definition via the user-defined type (UDT). Hierarchy within structured complex data offers an additional property, type inheritance. That is, a structured type can have subtypes that reuse all of its attributes and contain additional attributes specific to the subtype. Another advantage, the object behavior, is related with access to the program objects. Such program objects must be storable and transportable for database processing, therefore they usually are named as persistent objects. Inside a database, all the relations with a persistent program object are relations with its object identifier (OID). All of these points can be addressed in a proper relational system, although the SQL standard and its implementations impose arbitrary restrictions and additional complexity

In object-oriented programming (OOP), object behavior is described through the methods (object functions). The methods denoted by one name are distinguished by the type of their parameters and type of objects for which they attached (method signature). The OOP languages call this the polymorphism principle, which briefly is defined as "one interface, many implementations". Other OOP principles, inheritance and encapsulation, are related both to methods and attributes. Method inheritance is included in type inheritance. Encapsulation in OOP is a visibility degree declared, for example, through the public, private and protected access modifiers.

History

Object-relational database management systems grew out of research that occurred in the early 1990s. That research extended existing relational database concepts by adding object concepts. The researchers aimed to retain a declarative query-language based on predicate calculus as a central component of the architecture. Probably the most notable research project, Postgres (UC Berkeley), spawned two products tracing their lineage to that research: Illustra and PostgreSQL.

In the mid-1990s, early commercial products appeared. These included Illustra (Illustra Information Systems, acquired by Informix Software, which was in turn acquired by IBM), Omniscience (Omniscience Corporation, acquired by Oracle Corporation and became the original Oracle Lite), and UniSQL (UniSQL, Inc., acquired by KCOMS). Ukrainian developer Ruslan Zasukhin, founder of Paradigma Software, Inc., developed and shipped the first version of Valentina database in the mid-1990s as a C++ SDK. By the next decade, PostgreSQL had become a commercially viable database, and is the basis for several current products that maintain its ORDBMS features.

Computer scientists came to refer to these products as "object-relational database management systems" or ORDBMSs.

Many of the ideas of early object-relational database efforts have largely become incorporated into SQL:1999 via structured types. In fact, any product that adheres to the object-oriented aspects of SQL:1999 could be described as an object-relational database management product. For example, IBM's DB2, Oracle database, and Microsoft SQL Server, make claims to support this technology and do so with varying degrees of success.

Comparison to RDBMS

An RDBMS might commonly involve SQL statements such as these:

```
CREATE TABLE Customers (

   Id      CHAR(12)   NOT NULL PRIMARY KEY,
```

```
      Surname    VARCHAR(32) NOT NULL,

      FirstName  VARCHAR(32) NOT NULL,

      DOB        DATE    NOT NULL

    );

    SELECT InitCap(Surname) || ', ' || InitCap(FirstName)

      FROM Customers

      WHERE Month(DOB) = Month(getdate())

      AND Day(DOB) = Day(getdate())
```

Most current SQL databases allow the crafting of custom functions, which would allow the query to appear as:

```
    SELECT Formal(Id)

      FROM Customers

      WHERE Birthday(DOB) = Today()
```

In an object-relational database, one might see something like this, with user-defined data-types and expressions such as BirthDay():

```
    CREATE TABLE Customers (

      Id      Cust_Id   NOT NULL  PRIMARY KEY,

      Name      PersonName NOT NULL,

      DOB     DATE    NOT NULL

    );

    SELECT Formal( C.Id )

      FROM Customers C

      WHERE BirthDay ( C.DOB ) = TODAY;
```

The object-relational model can offer another advantage in that the database can make use of the relationships between data to easily collect related records. In an address book application, an additional table would be added to the ones above to hold zero or more addresses for each customer. Using a traditional RDBMS, collecting information for both the user and their address requires a "join":

```
    SELECT InitCap(C.Surname) || ', ' || InitCap(C.FirstName), A.city

      FROM Customers C join Addresses A ON A.Cust_Id=C.Id -- the join
```

    WHERE A.city="New York"

The same query in an object-relational database appears more simply:

    SELECT Formal(C.Name)

    FROM Customers C

    WHERE C.address.city="New York" -- the linkage is 'understood' by the ORDB

PostgreSQL

PostgreSQL, often simply Postgres, is an object-relational database (ORDBMS) – i.e. a RDBMS, with additional (optional use) "object" features – with an emphasis on extensibility and standards compliance. As a database server, its primary function is to store data securely, and to allow for retrieval at the request of other software applications. It can handle workloads ranging from small single-machine applications to large Internet-facing applications (or for data warehousing) with many concurrent users; on macOS, PostgreSQL is the default database – for web hosting – and it is also available for Microsoft Windows and Linux (supplied in most distributions).

PostgreSQL is ACID-compliant and transactional. PostgreSQL has updatable views and materialized views, triggers, foreign keys; supports functions and stored procedures, and other expandability.

PostgreSQL is developed by the PostgreSQL Global Development Group, a diverse group of many companies and individual contributors. It is free and open-source software, released under the terms of the PostgreSQL License, a permissive free-software license.

Name

PostgreSQL's developers pronounce PostgreSQL as. It is abbreviated as *Postgres* because of ubiquitous support for the SQL Standard among most relational databases. The community considered changing the name back to Postgres; however, the PostgreSQL Core Team announced in 2007 that the product would continue to use the name PostgreSQL. The name Postgres (Post Ingres) refers to the project's origins in that database which was developed at University of California, Berkeley.

History

PostgreSQL evolved from the Ingres project at the University of California, Berkeley. In 1982, the leader of the Ingres team, Michael Stonebraker, left Berkeley to make a proprietary version of Ingres. He returned to Berkeley in 1985, and started a post-Ingres project to address the problems with contemporary database systems that had become increasingly clear during the early 1980s. The new project, POSTGRES, aimed to add the fewest features needed to completely support types. These features included the ability to define types and to fully describe relationships – something used widely before but maintained entirely by the user. In POSTGRES, the database "understood" relationships, and could retrieve information in related tables in a natural way using *rules*. POSTGRES used many of the ideas of Ingres, but not its code.

Starting in 1986, the POSTGRES team published a number of papers describing the basis of the system, and by 1987 had a prototype version shown at the 1988 ACM SIGMOD Conference. The team released version 1 to a small number of users in June 1989, then version 2 with a re-written rules system in June 1990. Version 3, released in 1991, again re-wrote the rules system, and added support for multiple storage managers and an improved query engine. By 1993, the great number of users began to overwhelm the project with requests for support and features. After releasing version 4.2 on June 30, 1994 – primarily a cleanup – the project ended. Berkeley had released POSTGRES under an MIT-style license, which enabled other developers to use the code for any use. At the time, POSTGRES used an Ingres-influenced POSTQUEL query language interpreter, which could be interactively used with a console application named monitor.

In 1994, Berkeley graduate students Andrew Yu and Jolly Chen replaced the POSTQUEL query language interpreter with one for the SQL query language, creating Postgres95. The front-end program monitor was also replaced by psql. Yu and Chen announced the first version (0.01) to beta testers on May 5, 1995. Version 1.0 of Postgres95 was announced on September 5, 1995, with a more liberal license that enabled the software to be freely modifiable for any purpose.

On July 8, 1996, Marc Fournier at Hub.org Networking Services provided the first non-university development server for the open-source development effort. With the participation of Bruce Momjian and Vadim B. Mikheev, work began to stabilize the code inherited from Berkeley. The first open-source version was released on August 1, 1996.

In 1996, the project was renamed to PostgreSQL to reflect its support for SQL. The online presence at the website PostgreSQL.org began on October 22, 1996. The first PostgreSQL release formed version 6.0 on January 29, 1997. Since then a group of developers and volunteers around the world have maintained the software as The PostgreSQL Global Development Group.

The PostgreSQL project continues to make major releases (approximately annually) and minor "bugfix" releases, all available under its free and open-source software PostgreSQL License. Code comes from contributions from proprietary vendors, support companies, and open-source programmers at large.

Multiversion Concurrency Control (MVCC)

PostgreSQL manages concurrency through a system known as multiversion concurrency control (MVCC), which gives each transaction a "snapshot" of the database, allowing changes to be made without being visible to other transactions until the changes are committed. This largely eliminates the need for read locks, and ensures the database maintains the ACID (atomicity, consistency, isolation, durability) principles in an efficient manner. PostgreSQL offers three levels of transaction isolation: Read Committed, Repeatable Read and Serializable. Because PostgreSQL is immune to dirty reads, requesting a Read Uncommitted transaction isolation level provides read committed instead. PostgreSQL supports full serializability via the serializable snapshot isolation (SSI) technique.

Storage and Replication

Replication

PostgreSQL includes built-in binary replication based on shipping the changes (write-ahead logs) to replica nodes asynchronously, with the ability to run read-only queries against these replicated nodes. This allows splitting read traffic among multiple nodes efficiently. Earlier replication software that allowed similar read scaling normally relied on adding replication triggers to the master, introducing additional load onto it.

PostgreSQL also includes built-in synchronous replication that ensures that, for each write transaction, the master waits until at least one replica node has written the data to its transaction log. Unlike other database systems, the durability of a transaction (whether it is asynchronous or synchronous) can be specified per-database, per-user, per-session or even per-transaction. This can be useful for work loads that do not require such guarantees, and may not be wanted for all data as it will have some negative effect on performance due to the requirement of the confirmation of the transaction reaching the synchronous standby.

There can be a mixture of synchronous and asynchronous standby servers. A list of synchronous standby servers can be specified in the configuration which determines which servers are candidates for synchronous replication. The first in the list which is currently connected and actively streaming is the one that will be used as the current synchronous server. When this fails, it falls to the next in line.

Synchronous multi-master replication is currently not included in the PostgreSQL core. Postgres-XC which is based on PostgreSQL provides scalable synchronous multi-master replication, available in version 1.2.1 (April 2015 version) is licensed under the same license as PostgreSQL. A similar project is called Postgres-XL and is available under the Mozilla Public License. Postgres-R is yet another older fork. Bi-Directional Replication (BDR) is an asynchronous multi-master replication system for PostgreSQL.

The community has also written some tools to make managing replication clusters easier, such as repmgr.

There are also several asynchronous trigger-based replication packages for PostgreSQL. These remain useful even after introduction of the expanded core capabilities, for situations where binary replication of an entire database cluster is not the appropriate approach:

- Slony-I

- Londiste, part of SkyTools (developed by Skype)

- Bucardo multi-master replication (developed by Backcountry.com)

- SymmetricDS multi-master, multi-tier replication

Indexes

PostgreSQL includes built-in support for regular B-tree and hash indexes, and four index access methods: generalized search trees (GiST), generalized inverted indexes (GIN), Space-Partitioned GiST (SP-GiST) and Block Range Indexes (BRIN). Hash indexes are implemented, but discouraged because they cannot be recovered after a crash or power loss. In addition, user-defined index methods can be created, although this is quite an involved process. Indexes in PostgreSQL also support the following features:

- Expression indexes can be created with an index of the result of an expression or function, instead of simply the value of a column.

- Partial indexes, which only index part of a table, can be created by adding a WHERE clause to the end of the CREATE INDEX statement. This allows a smaller index to be created.

- The planner is capable of using multiple indexes together to satisfy complex queries, using temporary in-memory bitmap index operations (useful in data warehousing applications for joining a large fact table to smaller dimension tables such as those arranged in a star schema).

- k-nearest neighbors (k-NN) indexing (also referred to KNN-GiST) provides efficient searching of "closest values" to that specified, useful to finding similar words, or close objects or locations with geospatial data. This is achieved without exhaustive matching of values.

- In PostgreSQL 9.2 and later, index-only scans often allow the system to fetch data from indexes without ever having to access the main table.

- PostgreSQL 9.5 introduced Block Range Indexes (BRIN).

Schemas

In PostgreSQL, a schema holds all objects (with the exception of roles and tablespaces). Schemas effectively act like namespaces, allowing objects of the same name to co-exist in the same database. By default, newly created databases have a schema called "public", but any additional schemas can be added, and the public schema isn't mandatory.

A "search_path" setting determines the order in which PostgreSQL checks schemas for unqualified objects (those without a prefixed schema). By default, it is set to "$user, public" ($user refers to the currently connected database user). This default can be set on a database or role level, but as it is a session parameter, it can be freely changed (even multiple times) during a client session, affecting that session only.

Non-existent schemas listed in search_path are silently skipped during objects lookup.

New objects are created in whichever valid schema (one that presently exists) appears first in the search_path.

Data Types

A wide variety of native data types are supported, including:

- Boolean

- Arbitrary precision numerics

- Character (text, varchar, char)

- Binary

- Date/time (timestamp/time with/without timezone, date, interval)

- Money

- Enum

- Bit strings

- Text search type

- Composite

- HStore (an extension enabled key-value store within PostgreSQL)

- Arrays (variable length and can be of any data type, including text and composite types) up to 1 GB in total storage size

- Geometric primitives

- IPv4 and IPv6 addresses

- CIDR blocks and MAC addresses

- XML supporting XPath queries

- UUID

- JSON (since version 9.2), and a faster binary JSONB (since version 9.4; not the same as BSON)

In addition, users can create their own data types which can usually be made fully indexable via PostgreSQL's indexing infrastructures – GiST, GIN, SP-GiST. Examples of these include the geographic information system (GIS) data types from the PostGIS project for PostgreSQL.

There is also a data type called a "domain", which is the same as any other data type but with optional constraints defined by the creator of that domain. This means any data entered into a column using the domain will have to conform to whichever constraints were defined as part of the domain.

Starting with PostgreSQL 9.2, a data type that represents a range of data can be used which are called range types. These can be discrete ranges (e.g. all integer values 1 to 10) or continuous ranges (e.g. any point in time between 10:00 am and 11:00 am). The built-in range types available include ranges of integers, big integers, decimal numbers, time stamps (with and without time zone) and dates.

Custom range types can be created to make new types of ranges available, such as IP address ranges using the inet type as a base, or float ranges using the float data type as a base. Range types support inclusive and exclusive range boundaries using the [] and () characters respectively. (e.g. '[4,9)' represents all integers starting from and including 4 up to but not including 9.) Range types are also compatible with existing operators used to check for overlap, containment, right of etc.

User-defined Objects

New types of almost all objects inside the database can be created, including:

- Casts
- Conversions
- Data types
- Domains
- Functions, including aggregate functions and window functions
- Indexes including custom indexes for custom types
- Operators (existing ones can be overloaded)
- Procedural languages

Inheritance

Tables can be set to inherit their characteristics from a "parent" table. Data in child tables will appear to exist in the parent tables, unless data is selected from the parent table using the ONLY keyword, i.e. SELECT * FROM ONLY parent_table;. Adding a column in the parent table will cause that column to appear in the child table.

Inheritance can be used to implement table partitioning, using either triggers or rules to direct inserts to the parent table into the proper child tables.

As of 2010, this feature is not fully supported yet – in particular, table constraints are not currently inheritable. All check constraints and not-null constraints on a parent table are automatically inherited by its children. Other types of constraints (unique, primary key, and foreign key constraints) are not inherited.

Inheritance provides a way to map the features of generalization hierarchies depicted in entity relationship diagrams (ERDs) directly into the PostgreSQL database.

Other Storage Features

- Referential integrity constraints including foreign key constraints, column constraints, and row checks
- Binary and textual large-object storage
- Tablespaces
- Per-column collation
- Online backup
- Point-in-time recovery, implemented using write-ahead logging

- In-place upgrades with pg_upgrade for less downtime (supports upgrades from 8.3.x and later)

Control and Connectivity

Foreign Data Wrappers

PostgreSQL can link to other systems to retrieve data via foreign data wrappers (FDWs). These can take the form of any data source, such as a file system, another RDBMS, or a web service. This means that regular database queries can use these data sources like regular tables, and even join multiple data-sources together.

Interfaces

PostgreSQL has several interfaces available and is also widely supported among programming language libraries. Built-in interfaces include libpq (PostgreSQL's official C application interface) and ECPG (an embedded C system). External interfaces include:

- libpqxx: C++ interface
- PostgresDAC: PostgresDAC (for Embarcadero RadStudio/Delphi/CBuilder XE-XE3)
- DBD::Pg: Perl DBI driver
- JDBC: JDBC interface
- Lua: Lua interface
- Npgsql: .NET data provider
- ST-Links SpatialKit: Link Tool to ArcGIS
- PostgreSQL.jl: Julia interface
- node-postgres: Node.js interface
- pgoledb: OLEDB interface
- psqlODBC: ODBC interface
- psycopg2: Python interface (also used by HTSQL)
- pgtclng: Tcl interface
- pyODBC: Python library
- php5-pgsql: PHP driver based on libpq
- postmodern: A Common Lisp interface
- pq: A pure Go PostgreSQL driver for the Go database/sql package. The driver passes the compatibility test suite.

- dpq: D interface to libpq

- epgsql: Erlang interface

Procedural Languages

Procedural languages allow developers to extend the database with custom subroutines (functions), often called *stored procedures*. These functions can be used to build triggers (functions invoked upon modification of certain data) and custom aggregate functions. Procedural languages can also be invoked without defining a function, using the "DO" command at SQL level.

Languages are divided into two groups: "Safe" languages are sandboxed and can be safely used by any user. Procedures written in "unsafe" languages can only be created by superusers, because they allow bypassing the database's security restrictions, but can also access sources external to the database. Some languages like Perl provide both safe and unsafe versions.

PostgreSQL has built-in support for three procedural languages:

- Plain SQL (safe). Simpler SQL functions can get expanded inline into the calling (SQL) query, which saves function call overhead and allows the query optimizer to "see inside" the function.

- PL/pgSQL (safe), which resembles Oracle's PL/SQL procedural language and SQL/PSM.

- C (unsafe), which allows loading custom shared libraries into the database. Functions written in C offer the best performance, but bugs in code can crash and potentially corrupt the database. Most built-in functions are written in C.

In addition, PostgreSQL allows procedural languages to be loaded into the database through extensions. Three language extensions are included with PostgreSQL to support Perl, Python and Tcl. There are external projects to add support for many other languages, including Java, JavaScript (PL/V8), R, Ruby, and others.

Triggers

Triggers are events triggered by the action of SQL DML statements. For example, an INSERT statement might activate a trigger that checks if the values of the statement are valid. Most triggers are only activated by either INSERT or UPDATE statements.

Triggers are fully supported and can be attached to tables. Triggers can be per-column and conditional, in that UPDATE triggers can target specific columns of a table, and triggers can be told to execute under a set of conditions as specified in the trigger's WHERE clause. Triggers can be attached to views by using the INSTEAD OF condition. Multiple triggers are fired in alphabetical order. In addition to calling functions written in the native PL/pgSQL, triggers can also invoke functions written in other languages like PL/Python or PL/Perl.

Asynchronous Notifications

PostgreSQL provides an asynchronous messaging system that is accessed through the NOTIFY,

LISTEN and UNLISTEN commands. A session can issue a NOTIFY command, along with the user-specified channel and an optional payload, to mark a particular event occurring. Other sessions are able to detect these events by issuing a LISTEN command, which can listen to a particular channel. This functionality can be used for a wide variety of purposes, such as letting other sessions know when a table has updated or for separate applications to detect when a particular action has been performed. Such a system prevents the need for continuous polling by applications to see if anything has yet changed, and reducing unnecessary overhead. Notifications are fully transactional, in that messages are not sent until the transaction they were sent from is committed. This eliminates the problem of messages being sent for an action being performed which is then rolled back.

Many of the connectors for PostgreSQL provide support for this notification system (including libpq, JDBC, Npgsql, psycopg and node.js) so it can be used by external applications.

Rules

Rules allow the "query tree" of an incoming query to be rewritten. Rules, or more properly, "Query Re-Write Rules", are attached to a table/class and "Re-Write" the incoming DML (select, insert, update, and/or delete) into one or more queries that either replace the original DML statement or execute in addition to it. Query Re-Write occurs after DML statement parsing, but before query planning.

Other Querying Features

- Transactions

- Full text search

- Views

  - Materialized views

  - Updateable views

  - Recursive views

- Inner, outer (full, left and right), and cross joins

- Sub-selects

  - Correlated sub-queries

- Regular expressions

- Common table expressions and writable common table expressions

- Encrypted connections via TLS (current versions do not use vulnerable SSL, even with that configuration option)

- Domains

- Savepoints

- Two-phase commit

- TOAST (*The Oversized-Attribute Storage Technique*) is used to transparently store large table attributes (such as big MIME attachments or XML messages) in a separate area, with automatic compression.

- Embedded SQL is implemented using preprocessor. SQL code is first written embedded into C code. Then code is run through ECPG preprocessor, which replaces SQL with calls to code library. Then code can be compiled using a C compiler. Embedding works also with C++ but it does not recognize all C++ constructs.

Security

PostgreSQL manages its internal security on a per-role basis. A role is generally regarded to be a user (a role that can log in), or a group (a role of which other roles are members). Permissions can be granted or revoked on any object down to the column level, and can also allow/prevent the creation of new objects at the database, schema or table levels.

PostgreSQL's SECURITY LABEL feature (extension to SQL standards), allows for additional security; with a bundled loadable module that supports label-based mandatory access control (MAC) based on SELinux security policy.

PostgreSQL natively supports a broad number of external authentication mechanisms, including:

- password (either MD5 or plain-text)

- GSSAPI

- SSPI

- Kerberos

- ident (maps O/S user-name as provided by an ident server to database user-name)

- peer (maps local user name to database user name)

- LDAP

  o Active Directory

- RADIUS

- certificate

- PAM

The GSSAPI, SSPI, Kerberos, peer, ident and certificate methods can also use a specified "map" file that lists which users matched by that authentication system are allowed to connect as a specific database user.

These methods are specified in the cluster's host-based authentication configuration file (pg_hba. conf), which determines what connections are allowed. This allows control over which user can connect to which database, where they can connect from (IP address/IP address range/domain socket), which authentication system will be enforced, and whether the connection must use TLS.

Add-ons

- Apache MADlib: an open source analytics library for PostgreSQL providing mathematical, statistical and machine-learning methods for structured and unstructured data

- Ora2Pg: an OpenSource, GPL licensed Oracle and MySQL migration tool written in Perl Ora2Pg homepage

- MySQL migration wizard: included with EnterpriseDB's PostgreSQL installer (source code also available)

- Performance Wizard: included with EnterpriseDB's PostgreSQL installer (source code also available)

- pgRouting: extended PostGIS to provide geospatial routing functionality (GNU GPL)

- PostGIS: a popular add-on which provides support for geographic objects (GNU GPL)

- Postgres Enterprise Manager: a non-free tool consisting of a service, multiple agents, and a GUI which provides remote monitoring, management, reporting, capacity planning and tuning

- ST-Links SpatialKit: Extension for directly connecting to spatial databases

- Citus: an extension to turn Postgres into a distributed system to support real-time workloads on large data sets

Benchmarks and Performance

Many informal performance studies of PostgreSQL have been done. Performance improvements aimed at improving scalability started heavily with version 8.1. Simple benchmarks between version 8.0 and version 8.4 showed that the latter was more than 10 times faster on read-only workloads and at least 7.5 times faster on both read and write workloads.

The first industry-standard and peer-validated benchmark was completed in June 2007, using the Sun Java System Application Server (proprietary version of GlassFish) 9.0 Platform Edition, UltraSPARC T1-based Sun Fire server and PostgreSQL 8.2. This result of 778.14 SPECjAppServer2004 JOPS@Standard compares favourably with the 874 JOPS@Standard with Oracle 10 on an Itanium-based HP-UX system.

In August 2007, Sun submitted an improved benchmark score of 813.73 SPECjAppServer2004 JOPS@Standard. With the system under test at a reduced price, the price/performance improved from $84.98/JOPS to $70.57/JOPS.

The default configuration of PostgreSQL uses only a small amount of dedicated memory for performance-critical purposes such as caching database blocks and sorting. This limitation is primarily because older operating systems required kernel changes to allow allocating large blocks of shared memory. PostgreSQL.org provides advice on basic recommended performance practice in a wiki.

In April 2012, Robert Haas of EnterpriseDB demonstrated PostgreSQL 9.2's linear CPU scalability using a server with 64 cores.

Matloob Khushi performed benchmarking between Postgresql 9.0 and MySQL 5.6.15 for their ability to process genomic data. In his performance analysis he found that PostgreSQL extracts overlapping genomic regions eight times faster than MySQL using two datasets of 80,000 each forming random human DNA regions. Insertion and data uploads in PostgreSQL were also better, although general searching capability of both databases was almost equivalent.

Platforms

PostgreSQL is available for the following operating systems: Linux (all recent distributions), Windows (Windows 2000 SP4 and later; compilable by e.g. Visual Studio, now with up to most recent 2015 version), FreeBSD, OpenBSD, NetBSD, OS X (macOS), AIX, HP-UX, Solaris, and UnixWare; and not officially tested: DragonFly BSD, BSD/OS, IRIX, OpenIndiana, OpenSolaris, OpenServer, and Tru64 Unix. Most other Unix-like systems could also work; most modern do support.

PostgreSQL works on any of the following instruction set architectures: x86 and x86-64 on Windows and other operating systems; these are supported on other than Windows: IA-64 Itanium (external support for HP-UX), PowerPC, PowerPC 64, S/390, S/390x, SPARC, SPARC 64, ARMv8-A (64-bit) and older ARM (32-bit, including older such as ARMv6 in Raspberry Pi), MIPS, MIPSel, and PA-RISC. It is also known to work on Alpha (dropped in 9.5), M68k, M32R, NS32k, and VAX. In addition to these, it is possible to build PostgreSQL for an unsupported CPU by disabling spinlocks.

Database administration

Open source front-ends and tools for administering PostgreSQL include:

psql

> The primary front-end for PostgreSQL is the psql command-line program, which can be used to enter SQL queries directly, or execute them from a file. In addition, psql provides a number of meta-commands and various shell-like features to facilitate writing scripts and automating a wide variety of tasks; for example tab completion of object names and SQL syntax.

pgAdmin

> The pgAdmin package is a free and open source graphical user interface administration tool for PostgreSQL, which is supported on many computer platforms. The program is available in more than a dozen languages. The first prototype, named pgManager, was written for PostgreSQL 6.3.2 from 1998, and rewritten and released as pgAdmin under the GNU General Public License (GPL) in later months. The second incarnation (named

pgAdmin II) was a complete rewrite, first released on January 16, 2002. The third version, pgAdmin III, was originally released under the Artistic License and then released under the same license as PostgreSQL. Unlike prior versions that were written in Visual Basic, pgAdmin III is written in C++, using the wxWidgets framework allowing it to run on most common operating systems. The query tool includes a scripting language called pgScript for supporting admin and development tasks. In December 2014, Dave Page, the pgAdmin project founder and primary developer, announced that with the shift towards web-based models work has started on pgAdmin 4 with the aim of facilitating Cloud deployments. In 2016, pgAdmin 4 was released.

phpPgAdmin

phpPgAdmin is a web-based administration tool for PostgreSQL written in PHP and based on the popular phpMyAdmin interface originally written for MySQL administration.

PostgreSQL Studio

PostgreSQL Studio allows users to perform essential PostgreSQL database development tasks from a web-based console. PostgreSQL Studio allows users to work with cloud databases without the need to open firewalls.

TeamPostgreSQL

AJAX/JavaScript-driven web interface for PostgreSQL. Allows browsing, maintaining and creating data and database objects via a web browser. The interface offers tabbed SQL editor with auto-completion, row-editing widgets, click-through foreign key navigation between rows and tables, 'favorites' management for commonly used scripts, among other features. Supports SSH for both the web interface and the database connections. Installers are available for Windows, Mac and Linux, as well as a simple cross-platform archive that runs from a script.

SQLeo

SQLeo is a Visual query builder, that help users to create or understand SQL queries. It has a specific feature to avoid "ERROR: current transaction is aborted, commands ignored until end of transaction block". The source code is hosted on SourceForge.

LibreOffice/OpenOffice.org Base

LibreOffice/OpenOffice.org Base can be used as a front-end for PostgreSQL.

pgBadger

The pgBadger PostgreSQL log analyzer generates detailed reports from a PostgreSQL log file.

A number of companies offer proprietary tools for PostgreSQL. They often consist of a universal core that is adapted for various specific database products. These tools mostly share the administration features with the open source tools but offer improvements in data modeling, importing, exporting or reporting.

Prominent Users

Prominent organizations and products that use PostgreSQL as the primary database include:

- Yahoo! for web user behavioral analysis, storing two petabytes and purportedly the largest data warehouse, using a heavily modified version of PostgreSQL with an entirely different column-based storage engine and different query-processing layer. While in terms of performance, storage, and query the database bears little resemblance to PostgreSQL, the front-end maintains compatibility so that Yahoo can use many off-the-shelf tools already written to interact with PostgreSQL.

- In 2009, the social-networking website MySpace used Aster Data Systems's nCluster database for data warehousing, which was built on unmodified PostgreSQL.

- Geni.com uses PostgreSQL for their main genealogy database.

- OpenStreetMap, a collaborative project to create a free editable map of the world.

- Afilias, domain registries for .org, .info and others.

- Sony Online multiplayer online games.

- BASF, shopping platform for their agribusiness portal.

- Reddit social news website.

- Skype VoIP application, central business databases.

- Sun xVM, Sun's virtualization and datacenter automation suite.

- MusicBrainz, open online music encyclopedia.

- The International Space Station - for collecting telemetry data in orbit and replicating it to the ground.

- MyYearbook social-networking site.

- Instagram, a mobile photo-sharing service.

- Disqus, an online discussion and commenting service.

- TripAdvisor, travel-information website of mostly user-generated content.

- Yandex, a Russian internet company switched from Oracle to Postgres for its email offering.

- AWS Redshift, a columnar OLAP system based on ParAccel's Postgres modifications.

Service Implementations

Some major vendors offer PostgreSQLas software as a service:

- Heroku, a platform as a service provider, has supported PostgreSQL since the start in

2007. They offer value-add features like full database "roll-back" (ability to restore a database from any point in time), which is based on WAL-E, open-source software developed by Heroku.

- In January 2012, EnterpriseDB released a cloud version of both PostgreSQL and their own proprietary Postgres Plus Advanced Server with automated provisioning for failover, replication, load-balancing, and scaling. It runs on Amazon Web Services.

- VMware has offered vFabric Postgres (also known as vPostgres) for private clouds on vSphere since May 2012.

- In November 2013, Amazon.com announced the addition of PostgreSQL to their Relational Database Service offering.

- In November 2016, Amazon Web Services announced the addition of PostgreSQL compatibility to their cloud-native Amazon Aurora managed database offering.

Release History

Release	First release	Latest minor version	Latest release	End of Life	Milestones
6.0	1997-01-29	–	N/A	N/A	First formal release of PostgreSQL, unique indexes, pg_dumpall utility, ident authentication
6.1	1997-06-08	6.1.1	1997-07-22	N/A	Multi-column indexes, sequences, money data type, GEQO (GEnetic Query Optimizer)
6.2	1997-10-02	6.2.1	1997-10-17	N/A	JDBC interface, triggers, server programming interface, constraints
6.3	1998-03-01	6.3.2	1998-04-07	2003-04	SQL92 subselect capability, PL/pgTCL
6.4	1998-10-30	6.4.2	1998-12-20	2003-10	VIEWs (then only read-only) and RULEs, PL/pgSQL
6.5	1999-06-09	6.5.3	1999-10-13	2004-06	MVCC, temporary tables, more SQL statement support (CASE, INTERSECT, and EXCEPT)
7.0	2000-05-08	7.0.3	2000-11-11	2004-05	Foreign keys, SQL92 syntax for joins
7.1	2001-04-13	7.1.3	2001-08-15	2006-04	Write-ahead log, outer joins
7.2	2002-02-04	7.2.8	2005-05-09	2007-02	PL/Python, OIDs no longer required, internationalization of messages
7.3	2002-11-27	7.3.21	2008-01-07	2007-11	Schema, table function, prepared query
7.4	2003-11-17	7.4.30	2010-10-04	2010-10	Optimization on JOINs and data warehousing functions
8.0	2005-01-19	8.0.26	2010-10-04	2010-10	Native server on Microsoft Windows, savepoints, tablespaces, point-in-time recovery

8.1	2005-11-08	8.1.23	2010-12-16	2010-11	Performance optimization, two-phase commit, table partitioning, index bitmap scan, shared row locking, roles
8.2	2006-12-05	8.2.23	2011-09-26	2011-12	Performance optimization, online index builds, advisory locks, warm standby
8.3	2008-02-04	8.3.23	2013-02-07	2013-12	Heap-only tuples, full text search, SQL/XML, ENUM types, UUID types
8.4	2009-07-01	8.4.22	2014-07-24	2014-07	Windowing functions, column-level permissions, parallel database restore, per-database collation, common table expressions and recursive queries
9.0	2010-09-20	9.0.23	2015-10-08	2015-09	Built-in binary streaming replication, hot standby, 64-bit Windows, per-column triggers and conditional trigger execution, exclusion constraints, anonymous code blocks, named parameters, password rules
9.1	2011-09-12	9.1.24	2016-10-27	2016-09	Synchronous replication, per-column collations, unlogged tables, k-nearest neighbors (k-NN) indexing, serializable snapshot isolation, writeable common table expressions, SE-Linux integration, extensions, SQL/MED attached tables (Foreign Data Wrappers), triggers on views
9.2	2012-09-10	9.2.19	2016-10-27	2017-09	Cascading streaming replication, index-only scans, native JSON support, improved lock management, range types, pg_receivexlog tool, space-partitioned GiST indexes
9.3	2013-09-09	9.3.15	2016-10-27	2018-09	Custom background workers, data checksums, dedicated JSON operators, LATERAL JOIN, faster pg_dump, new pg_isready server monitoring tool, trigger features, view features, writeable foreign tables, materialized views, replication improvements
9.4	2014-12-18	9.4.10	2016-10-27	2019-12	JSONB data type, ALTER SYSTEM statement for changing config values, refresh materialized views without blocking reads, dynamic registration/start/stop of background worker processes, Logical Decoding API, GiN index improvements, Linux huge page support, database cache reloading via pg_prewarm
9.5	2016-01-07	9.5.5	2016-10-27	2021-01	UPSERT, row level security, TABLESAMPLE, CUBE/ROLLUP, GROUPING SETS, and new BRIN index
9.6	2016-09-29	9.6.1	2016-10-27	2021-09	Parallel query support, PostgreSQL foreign data wrapper (FDW) improvements with sort/join pushdown, multiple synchronous standbys, faster vacuuming of large table
10		10	TBD (2017)	TBD	

Legend:
Old version
Older version, still supported
Latest version
Latest preview version
Future release

Community-supported
Community support ended

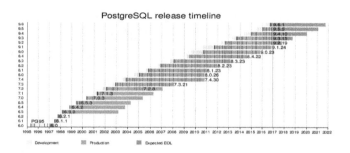
PostgreSQL release timeline

Oracle Database

Oracle Database (commonly referred to as Oracle RDBMS or simply as Oracle) is an object-relational database management system produced and marketed by Oracle Corporation.

Larry Ellison and his two friends and former co-workers, Bob Miner and Ed Oates, started a consultancy called Software Development Laboratories (SDL) in 1977. SDL developed the original version of the Oracle software. The name *Oracle* comes from the code-name of a CIA-funded project Ellison had worked on while formerly employed by Ampex.

Physical and Logical Structures

An Oracle database system—identified by an alphanumeric system identifier or SID—comprises at least one instance of the application, along with data storage. An instance—identified persistently by an instantiation number (or activation id: SYS.V_$DATABASE.ACTIVATION#)—comprises a set of operating-system processes and memory-structures that interact with the storage. Typical processes include PMON (the process monitor) and SMON (the system monitor). Oracle documentation can refer to an active database instance as a "shared memory realm".

Users of Oracle databases refer to the server-side memory-structure as the SGA (System Global Area). The SGA typically holds cache information such as data-buffers, SQL commands, and user information. In addition to storage, the database consists of online redo logs (or logs), which hold transactional history. Processes can in turn archive the online redo logs into archive logs (offline redo logs), which provide the basis for data recovery and for the physical-standby forms of data replication using Oracle Data Guard.

The Oracle RAC (Real Application Clusters) option uses multiple instances attached to a central storage array. In version 10*g*, grid computing introduced shared resources where an instance can use CPU resources from another node in the grid. The advantage of Oracle RAC is that the resources on both nodes are used by the database, and each node uses its own memory and CPU. Information is shared between nodes through the interconnect—the virtual private network.

The Oracle DBMS can store and execute stored procedures and functions within itself. PL/SQL (Oracle Corporation's proprietary procedural extension to SQL), or the object-oriented language Java can invoke such code objects and/or provide the programming structures for writing them.

Storage

The Oracle RDBMS stores data logically in the form of tablespaces and physically in the form of data files ("datafiles"). Tablespaces can contain various types of memory segments, such as Data Segments, Index Segments, etc. Segments in turn comprise one or more extents. Extents comprise groups of contiguous data blocks. Data blocks form the basic units of data storage.

A DBA can impose maximum quotas on storage per user within each tablespace.

Partitioning

The partitioning feature was introduced in Oracle 8. This allows the partitioning of tables based on different set of keys. Specific partitions can then be added or dropped to help manage large data sets.

Monitoring

Oracle database management tracks its computer data storage with the help of information stored in the SYSTEM tablespace. The SYSTEM tablespace contains the data dictionary, indexes and clusters. A data dictionary consists of a special collection of tables that contains information about all user-objects in the database. Since version 8i, the Oracle RDBMS also supports "locally managed" tablespaces that store space management information in bitmaps in their own headers rather than in the SYSTEM tablespace (as happens with the default "dictionary-managed" tablespaces). Version 10g and later introduced the SYSAUX tablespace, which contains some of the tables formerly stored in the SYSTEM tablespace, along with objects for other tools such as OEM, which previously required its own tablespace.

Disk Files

Disk files primarily represent one of the following structures:

- Data and index files: These files provide the physical storage of data, which can consist of the data-dictionary data (associated to the tablespace SYSTEM), user data, or index data. These files can be managed manually or managed by Oracle itself. Note that a datafile has to belong to exactly one tablespace, whereas a tablespace can consist of multiple datafiles.

- Redo log files, consisting of all changes to the database, used to recover from an instance failure. Note that often a database will store these files multiple times, for extra security in case of disk failure. The identical redo log files are said to belong to the same group.

- Undo files: These special datafiles, which can only contain undo information, aid in recovery, rollbacks, and read-consistency.

- Archive log files: These files, copies of the redo log files, are usually stored at different locations. They are necessary (for example) when applying changes to a standby database, or when performing recovery after a media failure. It is possible to archive to multiple locations.

- Tempfiles: These special datafiles serve exclusively for temporary storage data (used for example for large sorts or for global temporary tables)

- Control file, necessary for database startup. "A binary file that records the physical structure of a database and contains the names and locations of redo log files, the time stamp of the database creation, the current log sequence number, checkpoint information, and so on."

At the physical level, data files comprise one or more data blocks, where the block size can vary between data files.

Data files can occupy pre-allocated space in the file system of a computer server, utilize raw disk directly, or exist within ASM logical volumes.

Database Schema

Most Oracle database installations traditionally came with a default schema called SCOTT. After the installation process sets up sample tables, the user can log into the database with the username scott and the password tiger. The name of the SCOTT schema originated with Bruce Scott, one of the first employees at Oracle (then Software Development Laboratories), who had a cat named Tiger.

Oracle Corporation now de-emphasizes the SCOTT schema, as it uses few features of more recent Oracle releases. Most recent examples supplied by Oracle Corporation reference the default HR or OE schemas.

Other default schemas include:

- SYS (essential core database structures and utilities)

- SYSTEM (additional core database structures and utilities, and privileged account)

- OUTLN (utilized to store metadata for stored outlines for stable query-optimizer execution plans.)

- BI, IX, HR, OE, PM, and SH (expanded sample schemas containing more data and structures than the older SCOTT schema).

System Global Area

Each Oracle instance uses a System Global Area or SGA—a shared-memory area—to store its data and control-information.

Each Oracle instance allocates itself an SGA when it starts and de-allocates it at shut-down time. The information in the SGA consists of the following elements, each of which has a fixed size, established at instance startup:

- Datafiles

Every Oracle database has one or more physical datafiles, which contain all the database data. The data of logical database structures, such as tables and indexes, is physically stored in the datafiles allocated for a database.

Datafiles have the following characteristics:

- One or more datafiles form a logical unit of database storage called a tablespace.

- A datafile can be associated with only one tablespace.

- Datafiles can be defined to extend automatically when they are full.

Data in a datafile is read, as needed, during normal database operation and stored in the memory cache of Oracle Database. For example, if a user wants to access some data in a table of a database, and if the requested information is not already in the memory cache for the database, then it is read from the appropriate datafiles and stored in memory.

Modified or new data is not necessarily written to a datafile immediately. To reduce the amount of disk access and to increase performance, data is pooled in memory and written to the appropriate datafiles all at once.

- the redo log buffer: this stores redo entries—a log of changes made to the database. The instance writes redo log buffers to the redo log as quickly and efficiently as possible. The redo log aids in instance recovery in the event of a system failure.

- the shared pool: this area of the SGA stores shared-memory structures such as shared SQL areas in the library cache and internal information in the data dictionary. An insufficient amount of memory allocated to the shared pool can cause performance degradation.

- the Large pool Optional area that provides large memory allocations for certain large processes, such as Oracle backup and recovery operations, and I/O server processes

- Database buffer cache: Caches blocks of data retrieved from the database

- KEEP *buffer pool*: A specialized type of database buffer cache that is tuned to retain blocks of data in memory for long periods of time

- RECYCLE buffer pool: A specialized type of database buffer cache that is tuned to recycle or remove block from memory quickly

- nK buffer cache: One of several specialized database buffer caches designed to hold block sizes different from the default database block size

- Java pool:Used for all session-specific Java code and data in the Java Virtual Machine (JVM)

- Streams pool: Used by Oracle Streams to store information required by capture and apply

When you start the instance by using Enterprise Manager or SQL*Plus, the amount of memory allocated for the SGA is displayed.

Library Cache

The library cache stores shared SQL, caching the parse tree and the execution plan for every unique SQL statement. If multiple applications issue the same SQL statement, each application can access the shared SQL area. This reduces the amount of memory needed and reduces the processing-time used for parsing and execution planning.

Data Dictionary Cache

The data dictionary comprises a set of tables and views that map the structure of the database.

Oracle databases store information here about the logical and physical structure of the database. The data dictionary contains information such as:

- user information, such as user privileges

- integrity constraints defined for tables in the database

- names and datatypes of all columns in database tables

- information on space allocated and used for schema objects

The Oracle instance frequently accesses the data dictionary to parse SQL statements. Oracle operation depends on ready access to the data dictionary—performance bottlenecks in the data dictionary affect all Oracle users. Because of this, database administrators must make sure that the data dictionary cache has sufficient capacity to cache this data. Without enough memory for the data-dictionary cache, users see a severe performance degradation. Allocating sufficient memory to the shared pool where the data dictionary cache resides precludes this particular performance problem.

Program Global Area

The Program Global Area or PGA memory-area of an Oracle instance contains data and control-information for Oracle's server-processes or background process. Every server or background process has its own PGA, the total of PGA elements is call Instance PGA.

The size and content of the PGA depends on the Oracle-server options installed. This area consists of the following components:

- stack-space: the memory that holds the session's variables, arrays, and so on

- session-information: unless using the multithreaded server, the instance stores its session-information in the PGA. In a multithreaded server, the session-information goes in the SGA.)

- private SQL-area: an area that holds information such as bind-variables and runtime-buffers

- sorting area: an area in the PGA that holds information on sorts, hash-joins, etc.

DBAs can monitor PGA usage via the system view.

Dynamic Performance Views

The dynamic performance views (also known as "fixed views") within an Oracle database present information from virtual tables (X$ tables) built on the basis of database memory. Database users can access the V$ views (named after the prefix of their synonyms) to obtain information on database structures and performance.

Process Architectures

Oracle Processes

The Oracle RDBMS typically relies on a group of processes running simultaneously in the background and interacting to monitor and expedite database operations. Typical operating environments might include - temporarily or permanently - some of the following individual processes (shown along with their abbreviated nomenclature):

- advanced queueing processes (Qnnn)

- archiver processes (ARCn)

- checkpoint process (CKPT) *REQUIRED*

- coordinator-of-job-queues process (CJQn): dynamically spawns slave processes for job-queues

- database writer processes (DBWn) *REQUIRED*

- Data Pump master process (DMnn)

- Data Pump worker processes (DWnn)

- dispatcher processes (Dnnn): multiplex server-processes on behalf of users

- main Data Guard Broker monitor process (DMON)

- job-queue slave processes (Jnnn)

- log-writer process (LGWR) *REQUIRED*

- log-write network-server (LNSn): transmits redo logs in Data Guard environments

- logical standby coordinator process (LSP0): controls Data Guard log-application

- media-recovery process (MRP): detached recovery-server process

- memory-manager process (MMAN): used for internal database tasks such as Automatic Shared Memory Management (ASMM)

- memory-monitor process (MMON): process for automatic problem-detection, self-tuning and statistics-gathering

- memory-monitor light process (MMNL): gathers and stores Automatic Workload Repository (AWR) data

- mmon slaves (Mnnnn—M0000, M0001, etc.): background slaves of the MMON process

- netslave processes (NSVn): Data Guard Broker inter-database communication processes

- parallel query execution servers (Pnnn)

- process-monitor process (PMON) *REQUIRED*

- process-spawner process (PSPo): spawns Oracle background processes after initial instance startup

- queue-monitor coordinator process (QMNC): dynamically spawns queue monitor slaves

- queue-monitor processes (QMNn)

- recoverer process (RECO)

- remote file-server process (RFS): in Oracle Data Guard, a standby recipient of primary redo-logs

- monitor for Data Guard management (RSMo): Data Guard Broker Worker process

- shared server processes (Snnn): serve client-requests

- space-management coordinator process (SMCO): coordinates space management (from release 11g)

- system monitor process (SMON) *REQUIRED*

User Processes, Connections and Sessions

Oracle Database terminology distinguishes different computer-science terms in describing how end-users interact with the database:

- user processes involve the invocation of application software

- a connection refers to the pathway linking a user process to an Oracle instance

- sessions consist of specific established groups of interactions, with each group involving a client process and an Oracle instance.

Each session within an instance has a session identifier - a session ID or "SID" (distinct from the Oracle system-identifier SID), and may also have an associated SPID (operating-system process identifier).

Concurrency and Locking

Oracle databases control simultaneous access to data resources with locks (alternatively documented as "enqueues"). The databases also utilize "latches" - low-level serialization mechanisms to protect shared data structures in the System Global Area.

Oracle locks fall into three categories:

- DML locks (or data locks) protect data

- DDL locks (or data dictionary locks) protect the structure of schema objects

- System locks (including latches, mutexes and internal locks) protect internal database structures like data files.

Configuration

Database administrators control many of the tunable variations in an Oracle instance by means of values in a parameter file. This file in its ASCII default form ("pfile") normally has a name of the format init<SID-name>.ora. The default binary equivalent server parameter file ("spfile") (dynamically reconfigurable to some extent) defaults to the format spfile<SID-name>.ora. Within an SQL-based environment, the views V$PARAMETER and V$SPPARAMETER give access to reading parameter values.

Implementation

The Oracle DBMS kernel code depends on C programming. Database administrators have limited access to Oracle-internal C structures via V$ views and their underlying X$ "tables".

Layers or modules in the kernel (depending on different releases) may include the following (given with their inferred meaning):

K: Kernel

KA: Kernel Access

KC: Kernel Cache

KCB: Kernel Cache Buffer

KCBW: Kernel Cache Buffer Wait

KCC: Kernel Cache Control file

KCCB: Kernel Cache Control file Backup

KCCCF: Kernel Cache Copy Flash recovery area

KCCDC: Kernel cache Control file Copy

KCP: Kernel Cache transPortable tablespace

KCR: Kernel Cache Redo

KCT: Kernel Cache insTance

KD: Kernel Data

KG: Kernel Generic

KGL: Kernel Generic library cache

KGLJ: Kernel Generic library cache Java

KJ: Kernel Locking

KK: Kernel Compilation

KQ: Kernel Query

KS: Kernel Service(s)

KSB: Kernel Service Background

KSM: Kernel Service Memory

KSR: Kernel Service Reliable message

KSU: Kernel Service User

KSUSE: Kernel Service User SEssion

KSUSECON: Kernel Service User SEssion CONnection

KSUSEH: Kernel Service User SEssion History

KT: Kernel Transaction(s)

KTU: Kernel Transaction Undo

KX: Kernel Execution

KXS: Kernel eXecution Sql

KZ: Kernel Security

K2: Kernel Distributed Transactions

Administration

The "Scheduler" (DBMS_SCHEDULER package, available from Oracle 10g onwards) and the Job subsystem (DBMS_JOB package) permit the automation of predictable processing.

Oracle Resource Manager aims to allocate CPU resources between users and groups of users when such resources become scarce.

Oracle Corporation has stated in product announcements that manageability for DBAs had improved from Oracle9i to 10g. Lungu and Vătuiu (2008) assessed relative manageability by performing common DBA tasks and measuring timings. They performed their tests on a single Pentium CPU (1.7 GHz) with 512 MB RAM, running Windows Server 2000. From Oracle9i to 10g, installation improved 36%, day-to-day administration 63%, backup and recovery 63%, and performance diagnostics and tuning 74%, for a weighted total improvement of 56%. The researchers concluded that "Oracle10g represents a giant step forward from Oracle9i in making the database easier to use and manage".

Logging and Tracing

Various file-system structures hold logs and trace files which record different aspects of database activity. Configurable destinations for such records may include:

- background dump (bdump) destination: contains files generated when an Oracle process experiences unexpected problems. Also holds the "alert log".

- core dump (cdump) destination

- user dump (udump) destination

Network Access

Oracle Net Services allow client or remote applications to access Oracle databases via network sessions using various protocols.

Internationalization

Oracle Database software comes in 63 language-versions (including regional variations such as British English and American English). Variations between versions cover the names of days and months, abbreviations, time-symbols (such as A.M. and A.D.), and sorting.

Oracle Corporation has translated Oracle Database error-messages into Arabic, Catalan, Chinese, Czech, Danish, Dutch, English, Finnish, French, German, Greek, Hebrew, Hungarian, Italian, Japanese, Korean, Norwegian, Polish, Portuguese, Romanian, Russian, Slovak, Spanish, Swedish, Thai and Turkish.

Oracle Corporation provides database developers with tools and mechanisms for producing internationalized database applications: referred to internally as "Globalization".

History

Patch Updates and Security Alerts

Oracle Corporation releases Critical Patch Updates (CPUs) or Security Patch Updates (SPUs) and Security Alerts to close security holes that could be used for data theft.Critical Patch Updates (CPUs) and Security Alerts come out quarterly on the Tuesday closest to 17th day of the month.

- Customers may receive release notification by email.

- White Paper: Critical Patch Update Implementation Best Practices

Version Numbering

Oracle products follow a custom release numbering and naming convention. With the Oracle RDBMS 10*g* release, Oracle Corporation began using the "10*g*" label in all versions of its major products, although some sources refer to Oracle Applications Release 11*i* as Oracle 11*i*. The suffixes "i", "g" and "c" do not actually represent a low-order part of the version number, as letters typically represent in software industry version numbering; that is, there is no predecessor version of Oracle 10*g* called Oracle 10*f*. Instead, the letters stand for "internet", "grid" and "cloud", respectively. Consequently, many simply drop the "g" or "i" suffix when referring to specific versions of an Oracle product.

Major database-related products and some of their versions include:

- Oracle Application Server 10*g* (also known as "Oracle AS 10*g*"): a middleware product;

- Oracle Applications Release 11*i* (aka Oracle e-Business Suite, Oracle Financials or Oracle 11i): a suite of business applications;

- Oracle Developer Suite 10*g* (9.0.4);

- Oracle JDeveloper 10*g*: a Java integrated development environment;

Since version 2, Oracle's RDBMS release numbering has used the following codes:

- Oracle v2 : 2.3

- Oracle v3 : 3.1.3

- Oracle v4 : 4.1.4.0-4.1.4.4

- Oracle v5 : 5.0.22, 5.1.17, 5.1.22

- Oracle v6 : 6.0.17-6.0.36 (no OPS code), 6.0.37 (with OPS)

- Oracle7: 7.0.12–7.3.4

- Oracle8 Database: 8.0.3–8.0.6

- Oracle8*i* Database Release 1: 8.1.5.0–8.1.5.1

- Oracle8*i* Database Release 2: 8.1.6.0–8.1.6.3

- Oracle8*i* Database Release 3: 8.1.7.0–8.1.7.4

- Oracle9*i* Database Release 1: 9.0.1.0–9.0.1.5 (Patchset as of December 2003)

- Oracle9*i* Database Release 2: 9.2.0.1–9.2.0.8 (Patchset as of April 2007)

- Oracle Database 10*g* Release 1: 10.1.0.2–10.1.0.5 (Patchset as of February 2006)

- Oracle Database 10*g* Release 2: 10.2.0.1–10.2.0.5 (Patchset as of April 2010)

- Oracle Database 11*g* Release 1: 11.1.0.6–11.1.0.7 (Patchset as of September 2008)

- Oracle Database 11*g* Release 2: 11.2.0.1–11.2.0.4 (Patchset as of August 2013)

- Oracle Database 12*c* Release 1: 12.1.0.1 (Patchset as of June 2013)

- Oracle Database 12*c* Release 1: 12.1.0.2 (Patchset as of July 2014)

The version-numbering syntax within each release follows the pattern: major.maintenance.application-server.component-specific.platform-specific.

For example, "10.2.0.1 for 64-bit Solaris" means: 10th major version of Oracle, maintenance level 2, Oracle Application Server (OracleAS) 0, level 1 for Solaris 64-bit.

Oracle Database Product Family

Based on licensing and pricing, Oracle Corporation groups its Oracle Database-related product portfolio into the "Oracle Database product family", which consists of the following:

- Oracle Database editions: variations of the software designed for different scenarios.

- Database options: extra cost offers providing additional database functionality.

- Oracle data models: database schemas, offering pre-built data models with database analytics and business intelligence capabilities for specific industries.

- Management packs: integrated set of Oracle Enterprise Manager tools for maintaining various aspects of Oracle Database.

- Some of Oracle engineered systems, either specifically built for Oracle Database deployment or supporting such capability.

- Other related products intended for use with Oracle Database.

Database Editions

As of 2016 the latest Oracle Database version (12.1.0.2) comes in two editions:

- Oracle Database 12c Enterprise Edition (EE): Oracle Corporation's flagship database product. A fully featured edition of Oracle Database, it also allows purchase of add-on features in the form of Database Options and Management packs and imposes no limitation on server resources available to the database.

- Oracle Database 12c Standard Edition 2 (SE2): intended for small- to medium-sized implementations, this edition comes with Real Application Clusters option included, a reduced set of database features, and the licensing restriction to run on servers or clusters with a maximum of 2 sockets total and capped to use a maximum of 16 concurrent user threads. Oracle positions SE2 as a starter edition, stressing complete upward compatibility and ease of upgrade to the more costly Enterprise Edition.

Oracle Corporation also makes the following editions available:

- Oracle Database Express Edition 11gR2 (Oracle Database XE), a free-to-use entry-level version of Oracle Database 11gR2 available for Windows and Linux platforms limited to using only one CPU, up to 1 GB of RAM and storing up to 11 GB of user data. Oracle Database XE is a separate product from the rest of Oracle Database product family. It provides a subset of Standard Edition functionality (lacking features such as Java Virtual Machine, managed backup and recovery and high availability), is community-supported and comes with its own license terms. Express Edition was first introduced in 2005 with Oracle 10g release with a limitation to a maximum of 4 GB of user data. Oracle 11g Express Edition, released on 24 September 2011, increased user data cap to 11 GB.

- Oracle Database Personal Edition, a single-user, single-machine development and deployment license, allows use of all database features and extra-cost database options (with the exception of the Oracle RAC option). It is available for purchase for Windows and Linux platforms only and does not include management packs.

Up to and including Oracle Database 12.1.0.1, Oracle also offered the following:

- Standard Edition (SE) ran on single or clustered servers with a maximum capacity of 4 CPU sockets. It was largely the same as the current SE2 offer, including Real Application Clusters option at no additional cost, however allowing twice as much CPU sockets in a server or a cluster.

- Standard Edition One (SE1), introduced with Oracle 10*g*, offered the same features as SE and was licensed to run on single servers with a maximum of two CPU sockets.

Oracle Corporation discontinued SE and SE1 with the 12.1.0.2 release and stopped offering new licenses for these editions on December 1, 2015. Industry journalists and some ISVs perceived Oracle's desupport of affordable SE1 and restrictive updates to SE in the form of SE2 (specifically, the introduction of thread throttling and halving the number of licensable CPU sockets without changing price-per-socket) as an attempt to repress customers' efforts to scale SE/SE1 installations up to "enterprise" class by means of virtualization, while at the same time pushing them towards the more expensive Enterprise Edition or to Oracle Cloud Database as a service.

Database Options

Oracle Corporation refers to a number of add-on database features as "database options". These aim to enhance and complement existing database functionality to meet customer-specific requirements. All Database Options are only available for Enterprise Edition and offered for an extra cost. The one exception to these two rules is Oracle Real Application Clusters option which comes included with Oracle Database 12c Standard Edition 2 at no additional cost.

- Oracle Active Data Guard extends Oracle Data Guard functionality with advanced features, allowing read-only access to data in a physical standby database to offload primary of such tasks as reporting, ad-hoc queries, data extraction and backup, offloading redo transport and minimizing standby impact on commit response times (using Far Sync feature), providing option for rolling upgrades for non-RAC customers, managing clients workload across replicated database and improving automated service failover (using Global Data Services), etc.

- Oracle Advanced Analytics allows access to in-database data mining algorithms and use of Oracle R Enterprise functionality, an integration with open-source R statistical programming language and environment.

- Oracle Advanced Compression complements Enterprise Edition basic table compression feature with comprehensive data compression and Information Lifecycle Management capabilities, including those specifically tailored to Oracle's engineered systems, like Oracle Exadata.

- Oracle Advanced Security provides Transparent Data Encryption and Data Redaction security features, the former allowing encryption of data stored in a database (all or a subset of it), exported using Data Pump, or backed up using Oracle Recovery Manager, and the latter allowing redaction of sensitive database data (e.g., credit card or social security numbers) returned to database applications.

- Oracle Database In-Memory, an in-memory, column-oriented data store, has been seamlessly integrated into the Oracle Database. This technology aims to improve the performance of analytic workloads without impacting the performance of transactions that continue to use Oracle's traditional row format in memory. Note: data is persisted on disk only in a row format, so no additional storage is required. The product's performance comes through the in-memory columnar format and through the use of SIMD vector processing (Single Instruction processing Multiple Data values). Database In-Memory features include:

  o An In-Memory column store, a new component of the SGA called the In-Memory Area. One can allocate a little or a lot of memory to the In-Memory Area. The larger the In-Memory Area, the greater the number of objects that can be brought into memory in the In-Memory columnar format. Unlike in a pure in-memory database not all of the data in the Oracle Database requires populating into memory in the columnar format.

  o Only objects with the INMEMORY attribute get populated into the In-Memory column store. The INMEMORY attribute can be specified on a tablespace, table, (sub) partition, or materialized view. If it is enabled at the tablespace level, then all tables and materialized views in the tablespace are enabled for In-Memory by default.

  o Data is populated into a new In-Memory column store by a set of background processes referred to as worker processes (ora_w001_orcl). Each worker process receives a subset of database blocks from the object to populate into the In-Memory column store. Population is a streaming mechanism, simultaneously columnizing and compressing the data.

  o Oracle takes advantage of SIMD vector processing to scan the data in the columnar format. Instead of evaluating each entry in the column one at a time, SIMD vector processing allows a set of column values to be evaluated together in a single CPU instruction. The column format used in the IM column store has been specifically designed to maximize the number of column entries that can be loaded into the vector registers on the CPU and evaluated in a single CPU instruction.

  o Fault tolerance for In-Memory Column Store runs on Oracle Engineered Systems (Oracle Exadata, Oracle Database Appliance and Oracle Supercluster), mirroring the data in memory across RAC nodes. If one RAC node fails, the database simply reads from the other side of the mirror.

  o In-Memory Aggregation improves performance of typical analytic queries using efficient in-memory arrays for joins and aggregation.

- Oracle Database Vault enforces segregation of duties, principle of least privilege and other data access controls, allowing protection of application data from access by privileged database users.

- Oracle Label Security is a sophisticated and flexible framework for a fine-grained label based access control (LBAC) implementation.

- Oracle Multitenant is the capability that allows database consolidation and provides additional abstraction layer. In a Multitenant configuration, one Oracle database instance known as "container database" (CDB) acts as a federated database system for a collection of up to 252 distinct portable collections of database objects, referred to as "pluggable databases" (PDB), each appearing to an outside client as a regular non-CDB Oracle database.

- Oracle On-Line Analytical Processing (OLAP) is Oracle implementation of online analytical processing.

- Oracle Partitioning allows partitioning of tables and indices, where large objects are stored in database as a collection of individual smaller pieces at the same time appearing on application level as a uniform data object.

- Oracle RAC One Node is a one-node version of Oracle Real Application Clusters, providing capabilities for database failover and high availability in the form of rolling upgrades, online instance migration, application continuity and automated quality of service management.

- Oracle Real Application Clusters (Oracle RAC) is the cluster solution for Oracle Database.

- Oracle Real Application Testing is a suite of features that enable comprehensive testing of system changes in a simulation of production-level workload and use. The option includes Database Replay, SQL Performance Analyzer, Database Consolidation Workbench and SQL Tuning Sets.

- Oracle Spatial and Graph complements the Oracle Locator feature (available in all editions of Oracle Database) with advanced spatial capabilities enabling the development of complex geographic information systems and includes network data model and RDF/OWL Semantic graphs.

- Oracle TimesTen Application-Tier Database Cache allows caching subsets of a database in the application tier for improved response time. It is built using Oracle TimesTen In-Memory Database.

Supported Platforms

Oracle Database 12c is supported on the following OS and architecture combinations:

- Linux on x86-64 (only Red Hat Enterprise Linux, Oracle Linux and SUSE distributions are supported)

- Microsoft Windows on x86-64

- Oracle Solaris on SPARC and x86-64

- IBM AIX on POWER Systems

- IBM Linux on z Systems

- HP-UX on Itanium

In 2011, Oracle Corporation announced the availability of Oracle Database Appliance, a pre-built, pre-tuned, highly available clustered database server built using two SunFire X86 servers and direct attached storage.

Some Oracle Enterprise edition databases running on certain Oracle-supplied hardware can utilize Hybrid Columnar Compression for more efficient storage.

Database Features

Apart from the clearly defined database options, Oracle databases may include many semi-autonomous software sub-systems, which Oracle Corporation sometimes refers to as "features" in a sense subtly different from the normal usage of the word. For example, Oracle Data Guard counts officially as a feature, but the command-stack within SQL*Plus, though a usability feature, does not appear in the list of "features" in Oracle's list. Such "features" may include (for example):

- Active Session History (ASH), the collection of data for immediate monitoring of very recent database activity.

- Automatic Workload Repository (AWR)], providing monitoring and statistical services to Oracle database installations from Oracle version 10. Prior to the release of Oracle version 10, the Statspack facility provided similar functionality.

- Clusterware

- Data Aggregation and Consolidation

- Data Guard for high availability

- Generic Connectivity for connecting to non-Oracle systems.

- Data Pump utilities, which aid in importing and exporting data and metadata between databases

- SQL*Loader, utility that facilitates high performance data loading.

- Database Resource Manager (DRM), which controls the use of computing resources.

- Fast-start parallel rollback

- Fine-grained auditing (FGA) (in Oracle Enterprise Edition) supplements standard security-auditing features

- Flashback for selective data recovery and reconstruction

- iSQL*Plus, a web-browser-based graphical user interface (GUI) for Oracle database data-manipulation (compare SQL*Plus)

- Oracle Data Access Components (ODAC), tools that consist of:

  - Oracle Data Provider for .NET (ODP.NET)

  - Oracle Developer Tools (ODT) for Visual Studio

  - Oracle Providers for ASP.NET

  - Oracle Database Extensions for .NET

  - Oracle Provider for OLE DB

  - Oracle Objects for OLE

  - Oracle Services for Microsoft Transaction Server

- Oracle-managed files (OMF) - a feature allowing automated naming, creation and deletion of datafiles at the operating-system level.

- Oracle Multimedia (known as "Oracle *inter*Media" before Oracle 11g) for storing and integrating multimedia data within a database

- Oracle Spatial and Graph

- Recovery Manager (rman) for database backup, restoration and recovery

- SQL*Plus, a program that allows users to interact with Oracle database(s) via SQL and PL/SQL commands on a command-line. Compare iSQL*Plus.

- SQLcl, a command-line interface for queries, developed on the basis of Oracle SQL Developer

- Universal Connection Pool (UCP), a connection pool based on Java and supporting JDBC, LDAP, and JCA

- Virtual Private Database (VPD), an implementation of fine-grained access control.

- Oracle Application Express, a no-cost environment for database-oriented software-development

- Oracle XML DB, or XDB, a no-cost component in each edition of the database, provides high-performance technology for storing and retrieving native XML.

- Oracle GoldenGate 11*g* (distributed real-time data acquisition)

- Oracle Text uses standard SQL to index, search, and analyze text and documents stored in the Oracle database.

Utilities

Oracle Corporation classifies as "utilities" bundled software supporting data transfer, data maintenance and database administration.

Utilities included in Oracle database distributions include:

- oradebug - interfaces with Oracle session tracing

Tools

Users can develop their own applications in Java and in PL/SQL, using tools such as:

- Oracle Forms
- Oracle JDeveloper
- Oracle Reports

As of 2007 Oracle Corporation had started a drive toward "wizard"-driven environments with a view to enabling non-programmers to produce simple data-driven applications.

The Database Upgrade Assistant (DBUA) provides a GUI for the upgrading of an Oracle database.

JAccelerator (NCOMP) - a native-compilation Java "accelerator", integrates hardware-optimized Java code into an Oracle 10g database.

Oracle SQL Developer, a free graphical tool for database development, allows developers to browse database objects, to run SQL statements and SQL scripts, and to edit and debug PL/SQL statements. It incorporates standard and customized reporting.

Oracle REST Data Services (ORDS) function as a Java EE-based alternative to Oracle HTTP Server, providing a REST-based interface to relational data.

Oracle's OPatch provides patch management for Oracle databases.

The SQLTXPLAIN tool (or SQLT) offers tuning assistance for Oracle SQL queries.

Testing

- Oracle Live SQL makes available a test environment for Oracle Database users.

External Routines

PL/SQL routines within Oracle databases can access external routines registered in operating-system shared libraries.

Use

The Oracle RDBMS has had a reputation among novice users as difficult to install on Linux systems. Oracle Corporation has packaged recent versions for several popular Linux distributions in an attempt to minimize installation challenges beyond the level of technical expertise required to install a database server.

Official Support

Users who have Oracle support contracts can use Oracle's "My Oracle Support" or "MOS" web site

- known as "MetaLink" until a re-branding exercise completed in October 2010. The support site provides users of Oracle Corporation products with a repository of reported problems, diagnostic scripts and solutions. It also integrates with the provision of support tools, patches and upgrades.

The *Remote Diagnostic Agent* or *RDA* can operate as a command-line diagnostic tool executing a script. The data captured provides an overview of the Oracle Database environment intended for diagnostic and trouble-shooting. Within RDA, the *HCVE* (Health Check Validation Engine) can verify and isolate host system environmental issues that may affect the performance of Oracle software.

Database-related Guidelines

Oracle Corporation also endorses certain practices and conventions as enhancing the use of its database products. These include:

- Oracle Maximum Availability Architecture (MAA) guidelines on developing high-availability systems

- Optimal Flexible Architecture (OFA), blueprints for mapping Oracle-database objects to file-systems

Oracle Certification Program

The Oracle Certification Program, a professional certification program, includes the administration of Oracle Databases as one of its main certification paths. It contains three levels:

1. Oracle Certified Associate (OCA)

2. Oracle Certified Professional (OCP)

3. Oracle Certified Master (OCM)

User Groups

A variety of official (Oracle-sponsored) and unofficial Oracle User Groups has grown up of users and developers of Oracle databases. They include:

- Geographical/regional user groups

- Independent Oracle Users Group

- Industry-centric user groups

- Oracle Technology Network

- Oracle Health Sciences User Group

- Product-centric user groups

- The OakTable Network

- Usenet newsgroups

Market Position

As of 2013 Oracle holds #1 DBMS market share worldwide based on the revenue share ahead of its four closest competitors - IBM , Microsoft, SAP and Teradata.

Competition

In the market for relational databases, Oracle Database competes against commercial products such as IBM's DB2 UDB and Microsoft SQL Server. Oracle and IBM tend to battle for the mid-range database market on UNIX and Linux platforms, while Microsoft dominates the mid-range database market on Microsoft Windows platforms. However, since they share many of the same customers, Oracle and IBM tend to support each other's products in many middleware and application categories (for example: WebSphere, PeopleSoft, and Siebel Systems CRM), and IBM's hardware divisions work closely with Oracle on performance-optimizing server-technologies (for example, Linux on z Systems). Niche commercial competitors include Teradata (in data warehousing and business intelligence), Software AG's ADABAS, Sybase, and IBM's Informix, among many others.

Increasingly, the Oracle database products compete against such open-source software relational database systems as PostgreSQL, Firebird, and MySQL. Oracle acquired Innobase, supplier of the InnoDB codebase to MySQL, in part to compete better against open source alternatives, and acquired Sun Microsystems, owner of MySQL, in 2010. Database products licensed as open source are, by the legal terms of the Open Source Definition, free to distribute and free of royalty or other licensing fees.

Pricing

Oracle Corporation offers term licensing for all Oracle products. It bases the list price for a term-license on a specific percentage of the perpetual license price. Prospective purchasers can obtain licenses based either on the number of processors in their target machines or on the number of potential seats ("named users").

Enterprise Edition (DB EE)

> As of July 2010, the database that costs the most per machine-processor among Oracle database editions, at $47,500 per processor. The term "per processor" for Enterprise Edition is defined with respect to physical cores and a processor core multiplier (common processors = 0.5*cores). e.g. An 8-processor, 32-core server using Intel Xeon 56XX CPUs would require 16 processor licenses.

Standard Edition (DB SE)

> Cheaper: it can run on up to four processors but has fewer features than Enterprise Edition—it lacks proper parallelization, etc.; but remains quite suitable for running medium-sized applications. There are not additional cost for Oracle RAC on the latest Oracle 11g R2 standard edition release.

Standard ONE (DB SE1 or DB SEO)

> Sells even more cheaply, but remains limited to two CPUs. Standard Edition ONE sells on a

per-seat basis with a five-user minimum. Oracle Corporation usually sells the licenses with an extra 22% cost for support and upgrades (access to My Oracle Support—Oracle Corporation's support site), which customers must renew annually.

Oracle Express Edition (DB XE) (Oracle XE)

An addition to the Oracle database product family (beta version released in 2005, production version released in February 2006), offers a free version of the Oracle RDBMS, but one limited to 11 GB of user data and to 1 GB of memory used by the database (SGA+PGA). XE will use no more than one CPU and lacks an internal JVM. XE runs on 32-bit and 64-bit Windows and 64-bit Linux, but not on AIX, Solaris, HP-UX and the other operating systems available for other editions. Support is via a free Oracle Discussion Forum only.

Document-oriented Database

A document-oriented database, or document store, is a computer program designed for storing, retrieving, and managing document-oriented information, also known as semi-structured data. Document-oriented databases are one of the main categories of NoSQL databases, and the popularity of the term "document-oriented database" has grown with the use of the term NoSQL itself. XML databases are a subclass of document-oriented databases that are optimized to work with XML documents. Graph databases are similar, but add another layer, the *relationship*, which allows them to link documents for rapid traversal.

Document-oriented databases are inherently a subclass of the key-value store, another NoSQL database concept. The difference lies in the way the data is processed; in a key-value store the data is considered to be inherently opaque to the database, whereas a document-oriented system relies on internal structure in the *document* in order to extract metadata that the database engine uses for further optimization. Although the difference is often moot due to tools in the systems, conceptually the document-store is designed to offer a richer experience with modern programming techniques.

Document databases contrast strongly with the traditional relational database (RDB). Relational databases generally store data in separate *tables* that are defined by the programmer, and a single object may be spread across several tables. Document databases store all information for a given object in a single instance in the database, and every stored object can be different from every other. This makes mapping objects into the database a simple task, normally eliminating anything similar to an object-relational mapping. This makes document stores attractive for programming web applications, which are subject to continual change in place, and where speed of deployment is an important issue.

Documents

The central concept of a document-oriented database is the notion of a *document*. While each document-oriented database implementation differs on the details of this definition, in general, they all assume documents encapsulate and encode data (or information) in some standard formats or encodings. Encodings in use include XML, YAML, JSON, and BSON, as well as binary forms like PDF and Microsoft Office documents (MS Word, Excel, and so on).

Documents in a document store are roughly equivalent to the programming concept of an object. They are not required to adhere to a standard schema, nor will they have all the same sections, slots, parts, or keys. Generally, programs using objects have many different types of objects, and those objects often have many optional fields. Every object, even those of the same class, can look very different. Document stores are similar in that they allow different types of documents in a single store, allow the fields within them to be optional, and often allow them to be encoded using different encoding systems. For example, the following is a document, encoded in JSON:

```
{

    FirstName: "Bob",

    Address: "5 Oak St.",

    Hobby: "sailing"

}
```

A second document might be encoded in XML as:

```
 <contact>

   <firstname>Bob</firstname>

   <lastname>Smith</lastname>

   <phone type="Cell">(123) 555-0178</phone>

   <phone type="Work">(890) 555-0133</phone>

   <address>

    <type>Home</type>

    <street1>123 Back St.</street1>

    <city>Boys</city>

    <state>AR</state>

    <zip>32225</zip>

    <country>US</country>

   </address>

 </contact>
```

These two documents share some structural elements with one another, but each also has unique elements. The structure and text and other data inside the document are usually referred to as the document's *content* and may be referenced via retrieval or editing methods, Unlike a relational database where every record contains the same fields, leaving unused fields empty; there are no empty 'fields' in either document (record) in the above example. This approach allows new information to be added to some records without requiring that every other record in the database share the same structure.

Document databases typically provide for additional metadata to be associated with and stored along with the document content. That metadata may be related to facilities the datastore provides for organizing documents, providing security, or other implementation specific features.

CRUD Operations

The core operations a document-oriented database supports on documents are similar to other databases and while the terminology isn't perfectly standardized, most practitioners will recognize them as CRUD

- Creation (or insertion)

- Retrieval (or query, search, finds)

- Update (or edit)

- Deletion (or removal)

Keys

Documents are addressed in the database via a unique *key* that represents that document. This key is a simple identifier (or ID), typically a string, a URI, or a path. The key can be used to retrieve the document from the database. Typically the database retains an index on the key to speed up document retrieval, and in some cases the key is required to create or insert the document into the database.

Retrieval

Another defining characteristic of a document-oriented database is that, beyond the simple key-to-document lookup that can be used to retrieve a document, the database offers an API or query language that allows the user to retrieve documents based on content (or metadata). For example, you may want a query that retrieves all the documents with a certain field set to a certain value. The set of query APIs or query language features available, as well as the expected performance of the queries, varies significantly from one implementation to another. Likewise, the specific set of indexing options and configuration that are available vary greatly by implementation.

It is here that the document store varies most from the key-value store. In theory, the values in a key-value store are opaque to the store, they are essentially black boxes. They may offer search systems similar to those of a document store, but may have less understanding about the organization of the content. Document stores use the metadata in the document to classify the content, allowing them, for instance, to understand that one series of digits is a phone number, and another is a postal code. This allows them to search on those types of data, for instance, all phone numbers containing 555, which would ignore the zip code 55555.

Editing

Document databases typically provide some mechanism for updating or editing the content (or other metadata) of a document, either by allowing for replacement of the entire document, or individual structural pieces of the document.

Organization

Document database implementations offer a variety of ways of organizing documents, including notions of

- Collections: groups of documents, where depending on implementation, a document may be enforced to live inside one collection, or may be allowed to live in multiple collections

- Tags and non-visible metadata: additional data outside the document content

- Directory hierarchies: groups of documents organized in a tree-like structure, typically based on path or URI

Sometimes these organizational notions vary in how much they are logical vs physical, (e.g. on disk or in memory), representations.

Relationship to Other Databases

Relationship to Key-value stores

A document-oriented database is a specialized key-value store, which itself is another NoSQL database category. In a simple key-value store, the document content is opaque. A document-oriented database provides APIs or a query/update language that exposes the ability to query or update based on the internal structure in the *document*. This difference may be moot for users that do not need richer query, retrieval, or editing APIs that are typically provided by document databases. Modern key-value stores often include features for working with metadata, blurring the lines between document stores.

Relationship to Search Engines

Some search engines (aka information retrieval) systems like Elasticsearch provide enough of the core operations on documents to fit the definition of a document-oriented database.

Relationship to Relational Databases

In a relational database, data is first categorized into a number of predefined types, and *tables* are created to hold individual entries, or *records*, of each type. The tables define the data within each record's *fields*, meaning that every record in the table has the same overall form. The administrator also defines the *relationships* between the tables, and selects certain fields that they believe will be most commonly used for searching and defines *indexes* on them. A key concept in the relational design is that any data that may be repeated is normally placed in its own table, and if these instances are related to each other, a column is selected to group them together, the *foreign key*. This design is known as *database normalization*.

For example, an address book application will generally need to store the contact name, an optional image, one or more phone numbers, one or more mailing addresses, and one or more email addresses. In a canonical relational database solution, tables would be created for each of these rows with predefined fields for each bit of data: the CONTACT table might include FIRST_NAME, LAST_NAME and IMAGE columns, while the PHONE_NUMBER table might include COUNTRY_CODE, AREA_CODE, PHONE_NUMBER and TYPE (home, work, etc.). The PHONE_NUMBER table also contains a foreign key column, "CONTACT_ID", which holds the unique ID number assigned to the contact when it was created. In order to recreate the original contact, the database engine uses the foreign keys to look for the related items across the group of tables and reconstruct the original data.

In contrast, in a document-oriented database there may be no internal structure that maps directly onto the concept of a table, and the fields and relationships generally don't exist as predefined concepts. Instead, all of the data for an object is placed in a single document, and stored in the database as a single entry. In the address book example, the document would contain the contact's name, image, and any contact info, all in a single record. That entry is accessed through its key, which allows the database to retrieve and return the document to the application. No additional work is needed to retrieve the related data; all of this is returned in a single object.

A key difference between the document-oriented and relational models is that the data formats are not predefined in the document case. In most cases, any sort of document can be stored in any database, and those documents can change in type and form at any time. If one wishes to add a COUNTRY_FLAG to a CONTACT, this field can be added to new documents as they are inserted, this will have no effect on the database or the existing documents already stored. To aid retrieval of information from the database, document-oriented systems generally allow the administrator to provide *hints* to the database to look for certain types of information. These work in a similar fashion to indexes in the relational case. Most also offer the ability to add additional metadata outside of the content of the document itself, for instance, tagging entries as being part of an address book, which allows the programmer to retrieve related types of information, like "all the address book entries". This provides functionality similar to a table, but separates the concept (categories of data) from its physical implementation (tables).

In the classic normalized relational model, objects in the database are represented as separate rows of data with no inherent structure beyond that given to them as they are retrieved. This leads to problems when trying to translate programming objects to and from their associated database rows, a problem known as object-relational impedance mismatch. Document stores more closely, or in some cases directly, map programming objects into the store. This eliminates the impedance mismatch problem, and is offered as one of the main advantages of the NoSQL approach.

Implementations

Name	Publisher	License	Languages supported	Notes	RESTful API
BaseX	BaseX Team	BSD License	Java, XQuery	Support for XML, JSON and binary formats; client-/server based architecture; concurrent structural and full-text searches and updates.	Yes

Caché	InterSystems Corporation	Proprietary	Java, C#, Node.js	Commonly used in Health, Business and Government applications.	Yes
Cloudant	Cloudant, Inc.	Proprietary	Erlang, Java, Scala, and C	Distributed database service based on Big-Couch, the company's open source fork of the Apache-backed CouchDB project. Uses JSON model.	Yes
Clusterpoint Database	Clusterpoint Ltd.	Proprietary with free download	JavaScript, SQL, PHP, .NET, Java, Python, Node.js, C, C++,	Distributed document-oriented XML / JSON database platform with ACID-compliant transactions; high-availability data replication and sharding; built-in full text search engine with relevance ranking; JS/SQL query language; GIS; Available as pay-per-use database as a service or as an on-premise free software download.	Yes
Couchbase Server	Couchbase, Inc.	Apache License	C, .NET, Java, Python, Node.js, PHP, SQL, GoLang, Spring Framework, LINQ	Distributed NoSQL Document Database, JSON model and SQL based Query Language.	Yes
CouchDB	Apache Software Foundation	Apache License	Any language that can make HTTP requests	JSON over REST/HTTP with Multi-Version Concurrency Control and limited ACID properties. Uses map and reduce for views and queries.	Yes
CrateIO	CRATE Technology GmbH	Apache License	Java	Use familiar SQL syntax for real time distributed queries across a cluster. Based on Lucene / Elasticsearch ecosystem with built-in support for binary objects (BLOBs).	Yes
djondb	djondb.com	GNU GPL and Commercial	C, .Net, Java, Python, Node-JS, PHP.	Document Store with support to transactions.	No
DocumentDB	Microsoft	Proprietary	.NET, Java, Python, Node.js, JavaScript, SQL	Platform-as-a-Service offering, part of the Microsoft Azure platform.	Yes
Elasticsearch	Shay Banon	Apache License	Java	JSON, Search engine.	Yes

eXist	eXist	LGPL	XQuery, Java	XML over REST/HTTP, WebDAV, Lucene Fulltext search, binary data support, validation, versioning, clustering, triggers, URL rewriting, collections, ACLS, XQuery Update	Yes
HyperDex	hyperdex.org	BSD License	C, C++, Go, Node.js, Python, Ruby	Support for JSON and binary documents.	No
Informix	IBM	Proprietary, with no-cost editions	Various (Compatible with MongoDB API)	RDBMS with JSON, replication, sharding and ACID compliance.	Yes
Jackrabbit	Apache Foundation	Apache License	Java	Java Content Repository implementation	?
Lotus Notes (IBM Lotus Domino)	IBM	Proprietary	LotusScript, Java, Lotus @ Formula	MultiValue	Yes
MarkLogic	MarkLogic Corporation	Free Developer license or Commercial	REST, Java, JavaScript, Node.js, XQuery, SPARQL, XSLT, C++	Distributed document-oriented database for JSON, XML, and RDF triples. Built-in Full text search, ACID transactions, High availability and Disaster recovery, certified security.	Yes
MongoDB	MongoDB, Inc	GNU AGPL v3.0 for the DBMS, Apache 2 License for the client drivers	C, C++, C#, Java, Perl, PHP, Python, Node.js, Ruby, Scala	Document database with replication and sharding, BSON store (binary format JSON).	Yes
MUMPS Database	?	Proprietary and Affero GPL	MUMPS	Commonly used in health applications.	?
ObjectDatabase++	Ekky Software	Proprietary	C++, C#, TScript	Binary Native C++ class structures	?
OrientDB	Orient Technologies	Apache License	Java	JSON over HTTP, SQL support, ACID transactions	Yes
PostgreSQL	PostgreSQL	PostgreSQL Free License	C	HStore, JSON store (9.2+), JSON function (9.3+), HStore2 (9.4+), JSONB (9.4+)	No
Qizx	Qualcomm	Commercial	REST, Java, XQuery, XSLT, C, C++, Python	Distributed document-oriented XML database with integrated full text search; support for JSON, text, and binaries.	Yes

RethinkDB	?	GNU AGPL for the DBMS, Apache 2 License for the client drivers	C++, Python, JavaScript, Ruby, Java	Distributed document-oriented JSON database with replication and sharding.	No
Rocket U2	Rocket Software	Proprietary	?	UniData, UniVerse	Yes (Beta)
Sedna	sedna.org	Apache License	C++, XQuery	XML database	No
SimpleDB	Amazon	Proprietary on-line service	Erlang		?
Solr	Apache	Apache License	Java	Search engine	Yes
TokuMX	Tokutek	GNU Affero General Public License	C++, C#, Go	MongoDB with Fractal Tree indexing	?
OpenLink Virtuoso	OpenLink Software	GPLv2 and proprietary	C++, C#, Java, SPARQL	Middleware and database engine hybrid	Yes

XML Database Implementations

Most XML databases are document-oriented databases.

MongoDB

MongoDB (from *humongous*) is a free and open-source cross-platform document-oriented database program. Classified as a NoSQL database program, MongoDB uses JSON-like documents with schemas. MongoDB is developed by MongoDB Inc. and is free and open-source, published under a combination of the GNU Affero General Public License and the Apache License.

History

The software company 10gen began developing MongoDB in 2007 as a component of a planned platform as a service product. In 2009, the company shifted to an open source development model, with the company offering commercial support and other services. In 2013, 10gen changed its name to MongoDB Inc.

Main Features

Ad hoc queries

MongoDB supports field, range queries, regular expression searches. Queries can return specific fields of documents and also include user-defined JavaScript functions. Queries can also be configured to return a random sample of results of a given size.

Indexing

Fields in a MongoDB document can be indexed with primary and secondary indices.

Replication

MongoDB provides high availability with replica sets. A replica set consists of two or more copies of the data. Each replica set member may act in the role of primary or secondary replica at any time. All writes and reads are done on the primary replica by default. Secondary replicas maintain a copy of the data of the primary using built-in replication. When a primary replica fails, the replica set automatically conducts an election process to determine which secondary should become the primary. Secondaries can optionally serve read operations, but that data is only eventually consistent by default.

Load balancing

MongoDB scales horizontally using sharding. The user chooses a shard key, which determines how the data in a collection will be distributed. The data is split into ranges (based on the shard key) and distributed across multiple shards. (A shard is a master with one or more slaves.). Alternatively, the shard key can be hashed to map to a shard – enabling an even data distribution.

MongoDB can run over multiple servers, balancing the load or duplicating data to keep the system up and running in case of hardware failure.

File storage

MongoDB can be used as a file system with load balancing and data replication features over multiple machines for storing files.

This function, called Grid File System, is included with MongoDB drivers. MongoDB exposes functions for file manipulation and content to developers. GridFS is used in plugins for NGINX and lighttpd. GridFS divides a file into parts, or chunks, and stores each of those chunks as a separate document.

Aggregation

MapReduce can be used for batch processing of data and aggregation operations.

The aggregation framework enables users to obtain the kind of results for which the SQL GROUP BY clause is used. Aggregation operators can be strung together to form a pipeline – analogous to Unix pipes. The aggregation framework includes the $lookup operator which can join documents from multiple documents, as well as statistical operators such as standard deviation.

Server-side JavaScript execution

JavaScript can be used in queries, aggregation functions (such as MapReduce), and sent directly to the database to be executed.

Capped collections

MongoDB supports fixed-size collections called capped collections. This type of collection maintains insertion order and, once the specified size has been reached, behaves like a circular queue.

Bug Reports and Criticisms

In some failure scenarios where an application can access two distinct MongoDB processes, but these processes cannot access each other, it is possible for MongoDB to return stale reads. In this scenario it is also possible for MongoDB to roll back writes that have been acknowledged.

Before version 2.2, concurrency control was implemented on a per-mongod basis. With version 2.2, concurrency control was implemented at the database level. Since version 3.0, pluggable storage engines were introduced, and each storage engine may implement concurrency control differently. With MongoDB 3.0 concurrency control is implemented at the collection level for the MMAPv1 storage engine, and at the document level with the WiredTiger storage engine. With versions prior to 3.0, one approach to increase concurrency is to use sharding. In some situations, reads and writes will yield their locks. If MongoDB predicts a page is unlikely to be in memory, operations will yield their lock while the pages load. The use of lock yielding expanded greatly in 2.2.

Another criticism is related to the limitations of MongoDB when used on 32-bit systems. In some cases, this was due to inherent memory limitations. MongoDB recommends 64-bit systems and that users provide sufficient RAM for their working set.

Up until version 3.3.11, MongoDB could not do collation-based sorting and was limited to bytewise comparison via memcmp, which would not provide correct ordering for many non-English languages when used with a Unicode encoding. The issue was fixed on August 23, 2016.

MongoDB queries against an index are not atomic and can miss documents which are being updated while the query is running and match the query both before and after an update.

Architecture

Programming Language Accessibility

MongoDB has official drivers for a variety of popular programming languages and development environments. There are also a large number of unofficial or community-supported drivers for other programming languages and frameworks.

Management and Graphical Front-ends

Record insertion in MongoDB with Robomongo 0.8.5.

Most administration is done from command line tools such as the mongo shell because MongoDB does not include a GUI-style administrative interface. There are products and third-party projects that offer user interfaces for administration and data viewing.

Licensing

MongoDB is available at no cost under the GNU Affero General Public License, version 3. The language drivers are available under an Apache License. In addition, MongoDB Inc. offers proprietary licenses for MongoDB.

MongoDB World

MongoDB World is an annual developer conference hosted by MongoDB, Inc.

Object Database

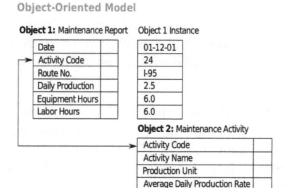

Example of an object-oriented model

An object database (also object-oriented database management system, OODBMS) is a database management system in which information is represented in the form of objects as used in object-oriented programming. Object databases are different from relational databases which are table-oriented. Object-relational databases are a hybrid of both approaches.

Object databases have been considered since the early 1980s.

Overview

Object-oriented database management systems (OODBMSs) combine database capabilities with object-oriented programming language capabilities. OODBMSs allow object-oriented programmers to develop the product, store them as objects, and replicate or modify existing objects to make new objects within the OODBMS. Because the database is integrated with the programming language, the programmer can maintain consistency within one environment, in that both the OODBMS and the programming language will use the same model of representation. Relational

DBMS projects, by way of contrast, maintain a clearer division between the database model and the application.

As the usage of web-based technology increases with the implementation of Intranets and extranets, companies have a vested interest in OODBMSs to display their complex data. Using a DBMS that has been specifically designed to store data as objects gives an advantage to those companies that are geared towards multimedia presentation or organizations that utilize computer-aided design (CAD).

Some object-oriented databases are designed to work well with object-oriented programming languages such as Delphi, Ruby, Python, Perl, Java, C#, Visual Basic .NET, C++, Objective-C and Smalltalk; others such as JADE have their own programming languages. OODBMSs use exactly the same model as object-oriented programming languages.

History

Object database management systems grew out of research during the early to mid-1970s into having intrinsic database management support for graph-structured objects. The term "object-oriented database system" first appeared around 1985. Notable research projects included Encore-Ob/Server (Brown University), EXODUS (University of Wisconsin–Madison), IRIS (Hewlett-Packard), ODE (Bell Labs), ORION (Microelectronics and Computer Technology Corporation or MCC), Vodak (GMD-IPSI), and Zeitgeist (Texas Instruments). The ORION project had more published papers than any of the other efforts. Won Kim of MCC compiled the best of those papers in a book published by The MIT Press.

Early commercial products included Gemstone (Servio Logic, name changed to GemStone Systems), Gbase (Graphael), and Vbase (Ontologic). The early to mid-1990s saw additional commercial products enter the market. These included ITASCA (Itasca Systems), Jasmine (Fujitsu, marketed by Computer Associates), Matisse (Matisse Software), Objectivity/DB (Objectivity, Inc.), ObjectStore (Progress Software, acquired from eXcelon which was originally Object Design), ONTOS (Ontos, Inc., name changed from Ontologic), O_2 (O_2 Technology, merged with several companies, acquired by Informix, which was in turn acquired by IBM), POET (now FastObjects from Versant which acquired Poet Software), Versant Object Database (Versant Corporation), VOSS (Logic Arts) and JADE (Jade Software Corporation). Some of these products remain on the market and have been joined by new open source and commercial products such as InterSystems Caché.

Object database management systems added the concept of persistence to object programming languages. The early commercial products were integrated with various languages: GemStone (Smalltalk), Gbase (LISP), Vbase (COP) and VOSS (Virtual Object Storage System for Smalltalk). For much of the 1990s, C++ dominated the commercial object database management market. Vendors added Java in the late 1990s and more recently, C#.

Starting in 2004, object databases have seen a second growth period when open source object databases emerged that were widely affordable and easy to use, because they are entirely written in OOP languages like Smalltalk, Java, or C#, such as Versant's db4o (db4objects), DTS/S1 from Obsidian Dynamics and Perst (McObject), available under dual open source and commercial licensing.

Timeline

- 1966
  - MUMPS
- 1979
  - InterSystems M
- 1980
  - TORNADO – an object database for CAD/CAM
- 1982
  - Gemstone started (as Servio Logic) to build a set theoretic model data base machine.
- 1985 – Term Object Database first introduced
- 1986
  - Servio Logic (Gemstone Systems) Ships Gemstone 1.0
- 1988
  - Versant Corporation started (as Object Sciences Corp)
  - Objectivity, Inc. founded
- Early 1990s
  - Servio Logic changes name to Gemstone Systems
  - Gemstone (Smalltalk)-(C++)-(Java)
  - GBase (LISP)
  - VBase (O2- ONTOS – INFORMIX)
  - Objectivity/DB
- Mid 1990s
  - InterSystems Caché
  - Versant Object Database
  - ObjectStore
  - ODABA
  - ZODB

- o   Poet

- o   JADE

- o   Matisse

- o   Illustra Informix

- o   Webcrossing

- 2000s

  - o   db4o project started by Carl Rosenberger

  - o   ObjectDB

- 2001 IBM acquires Informix

- 2003 odbpp public release

- 2004 db4o's commercial launch as db4objects, Inc.

- 2008 db4o acquired by Versant Corporation

- 2010 VMware acquires GemStone

- 2012 Wakanda first production versions with open source and commercial licenses

- 2013 GemTalk Systems acquires GemStone products from VMware

- 2014 Realm

Adoption of Object Databases

Object databases based on persistent programming acquired a niche in application areas such as engineering and spatial databases, telecommunications, and scientific areas such as high energy physics and molecular biology.

Another group of object databases focuses on embedded use in devices, packaged software, and real-time systems.

Technical Features

Most object databases also offer some kind of query language, allowing objects to be found using a declarative programming approach. It is in the area of object query languages, and the integration of the query and navigational interfaces, that the biggest differences between products are found. An attempt at standardization was made by the ODMG with the Object Query Language, OQL.

Access to data can be faster because joins are often not needed (as in a tabular implementation of a relational database). This is because an object can be retrieved directly without a search, by following pointers.

Another area of variation between products is in the way that the schema of a database is defined. A general characteristic, however, is that the programming language and the database schema use the same type definitions.

Multimedia applications are facilitated because the class methods associated with the data are responsible for its correct interpretation.

Many object databases, for example Gemstone or VOSS, offer support for versioning. An object can be viewed as the set of all its versions. Also, object versions can be treated as objects in their own right. Some object databases also provide systematic support for triggers and constraints which are the basis of active databases.

The efficiency of such a database is also greatly improved in areas which demand massive amounts of data about one item. For example, a banking institution could get the user's account information and provide them efficiently with extensive information such as transactions, account information entries etc.

Standards

The Object Data Management Group was a consortium of object database and object-relational mapping vendors, members of the academic community, and interested parties. Its goal was to create a set of specifications that would allow for portable applications that store objects in database management systems. It published several versions of its specification. The last release was ODMG 3.0. By 2001, most of the major object database and object-relational mapping vendors claimed conformance to the ODMG Java Language Binding. Compliance to the other components of the specification was mixed. In 2001, the ODMG Java Language Binding was submitted to the Java Community Process as a basis for the Java Data Objects specification. The ODMG member companies then decided to concentrate their efforts on the Java Data Objects specification. As a result, the ODMG disbanded in 2001.

Many object database ideas were also absorbed into SQL:1999 and have been implemented in varying degrees in object-relational database products.

In 2005 Cook, Rai, and Rosenberger proposed to drop all standardization efforts to introduce additional object-oriented query APIs but rather use the OO programming language itself, i.e., Java and .NET, to express queries. As a result, Native Queries emerged. Similarly, Microsoft announced Language Integrated Query (LINQ) and DLINQ, an implementation of LINQ, in September 2005, to provide close, language-integrated database query capabilities with its programming languages C# and VB.NET 9.

In February 2006, the Object Management Group (OMG) announced that they had been granted the right to develop new specifications based on the ODMG 3.0 specification and the formation of the Object Database Technology Working Group (ODBT WG). The ODBT WG planned to create a set of standards that would incorporate advances in object database technology (e.g., replication), data management (e.g., spatial indexing), and data formats (e.g., XML) and to include new features into these standards that support domains where object databases are being adopted (e.g., real-time systems). The work of the ODBT WG was suspended in March 2009 when, subsequent to the economic turmoil in late 2008, the ODB vendors involved in this effort decided to focus their resources elsewhere.

In January 2007 the World Wide Web Consortium gave final recommendation status to the XQuery language. XQuery uses XML as its data model. Some of the ideas developed originally for object databases found their way into XQuery, but XQuery is not intrinsically object-oriented. Because of the popularity of XML, XQuery engines compete with object databases as a vehicle for storage of data that is too complex or variable to hold conveniently in a relational database. XQuery also allows modules to be written to provide encapsulation features that have been provided by Object-Oriented systems.

XQuery v1 and XPath v2 are so complex (no FOSS software is implementing this standards after 10 years of its publication) when comparing with XPath v1 and XSLT v1 implementations, and XML not fitted all community demands as an open format. Since early 2000s JSON is gaining community and applications, overcoming XML in the 2010s. JSONiq, a query-analog of XQuery for JSON (sharing same XQuery core expressions and operations), demonstred the functional equivalence between JSON and XML formats. In this context, the main strategy of OODBMS maintainers was to retrofitting JSON (by using JSON as internal data type).

In January 2016, with the PostgreSQL 9.5 release was the first FOSS OODBMS to offer an effcient JSON internal datatype (JSONB) with a complete set of functions and operations, for all basic relational and non-relational manipulations.

Comparison With RDBMSs

An object database stores complex data and relationships between data directly, without mapping to relational rows and columns, and this makes them suitable for applications dealing with very complex data. Objects have a many to many relationship and are accessed by the use of pointers. Pointers are linked to objects to establish relationships. Another benefit of an OODBMS is that it can be programmed with small procedural differences without affecting the entire system.

In-memory Database

An in-memory database (IMDB, also main memory database system or MMDB or memory resident database) is a database management system that primarily relies on main memory for computer data storage. It is contrasted with database management systems that employ a disk storage mechanism. Main memory databases are faster than disk-optimized databases because the disk access is slower than memory access, the internal optimization algorithms are simpler and execute fewer CPU instructions. Accessing data in memory eliminates seek time when querying the data, which provides faster and more predictable performance than disk.

Applications where response time is critical, such as those running telecommunications network equipment and mobile advertising networks, often use main-memory databases. IMDBs have gained a lot of traction, especially in the data analytics space, starting in the mid-2000s – mainly due to multi-core processors that can address large memory and due to less expensive RAM.

With the introduction of non-volatile random access memory technology, in-memory databases will be able to run at full speed and maintain data in the event of power failure.

ACID Support

In its simplest form, main memory databases store data on volatile memory devices. These devices lose all stored information when the device loses power or is reset. In this case, IMDBs can be said to lack support for the "durability" portion of the ACID (atomicity, consistency, isolation, durability) properties. Volatile memory-based IMDBs can, and often do, support the other three ACID properties of atomicity, consistency and isolation.

Many IMDBs have added durability via the following mechanisms:

- Snapshot files, or, checkpoint images, which record the state of the database at a given moment in time. The system typically generates these periodically, or at least when the IMDB does a controlled shut-down. While they give a measure of persistence to the data (in that the database does not lose everything in the case of a system crash) they only offer partial durability (as 'recent" changes will be lost). For full durability, they need supplementing with one of the following:

- Transaction logging, which records changes to the database in a journal file and facilitates automatic recovery of an in-memory database.

- Non-Volatile DIMM (NVDIMM), a memory module that has a DRAM interface, often combined with NAND flash for the Non-Volatile data security. The first NVDIMM solutions were designed with supercapacitors instead of batteries for the backup power source. With this storage, IMDB can resume securely from its state upon reboot.

- Non-volatile random access memory (NVRAM), usually in the form of static RAM backed up with battery power (battery RAM), or an electrically erasable programmable ROM (EEPROM). With this storage, the re-booting IMDB system can recover the data store from its last consistent state.

- High availability implementations that rely on database replication, with automatic failover to an identical standby database in the event of primary database failure. To protect against loss of data in the case of a complete system crash, replication of an IMDB is normally used in addition to one or more of the mechanisms listed above.

Some IMDBs allow the database schema to specify different durability requirements for selected areas of the database - thus, faster-changing data that can easily be regenerated or that has no meaning after a system shut-down would not need to be journaled for durability (though it would have to be replicated for high availability), whereas configuration information would be flagged as needing preservation.

Hybrids With on-disk Databases

The first database engine to support both in-memory and on-disk tables in a single database, WebDNA, was released in 1995. The advantage to this approach is flexibility: the developer can strike a balance between:

- performance (which is enhanced by sorting, storing and retrieving specified data entirely in memory, rather than going to disk)

- cost, because a less costly hard disk can be substituted for more memory

- persistence

- form factor, because RAM chips cannot approach the density of a small hard drive

Manufacturing efficiency provides another reason for selecting a combined in-memory/on-disk database system. Some device product lines, especially in consumer electronics, include some units with permanent storage, and others that rely on memory for storage (set-top boxes, for example). If such devices require a database system, a manufacturer can adopt a hybrid database system at lower and *upper* cost, and with less customization of code, rather than using separate in-memory and on-disk databases, respectively, for its disk-less and disk-based products.

Storage Memory

Another variation involves large amounts of nonvolatile memory in the server, for example, flash memory chips as addressable memory rather than structured as disk arrays. A database in this form of memory combines very fast access speed with persistence over reboots and power losses.

Embedded Database

An embedded database system is a database management system (DBMS) which is tightly integrated with an application software that requires access to stored data, such that the database system is "hidden" from the application's end-user and requires little or no ongoing maintenance. It is actually a broad technology category that includes

- database systems with differing application programming interfaces (SQL as well as proprietary, native APIs),

- database architectures (client-server and in-process),

- storage modes (on-disk, in-memory, and combined),

- database models (relational, object-oriented, entity–attribute–value model, network/CODASYL), and

- target markets.

The term *embedded database* can be confusing because only a small subset of embedded database products are used in real-time embedded systems such as telecommunications switches and consumer electronics devices.

Implementations

Major embedded database products include, in alphabetical order:

- Advantage Database Server from Sybase Inc.

- Berkeley DB from Oracle Corporation

- CSQL from csqlcache.com

- Extensible Storage Engine from Microsoft

- eXtremeDB from McObject

- Firebird Embedded

- HSQLDB from HSQLDB.ORG,

- Informix Dynamic Server (IDS) from IBM

- InfinityDB from Boiler Bay Inc.

- InnoDB from Oracle Corporation

- InterBase (Both server and mobile friendly deeply embedded version) from Embarcadero Technologies

- RDM Embedded from Raima

- solidDB

- SQLite

- SQL Server Compact from Microsoft Corporation

- Sophia Embeddable key-value storage

Comparisons of Database Storage Engines

Advantage Database Server

Sybase's Advantage Database Server (ADS) is a full-featured embedded database management system. It provides both ISAM and relational data access and is compatible with multiple platforms including Windows, Linux, and Netware. It is available as a royalty-free local file-server database or a full client-server version. ADS has been around for many years and is highly scalable, with no administration, and has support for a variety of IDEs including .NET Framework (.NET), Object Pascal (Delphi), Visual FoxPro (FoxPro), PHP, Visual Basic (VB), Visual Objects (VO), Vulcan, Clipper, Perl, Java, xHarbour, etc.

Apache Derby

Derby is an embeddable SQL engine written entirely in Java. Fully transactional, multi-user with a decent SQL subset, Derby is a mature engine and freely available under the Apache license and is actively maintained. Derby project page. It is also distributed as part of Oracle's Java SE Development Kit (JDK) under the name of Java DB.

Empress Embedded Database

Empress Software, Inc., developer of the Empress Embedded Database, is a privately held company founded in 1979. Empress Embedded Database is a full-function, relational database that has been embedded into applications by organizations small to large, with deployment environments including medical systems, network routers, nuclear power plant monitors, satellite management systems, and other embedded system applications that require reliability and power. Empress is an ACID compliant, SQL database engine with C, C++, Java, JDBC, ODBC, SQL, ADO.NET and kernel level APIs. Applications developed using these APIs may be run in standalone and/or server modes. Empress Embedded Database runs on Linux, Unix, Microsoft Windows and real-time operating systems.

Extensible Storage Engine

ESE is an Indexed Sequential Access Method (ISAM) data storage technology from Microsoft. ESE is notably a core of Microsoft Exchange Server and Active Directory. Its purpose is to allow applications to store and retrieve data via indexed and sequential access. Windows Mail and Desktop Search in the Windows Vista operating system also make use of ESE to store indexes and property information respectively.

eXtremeDB

McObject launched eXtremeDB as the first in-memory embedded database designed from scratch for real-time embedded systems. The initial product was soon joined by eXtremeDB High Availability (HA) for fault tolerant applications. The product family now includes 64-bit and transaction logging editions, and the hybrid eXtremeDB Fusion, which combines in-memory and on-disk data storage. In 2008, McObject introduced eXtremeDB Kernel Mode, the first embedded DBMS designed to run in an operating system kernel. Today, eXtremeDB is used in millions of real-time and embedded systems worldwide. McObject also offers Perst, an open source, object-oriented embedded database for Java, Java ME, .NET, .NET Compact Framework and Silverlight.

Firebird Embedded

Firebird Embedded is a relational database engine. It's an open source fork of InterBase, is ACID compliant, supports triggers and stored procedures, and is available on Linux, OSX and Windows systems. It has the same features as the classic and superserver version of Firebird, two or more threads (and applications) can access the same database at the same time starting with Firebird 2.5. So Firebird embedded acts as a local server for one threaded client accessing its databases (that means it works properly for ASP.NET web applications, because there, each user has its own thread, which means two users could access the same database at the same time, but they would not be in the same thread, because ASP.NET opens a new thread for each user). It exports the standard Firebird API entrypoints. The main advantage of Firebird embedded databases is, that unlike SQlite or Access databases, they can be plugged into a full Firebird server without any modifications at all also is multiplatform (runs on Linux, OS X with full ASP.NET Mono support)

H2

Written in Java Open source very fast database engine. Embedded and Server mode, Clustering support, can run inside the Google App Engine. Supports encrypted database files (AES or XTEA). The development of H2 was started in May 2004, but it was first published on December 14, 2005.

H2 is dual licensed and available under a modified version of the MPL 1.1 (Mozilla Public License) or under the (unmodified) EPL 1.0 (Eclipse Public License).

HailDB, Formerly Embedded InnoDB

HailDB is a standalone, embeddable form of the InnoDB Storage Engine. Given that HailDB is based on the same code base as the InnoDB Storage Engine, it contains many of the same features: high-performance and scalability, multiversion concurrency control (MVCC), row-level locking, deadlock detection, fault tolerance, automatic crash recovery, etc. However, because the embedded engine is completely independent from MySQL, it lacks server components such as networking, object-level permissions, etc. By eliminating the MySQL server overhead, InnoDB has a small footprint and is well-suited for embedding in applications which require high-performance and concurrency. As with most embedded database systems, HailDB is designed to be accessed primarily with an ISAM-like C API rather than SQL (though an extremely rudimentary SQL variant is supported).

The project is no longer maintained.

HSQLDB

HSQLDB is an opensource relational database management system with a BSD-like license that runs in the same Java Virtual Machine as the embedded application. HSQLDB supports a variety of in-memory and disk-based table modes, Unicode and SQL:2008.

InfinityDB

InfinityDB is a multi-model Java embedded DBMS that upgrades DB's incrementally and has a very simple low-level API. Data structures supported are schemaless and flexible, including relational, EAV triples, ER, Key/Value with set values, text index, trees, DAGs, taxonomies, graphs, ordered sets, large sparse arrays, BLOB's/CLOB's and mixed or custom. The multi-core speed is patent-applied-for. InfinityDB is transactional, compressing, fast, safe, strongly typed, and self-maintaining. The flexibility comes from a trivial fast 'ItemSpace' API that avoids slow JSON and XML parsing and chunking as well as dangerous inflexible binary encodings like Java Object Serialization or POJOs. The database is a simple ordered set of 'Items' which are composites of binary-encoded self-describing primitives up to 1K long.

Informix Dynamic Server

Informix Dynamic Server (IDS) is characterized as an *enterprise class embeddable database server*, combining embeddable features such as low footprint, programmable and autonomic capabilities with enterprise class database features such as high availability and flexible replication features. IDS is used in deeply embedded scenarios such as IP telephony call-processing systems, point of sale applications and financial transaction processing systems.

InterBase

InterBase is an IoT Award winning cross-platform, Unicode enabled SQL database platform able to be embedded within turn-key applications. Out of the box SMP support and on disk AES strength 256bit encryption, SQL 92 & ACID compliance and support for Windows, Macintosh, Linux, Solaris, iOS and Android platforms. Ideal for small-to-medium enterprises supporting hundreds of users and mobile application development.

LevelDB

LevelDB is an ordered key/value store created by Google as a lightweight implementation of the BigTable storage design. As a library (which is the only way to use LevelDB), its native API is C++. It also includes official C wrappers for most functionality. Third-party API wrappers exist for Python, PHP, Go (pure Go LevelDB implementation exists but is in progress still), Node.js and Objective C. Google distributes LevelDB under the New BSD License.

LightningDB

LightningDB is a memory-mapped database for the OpenLDAP Project. It is written in C and the API is modeled after the Berkeley DB API, though much simplified. The library is extremely compact, compiling down to under 40KB of x86 object code, corruption proof, and orders of magnitude faster, more robust, more scalable, and more efficient than similar libraries like Berkeley DB, LevelDB, etc. The library implements B+trees with multiversion concurrency control (MVCC), Single level store, Copy on write and provides full ACID transactions with no deadlocks. The library is optimized for high read concurrency; readers need no locks at all. Readers don't block writers and writers don't block readers, so read performance scales perfectly linearly across arbitrarily many threads and CPUs. Third-party wrappers exist for C++, Erlang and Python. Lightning DB is distributed by the OpenLDAP Project under the OpenLDAP Public License. As of 2013 the OpenLDAP Project is deprecating the use of Berkeley DB, in favor of LightningDB.

MySQL Embedded Server Library

The libmysqld, MySQL Embedded Server Library provides most of the features of regular MySQL as a linkable library that can be run in the context of a client process. After initialization clients can use the same C API calls as when talking to a separate MySQL server but with less communication overhead and with no need for a separate database process.

NexusDB

NexusDB is the commercial successor to the FlashFiler database which is now open source. They can both be embedded in Delphi applications to create stand-alone executables with full database functionality.

Oracle Berkeley DB

As the name implies, Oracle's embedded database is actually Berkeley DB, which Oracle acquired from Sleepycat Software. It was originally developed at the University of California. Berkeley DB is a fast, open-source embedded database and is used in several well-known open-source products, including the Linux and BSD Unix operating systems, Apache Web server, OpenLDAP directory, OpenOffice productivity suite.

RDM Embedded

RDM Embedded, produced by Raima was one of the first database management systems to be categorized as an *embedded database'. According to Raima's definition, the product is embedded in two senses: first, it is embedded within an application, becoming an extension to the application, second, it is possible to use it in embedded computer/OS or real-time environments because of its small footprint and efficient operation. Its APIs (for C/C++ and SQL) have been designed to support the limited resources of embedded environments. Since its initial release, RDM Embedded has been continually evolving and is currently released as version 12.1. Today Raima produces two products under the product names RDM Embedded.*

ScimoreDB

Scimore is an embedded database running on Windows. It performs fast and can easily handle millions of rows. This database provides full data reliability (ACID properties), manages heavy loads and includes features such as support for T-SQL, Read/Merge replication with ScimoreDB server, full text search. Clients can access database via .NET provider or C++ library.

SolidDB

solidDB is a hybrid on-disk/in-memory, relational database and is often used as an embedded system database in telecommunications equipment, network software, and similar systems. In-memory database technology is used to achieve throughput of tens of thousands of transactions per second with response times measured in microseconds. High availability option maintains two copies of the data synchronized at all times. In case of system failure, applications can recover access to solidDB in less than a second without loss of data.

SQLite

SQLite is a software library that implements a self-contained, server-less, zero-configuration, transactional SQL database engine. SQLite is the most widely deployed SQL database engine in the world. The source code, chiefly C, for SQLite is in the public domain. It includes both a native C library and a simple command line client for its database. It's included in several operating systems; among them are Android, FreeBSD, iOS, OS X and Windows 10.

SQL Server Compact

Microsoft's SQL Server Compact is an embedded database with wide variety of features like multi-process connections, T-SQL, ADO.NET Sync Services to sync with any back end database, Merge Replication with SQL Server, Programming API: LINQ to SQL, LINQ to Entities, ADO. NET. The product runs on both Desktop and Mobile Windows platforms. It has been in the market for long time, used by many enterprises in production software (Case Studies). The product went through multiple re-brandings and was known with multiple names like: SQL CE, SQL Server CE, SQL Server Mobile, SQL Mobile.

Network Model

Network Model

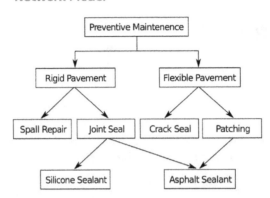

Example of a Network Model.

The network model is a database model conceived as a flexible way of representing objects and their relationships. Its distinguishing feature is that the schema, viewed as a graph in which object types are nodes and relationship types are arcs, is not restricted to being a hierarchy or lattice.

Overview

While the hierarchical database model structures data as a tree of records, with each record having one parent record and many children, the network model allows each record to have multiple parent and child records, forming a generalized graph structure. This property applies at two levels: the schema is a generalized graph of record types connected by relationship types (called "set types" in CODASYL), and the database itself is a generalized graph of record occurrences connected by relationships (CODASYL "sets"). Cycles are permitted at both levels. The chief argument in favour of the network model, in comparison to the hierarchical model, was that it allowed a more natural modeling of relationships between entities. Although the model was widely implemented and used, it failed to become dominant for two main reasons. Firstly, IBM chose to stick to the hierarchical model with semi-network extensions in their established products such as IMS and DL/I. Secondly, it was eventually displaced by the relational model, which offered a higher-level, more declarative interface. Until the early 1980s the performance benefits of the low-level navigational interfaces offered by hierarchical and network databases were persuasive for many large-scale applications, but as hardware became faster, the extra productivity and flexibility of the relational model led to the gradual obsolescence of the network model in corporate enterprise usage.

History

The network model's original inventor was Charles Bachman, and it was developed into a standard specification published in 1969 by the Conference on Data Systems Languages (CODASYL) Consortium. This was followed by a second publication in 1971, which became the basis for most implementations. Subsequent work continued into the early 1980s, culminating in an ISO specification, but this had little influence on products.

Database Systems

Some well-known database systems that use the network model include:

- Integrated Data Store (IDS)

- IDMS (Integrated Database Management System)

- RDM Embedded

- RDM Server

- TurboIMAGE

- Univac DMS-1100

Hierarchical Database Model

A hierarchical database model is a data model in which the data is organized into a tree-like structure. The data is stored as records which are connected to one another through links. A record is a collection of fields, with each field containing only one value. The entity type of a record defines which fields the record contains.

Hierarchical Model

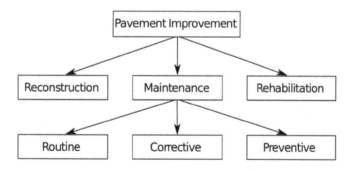

Example of a hierarchical model

A record in the hierarchical database model corresponds to a row (or tuple) in the relational database model and an entity type corresponds to a table (or relation).

The hierarchical database model mandates that each child record has only one parent, whereas each parent record can have one or more child records. In order to retrieve data from a hierarchical database the whole tree needs to be traversed starting from the root node. This model is recognized as the first database model created by IBM in the 1960s.

History

The hierarchical structure was developed by IBM in the 1960s, and used in early mainframe DBMS. Records' relationships form a treelike model. This structure is simple but inflexible because the relationship is confined to a one-to-many relationship. The IBM Information Management System (IMS) and the RDM Mobile are examples of a hierarchical database system with multiple hierarchies over the same data. RDM Mobile is a newly designed embedded database for a mobile computer system.

The hierarchical data model lost traction as Codd's relational model became the de facto standard used by virtually all mainstream database management systems. A relational-database implementation of a hierarchical model was first discussed in published form in 1992. Hierarchical data organization schemes resurfaced with the advent of XML in the late 1990s. The hierarchical structure is used primarily today for storing geographic information and file systems.

Currently hierarchical databases are still widely used especially in applications that require very high performance and availability such as banking and telecommunications. One of the most widely used commercial hierarchical databases is IMS. Another example of the use of hierarchical databases is Windows Registry in the Microsoft Windows operating systems.

Examples of Hierarchical Data Represented as Relational Tables

An organization could store employee information in a table that contains attributes/columns such as employee number, first name, last name, and department number. The organization provides each employee with computer hardware as needed, but computer equipment may only be used by the employee to which it is assigned. The organization could store the computer hardware information in a separate table that includes each part's serial number, type, and the employee that uses it. The tables might look like this:

employee table			
EmpNo	**First Name**	**Last Name**	**Dept. Num**
100	Rizmy	Muhammed	10-L
101	Hamadh	Hashim	10-L
102	Nirun	Ar	20-B
103	Thisara	Sandakelum	20-B

computer table		
Serial Num	**Type**	**User EmpNo**
3009734-4	Computer	100
3-23-283742	Monitor	100
2-22-723423	Monitor	100
232342	Printer	100

In this model, the employee data table represents the "parent" part of the hierarchy, while the computer table represents the "child" part of the hierarchy. In contrast to tree structures usually found in computer software algorithms, in this model the children point to the parents. As shown, each employee may possess several pieces of computer equipment, but each individual piece of computer equipment may have only one employee owner.

Consider the following structure:

EmpNo	Designation	ReportsTo
10	Director	
20	Senior Manager	10
30	Typist	20
40	Programmer	20

In this, the "child" is the same type as the "parent". The hierarchy stating EmpNo 10 is boss of 20, and 30 and 40 each report to 20 is represented by the "ReportsTo" column. In Relational database terms, the ReportsTo column is a foreign key referencing the EmpNo column. If the "child" data type were different, it would be in a different table, but there would still be a foreign key referencing the EmpNo column of the employees table.

This simple model is commonly known as the adjacency list model, and was introduced by Dr. Edgar F. Codd after initial criticisms surfaced that the relational model could not model hierarchical data.

Relational Model

The relational model (RM) for database management is an approach to managing data using a structure and language consistent with first-order predicate logic, first described in 1969 by Edgar F. Codd, where all data is represented in terms of tuples, grouped into relations. A database organized in terms of the relational model is a relational database.

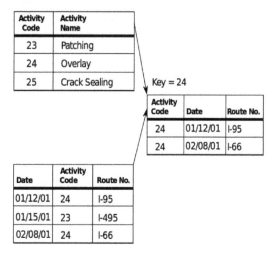

Diagram of an example database according to the relational model

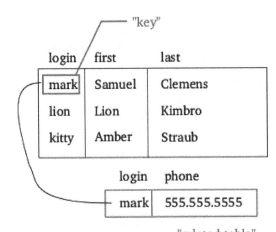

In the relational model, related records are linked together with a "key".

The purpose of the relational model is to provide a declarative method for specifying data and queries: users directly state what information the database contains and what information they want from it, and let the database management system software take care of describing data structures for storing the data and retrieval procedures for answering queries.

Most relational databases use the SQL data definition and query language; these systems implement what can be regarded as an engineering approximation to the relational model. A *table* in an SQL database schema corresponds to a predicate variable; the contents of a table to a relation; key constraints, other constraints, and SQL queries correspond to predicates. However, SQL databases deviate from the relational model in many details, and Codd fiercely argued against deviations that compromise the original principles.

Overview

The relational model's central idea is to describe a database as a collection of predicates over a finite set of predicate variables, describing constraints on the possible values and combinations of values. The content of the database at any given time is a finite (logical) model of the database, i.e. a set of relations, one per predicate variable, such that all predicates are satisfied. A request for information from the database (a database query) is also a predicate.

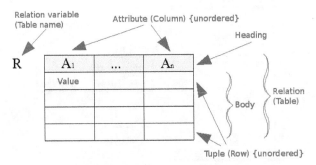

Relational model concepts.

Alternatives

Other models are the hierarchical model and network model. Some systems using these older

architectures are still in use today in data centers with high data volume needs, or where existing systems are so complex and abstract it would be cost-prohibitive to migrate to systems employing the relational model. Also of note are newer object-oriented databases.

Implementation

There have been several attempts to produce a true implementation of the relational database model as originally defined by Codd and explained by Date, Darwen and others, but none have been popular successes so far. As of October 2015 Rel is one of the more recent attempts to do this.

The relational model was the first database model to be described in formal mathematical terms. Hierarchical and network databases existed before relational databases, but their specifications were relatively informal. After the relational model was defined, there were many attempts to compare and contrast the different models, and this led to the emergence of more rigorous descriptions of the earlier models; though the procedural nature of the data manipulation interfaces for hierarchical and network databases limited the scope for formalization.

History

The relational model was invented by Edgar Codd as a general model of data, and subsequently maintained and developed by Chris Date and Hugh Darwen among others. In The Third Manifesto (first published in 1995) Date and Darwen show how the relational model can accommodate certain desired object-oriented features.

Controversies

Codd himself, some years after publication of his 1970 model, proposed a three-valued logic (True, False, Missing/NULL) version of it to deal with missing information, and in his *The Relational Model for Database Management Version 2* (1990) he went a step further with a four-valued logic (True, False, Missing but Applicable, Missing but Inapplicable) version. But these have never been implemented, presumably because of attending complexity. SQL's NULL construct was intended to be part of a three-valued logic system, but fell short of that due to logical errors in the standard and in its implementations.

Topics

The fundamental assumption of the relational model is that all data is represented as mathematical n-ary relations, an n-ary relation being a subset of the Cartesian product of n domains. In the mathematical model, reasoning about such data is done in two-valued predicate logic, meaning there are two possible evaluations for each proposition: either *true* or *false* (and in particular no third value such as *unknown*, or *not applicable*, either of which are often associated with the concept of NULL). Data are operated upon by means of a relational calculus or relational algebra, these being equivalent in expressive power.

The relational model of data permits the database designer to create a consistent, logical representation of information. Consistency is achieved by including declared *constraints* in the database design, which is usually referred to as the logical schema. The theory includes a process of database normalization whereby a design with certain desirable properties can be selected from a set of logically equivalent alternatives. The access plans and other implementation and operation details are handled by the DBMS engine, and are not reflected in the logical model. This contrasts with common practice for SQL DBMSs in which performance tuning often requires changes to the logical model.

The basic relational building block is the domain or data type, usually abbreviated nowadays to *type*. A *tuple* is an ordered set of *attribute values*. An attribute is an ordered pair of *attribute name* and *type name*. An attribute value is a specific valid value for the type of the attribute. This can be either a scalar value or a more complex type.

A relation consists of a *heading* and a *body*. A heading is a set of attributes. A body (of an n-ary relation) is a set of n-tuples. The heading of the relation is also the heading of each of its tuples.

A relation is defined as a set of n-tuples. In both mathematics and the relational database model, a set is an *unordered* collection of unique, non-duplicated items, although some DBMSs impose an order to their data. In mathematics, a tuple has an order, and allows for duplication. E. F. Codd originally defined tuples using this mathematical definition. Later, it was one of E. F. Codd's great insights that using attribute names instead of an ordering would be so much more convenient (in general) in a computer language based on relations. This insight is still being used today. Though the concept has changed, the name "tuple" has not. An immediate and important consequence of this distinguishing feature is that in the relational model the Cartesian product becomes commutative.

A table is an accepted visual representation of a relation; a tuple is similar to the concept of a *row*.

A *relvar* is a named variable of some specific relation type, to which at all times some relation of that type is assigned, though the relation may contain zero tuples.

The basic principle of the relational model is the Information Principle: all information is represented by data values in relations. In accordance with this Principle, a relational database is a set of relvars and the result of every query is presented as a relation.

The consistency of a relational database is enforced, not by rules built into the applications that use it, but rather by *constraints*, declared as part of the logical schema and enforced by the DBMS for all applications. In general, constraints are expressed using relational comparison operators, of which just one, "is subset of" ($\subseteq$), is theoretically sufficient. In practice, several useful shorthands are expected to be available, of which the most important are candidate key (really, superkey) and foreign key constraints.

Interpretation

To fully appreciate the relational model of data it is essential to understand the intended *interpretation* of a relation.

The body of a relation is sometimes called its extension. This is because it is to be interpreted as a representation of the extension of some predicate, this being the set of true propositions that can be formed by replacing each free variable in that predicate by a name (a term that designates something).

There is a one-to-one correspondence between the free variables of the predicate and the attribute names of the relation heading. Each tuple of the relation body provides attribute values to instantiate the predicate by substituting each of its free variables. The result is a proposition that is deemed, on account of the appearance of the tuple in the relation body, to be true. Contrariwise, every tuple whose heading conforms to that of the relation, but which does not appear in the body is deemed to be false. This assumption is known as the closed world assumption: it is often violated in practical databases, where the absence of a tuple might mean that the truth of the corresponding proposition is unknown. For example, the absence of the tuple ('John', 'Spanish') from a table of language skills cannot necessarily be taken as evidence that John does not speak Spanish.

Application to Databases

A data type as used in a typical relational database might be the set of integers, the set of character strings, the set of dates, or the two boolean values *true* and *false*, and so on. The corresponding type names for these types might be the strings "int", "char", "date", "boolean", etc. It is important to understand, though, that relational theory does not dictate what types are to be supported; indeed, nowadays provisions are expected to be available for *user-defined* types in addition to the *built-in* ones provided by the system.

Attribute is the term used in the theory for what is commonly referred to as a column. Similarly, table is commonly used in place of the theoretical term relation (though in SQL the term is by no means synonymous with relation). A table data structure is specified as a list of column definitions, each of which specifies a unique column name and the type of the values that are permitted for that column. An attribute *value* is the entry in a specific column and row, such as "John Doe" or "35".

A tuple is basically the same thing as a row, except in an SQL DBMS, where the column values in a row are ordered. (Tuples are not ordered; instead, each attribute value is identified solely by the attribute name and never by its ordinal position within the tuple.) An attribute name might be "name" or "age".

A relation is a table structure definition (a set of column definitions) along with the data appearing in that structure. The structure definition is the heading and the data appearing in it is the body, a set of rows. A database relvar (relation variable) is commonly known as a base table. The heading of its assigned value at any time is as specified in the table declaration and its body is that most recently assigned to it by invoking some update operator (typically, INSERT, UPDATE, or DELETE). The heading and body of the table resulting from evaluation of some query are determined by the definitions of the operators used in the expression of that query. (Note that in SQL the heading is not always a set of column definitions as described above, because it is possible for a column to have no name and also for two or more columns to have the same name. Also, the body is not always a set of rows because in SQL it is possible for the same row to appear more than once in the same body.)

SQL and the Relational Model

SQL, initially pushed as the standard language for relational databases, deviates from the relational model in several places. The current ISO SQL standard doesn't mention the relational model or use relational terms or concepts. However, it is possible to create a database conforming to the relational model using SQL if one does not use certain SQL features.

The following deviations from the relational model have been notedin SQL. Note that few database servers implement the entire SQL standard and in particular do not allow some of these deviations. Whereas NULL is ubiquitous, for example, allowing duplicate column names within a table or anonymous columns is uncommon.

Duplicate rows

> The same row can appear more than once in an SQL table. The same tuple cannot appear more than once in a relation.

Anonymous columns

> A column in an SQL table can be unnamed and thus unable to be referenced in expressions. The relational model requires every attribute to be named and referenceable.

Duplicate column names

> Two or more columns of the same SQL table can have the same name and therefore cannot be referenced, on account of the obvious ambiguity. The relational model requires every attribute to be referenceable.

Column order significance

> The order of columns in an SQL table is defined and significant, one consequence being that SQL's implementations of Cartesian product and union are both noncommutative. The relational model requires there to be no significance to any ordering of the attributes of a relation.

Views without CHECK OPTION

> Updates to a view defined without CHECK OPTION can be accepted but the resulting update to the database does not necessarily have the expressed effect on its target. For example, an invocation of INSERT can be accepted but the inserted rows might not all appear in the view, or an invocation of UPDATE can result in rows disappearing from the view. The relational model requires updates to a view to have the same effect as if the view were a base relvar.

Columnless tables unrecognized

> SQL requires every table to have at least one column, but there are two relations of degree zero (of cardinality one and zero) and they are needed to represent extensions of predicates that contain no free variables.

NULL

This special mark can appear instead of a value wherever a value can appear in SQL, in particular in place of a column value in some row. The deviation from the relational model arises from the fact that the implementation of this *ad hoc* concept in SQL involves the use of three-valued logic, under which the comparison of NULL with itself does not yield *true* but instead yields the third truth value, *unknown*; similarly the comparison NULL with something other than itself does not yield *false* but instead yields *unknown*. It is because of this behaviour in comparisons that NULL is described as a mark rather than a value. The relational model depends on the law of excluded middle under which anything that is not true is false and anything that is not false is true; it also requires every tuple in a relation body to have a value for every attribute of that relation. This particular deviation is disputed by some if only because E. F. Codd himself eventually advocated the use of special marks and a 4-valued logic, but this was based on his observation that there are two distinct reasons why one might want to use a special mark in place of a value, which led opponents of the use of such logics to discover more distinct reasons and at least as many as 19 have been noted, which would require a 21-valued logic. SQL itself uses NULL for several purposes other than to represent "value unknown". For example, the sum of the empty set is NULL, meaning zero, the average of the empty set is NULL, meaning undefined, and NULL appearing in the result of a LEFT JOIN can mean "no value because there is no matching row in the right-hand operand".

Relational Operations

Users (or programs) request data from a relational database by sending it a query that is written in a special language, usually a dialect of SQL. Although SQL was originally intended for end-users, it is much more common for SQL queries to be embedded into software that provides an easier user interface.

In response to a query, the database returns a result set, which is just a list of rows containing the answers. The simplest query is just to return all the rows from a table, but more often, the rows are filtered in some way to return just the answer wanted.

Often, data from multiple tables are combined into one, by doing a join. Conceptually, this is done by taking all possible combinations of rows (the Cartesian product), and then filtering out everything except the answer. In practice, relational database management systems rewrite ("optimize") queries to perform faster, using a variety of techniques.

There are a number of relational operations in addition to join. These include project (the process of eliminating some of the columns), restrict (the process of eliminating some of the rows), union (a way of combining two tables with similar structures), difference (that lists the rows in one table that are not found in the other), intersect (that lists the rows found in both tables), and product (mentioned above, which combines each row of one table with each row of the other). Depending on which other sources you consult, there are a number of other operators – many of which can be defined in terms of those listed above. These include semi-join, outer operators such as outer join and outer union, and various forms of division. Then there are operators to rename columns, and summarizing or aggregating operators, and if you permit relation values as attributes (RVA – relation-valued attribute), then operators such as group and ungroup. The SELECT statement in SQL serves to handle all of these except for the group and ungroup operators.

The flexibility of relational databases allows programmers to write queries that were not anticipated by the database designers. As a result, relational databases can be used by multiple applications in ways the original designers did not foresee, which is especially important for databases that might be used for a long time (perhaps several decades). This has made the idea and implementation of relational databases very popular with businesses.

Database Normalization

Relations are classified based upon the types of anomalies to which they're vulnerable. A database that's in the first normal form is vulnerable to all types of anomalies, while a database that's in the domain/key normal form has no modification anomalies. Normal forms are hierarchical in nature. That is, the lowest level is the first normal form, and the database cannot meet the requirements for higher level normal forms without first having met all the requirements of the lesser normal forms.

Examples

Database

An idealized, very simple example of a description of some relvars (relation variables) and their attributes:

- Customer (Customer ID, Tax ID, Name, Address, City, State, Zip, Phone, Email,Sex)

- Order (Order No, Customer ID, Invoice No, Date Placed, Date Promised, Terms, Status)

- Order Line (Order No, Order Line No, Product Code, Qty)

- Invoice (Invoice No, Customer ID, Order No, Date, Status)

- Invoice Line (Invoice No, Invoice Line No, Product Code, Qty Shipped)

- Product (Product Code, Product Description)

In this design we have six relvars: Customer, Order, Order Line, Invoice, Invoice Line and Product. The bold, underlined attributes are *candidate keys*. The non-bold, underlined attributes are *foreign keys*.

Usually one candidate key is chosen to be called the primary key and used in preference over the other candidate keys, which are then called alternate keys.

A *candidate key* is a unique identifier enforcing that no tuple will be duplicated; this would make the relation into something else, namely a bag, by violating the basic definition of a set. Both foreign keys and superkeys (that includes candidate keys) can be composite, that is, can be composed of several attributes. Below is a tabular depiction of a relation of our example Customer relvar; a relation can be thought of as a value that can be attributed to a relvar.

Customer Relation

Customer ID	Tax ID	Name	Address
1234567890	555-5512222	Munmun	323 Broadway
2223344556	555-5523232	Wile E.	1200 Main Street
3334445563	555-5533323	Ekta	871 1st Street
4232342432	555-5325523	E. F. Codd	123 It Way

If we attempted to *insert* a new customer with the ID *1234567890*, this would violate the design of the relvar since Customer ID is a *primary key* and we already have a customer *1234567890*. The DBMS must reject a transaction such as this that would render the database inconsistent by a violation of an integrity constraint.

Foreign keys are integrity constraints enforcing that the value of the attribute set is drawn from a *candidate key* in another relation. For example, in the Order relation the attribute Customer ID is a foreign key. A *join* is the operation that draws on information from several relations at once. By joining relvars from the example above we could *query* the database for all of the Customers, Orders, and Invoices. If we only wanted the tuples for a specific customer, we would specify this using a restriction condition.

If we wanted to retrieve all of the Orders for Customer *1234567890*, we could query the database to return every row in the Order table with Customer ID *1234567890* and join the Order table to the Order Line table based on Order No.

There is a flaw in our database design above. The Invoice relvar contains an Order No attribute. So, each tuple in the Invoice relvar will have one Order No, which implies that there is precisely one Order for each Invoice. But in reality an invoice can be created against many orders, or indeed for no particular order. Additionally the Order relvar contains an Invoice No attribute, implying that each Order has a corresponding Invoice. But again this is not always true in the real world. An order is sometimes paid through several invoices, and sometimes paid without an invoice. In other words, there can be many Invoices per Order and many Orders per Invoice. This is a many-to-many relationship between Order and Invoice (also called a *non-specific relationship*). To represent this relationship in the database a new relvar should be introduced whose role is to specify the correspondence between Orders and Invoices:

OrderInvoice (Order No, Invoice No)

Now, the Order relvar has a *one-to-many relationship* to the OrderInvoice table, as does the Invoice relvar. If we want to retrieve every Invoice for a particular Order, we can query for all orders where Order No in the Order relation equals the Order No in OrderInvoice, and where Invoice No in OrderInvoice equals the Invoice No in Invoice.

Set-theoretic Formulation

Basic notions in the relational model are *relation names* and *attribute names*. We will represent these as strings such as "Person" and "name" and we will usually use the variables $r, s, t, \ldots$ and a, b, c to range over them. Another basic notion is the set of *atomic values* that contains values such as numbers and strings.

Our first definition concerns the notion of *tuple*, which formalizes the notion of row or record in a table:

Tuple

> A tuple is a partial function from attribute names to atomic values.

Header

> A header is a finite set of attribute names.

Projection

> The projection of a tuple t on a finite set of attributes A is $t[A] = \{(a,v) : (a,v) \in t, a \in A\}$.

The next definition defines *relation* that formalizes the contents of a table as it is defined in the relational model.

Relation

> A relation is a tuple (H,B) with H, the header, and B, the body, a set of tuples that all have the domain H

Such a relation closely corresponds to what is usually called the extension of a predicate in first-order logic except that here we identify the places in the predicate with attribute names. Usually in the relational model a database schema is said to consist of a set of relation names, the headers that are associated with these names and the constraints that should hold for every instance of the database schema.

Relation universe

> A relation universe U over a header H is a non-empty set of relations with header H.

Relation schema

> A relation schema (H,C) consists of a header H and a predicate $C(R)$ that is defined for all relations R with header H. A relation satisfies a relation schema (H,C) if it has header H and satisfies C.

Key Constraints and Functional Dependencies

One of the simplest and most important types of relation constraints is the *key constraint*. It tells us that in every instance of a certain relational schema the tuples can be identified by their values for certain attributes.

Superkey

> A superkey is written as a finite set of attribute names.
>
> A superkey K holds in a relation (H,B) if:
>
> - $K \subseteq H$ and

- there exist no two distinct tuples $t_1, t_2 \in B$ such that $t_1[K] = t_2[K]$.

A superkey holds in a relation universe U if it holds in all relations in U.

Theorem: A superkey K holds in a relation universe   over H if and only if $K \subseteq H$ and $K \to H$ holds in U.

Candidate key

A superkey K holds as a candidate key for a relation universe U if it holds as a superkey for U and there is no proper subset of K that also holds as a superkey for U.

Functional dependency

A functional dependency (FD for short) is written as $X \to Y$ for X, Y finite sets of attribute names.

A functional dependency $X \to Y$ holds in a relation (H, B) if:

- $X, Y \subseteq H$ and

- $\forall$ tuples $t_1, t_2 \in B$, $t_1[X] = t_2[X] \Rightarrow t_1[Y] = t_2[Y]$

A functional dependency $X \to Y$ holds in a relation universe U if it holds in all relations in U.

Trivial functional dependency

A functional dependency is trivial under a header H if it holds in all relation universes over H.

Theorem: An FD $X \to Y$ is trivial under a header H if and only if $Y \subseteq X \subseteq H$.

Closure

Armstrong's axioms: The closure of a set of FDs S under a header H, written as S^+, is the smallest superset of S such that:

- $Y \subseteq X \subseteq H \Rightarrow X \to Y \in S^+$ (reflexivity)

- $X \to Y \in S^+ \wedge Y \to Z \in S^+ \Rightarrow X \to Z \in S^+$ (transitivity) and

- $X \to Y \in S^+ \wedge Z \subseteq H \Rightarrow (X \cup Z) \to (Y \cup Z) \in S^+$ (augmentation)

Theorem: Armstrong's axioms are sound and complete; given a header H and a set of FDs that only contain subsets of, S if and only if H, holds in all relation universes over in which all FDs in hold.

Completion

The completion of a finite set of attributes X under a finite set of FDs S, written as X^+, is the smallest superset of X such that:

- $Y \rightarrow Z \in S \wedge Y \subseteq X^+ \Rightarrow Z \subseteq X^+$

The completion of an attribute set can be used to compute if a certain dependency is in the closure of a set of FDs.

Theorem: Given a set S of FDs, $X \rightarrow Y \in S^+$ if and only if $Y \subseteq X^+$.

Irreducible cover

An irreducible cover of a set S of FDs is a set T of FDs such that:

- $S^+ = T^+$

- there exists no $U \subset T$ such that $S^+ = U^+$

- $X \rightarrow Y \in T \Rightarrow Y$ is a singleton set and

- $X \rightarrow Y \in T \wedge Z \subset X \Rightarrow Z \rightarrow Y \notin S^+$.

Algorithm to Derive Candidate Keys from Functional Dependencies

INPUT: a set S of FDs that contain only subsets of a header H

OUTPUT: the set C of superkeys that hold as candidate keys in

all relation universes over H in which all FDs in S hold

begin

  $C := \emptyset$;   // found candidate keys

  $Q := \{H\}$;   // superkeys that contain candidate keys

  while $Q <> \emptyset$ do

    let K be some element from Q;

    $Q := Q - \{K\}$;

    $minimal :=$ true;

    for each $X \rightarrow Y$ in S do

    $K' := (K - Y) \cup X$;   // derive new superkey

    if $K' \subset K$ then

      $minimal :=$ false;

      $Q := Q \cup \{K'\}$;

    end if

end for

if *minimal* and there is not a subset of K in C then

  remove all supersets of K from C;

   $C := C \cup \{K\}$;

  end if

 end while

end

Entity–relationship Model

An entity–relationship model (ER model) describes inter-related things of interest in a specific domain of knowledge. An ER model is composed of entity types (which classify the things of interest) and specifies relationships that can exist between instances of those entity types.

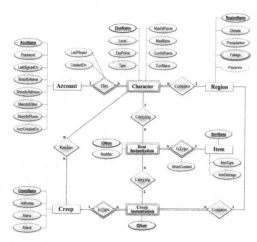

An entity–relationship diagram for an MMORPG using Chen's notation.

In software engineering an ER model is commonly formed to represent things that a business needs to remember in order to perform business processes. Consequently, the ER model becomes an abstract data model that defines a data or information structure that can be implemented in a database, typically a relational database.

Entity–relationship modeling was developed for database design by Peter Chen and published in a 1976 paper. However, variants of the idea existed previously, some ER modelers show super and subtype entities connected by generalization-specialization relationships, and an ER model can be used also in the specification of domain-specific ontology.

Introduction

An entity–relationship model is usually the result of systematic analysis to define and describe what is important to processes in an area of a business. It does not define the business processes; it only presents a business data schema in graphical form. It is usually drawn in a graphical form as boxes (*entities*) that are connected by lines (*relationships*) which express the associations and dependencies between entities. An ER model can also be expressed in a verbal form, for example: *one building may be divided into zero or more apartments, but one apartment can only be located in one building.*

Entities may be characterized not only by relationships, but also by additional properties (*attributes*), which include identifiers called "primary keys". Diagrams created to represent attributes as well as entities and relationships may be called entity-attribute-relationship diagrams, rather than entity-relationship models.

An ER model is typically implemented as a database. In a simple relational database implementation, each row of a table represents one instance of an entity type, and each field in a table represents an attribute type. In a relational database a relationship between entities is implemented by storing the primary key of one entity as a pointer or "foreign key" in the table of another entity

There is a tradition for ER/data models to be built at two or three levels of abstraction. Note that the conceptual-logical-physical hierarchy below is used in other kinds of specification, and is different from the three schema approach to software engineering.

Conceptual data model

> This is the highest level ER model in that it contains the least granular detail but establishes the overall scope of what is to be included within the model set. The conceptual ER model normally defines master reference data entities that are commonly used by the organization. Developing an enterprise-wide conceptual ER model is useful to support documenting the data architecture for an organization.
>
> A conceptual ER model may be used as the foundation for one or more *logical data models*. The purpose of the conceptual ER model is then to establish structural metadata commonality for the master data entities between the set of logical ER models. The conceptual data model may be used to form commonality relationships between ER models as a basis for data model integration.

Logical data model

> A logical ER model does not require a conceptual ER model, especially if the scope of the logical ER model includes only the development of a distinct information system. The logical ER model contains more detail than the conceptual ER model. In addition to master data entities, operational and transactional data entities are now defined. The details of each data entity are developed and the relationships between these data entities are established. The logical ER model is however developed independently of the specific database management system into which it can be implemented.

Physical data model

> One or more physical ER models may be developed from each logical ER model. The physical ER model is normally developed to be instantiated as a database. Therefore, each physical ER model must contain enough detail to produce a database and each physical ER model is technology dependent since each database management system is somewhat different.

The physical model is normally instantiated in the structural metadata of a database management system as relational database objects such as database tables, database indexes such as unique key indexes, and database constraints such as a foreign key constraint or a commonality constraint. The ER model is also normally used to design modifications to the relational database objects and to maintain the structural metadata of the database.

The first stage of information system design uses these models during the requirements analysis to describe information needs or the type of information that is to be stored in a database. The data modeling technique can be used to describe any ontology (i.e. an overview and classifications of used terms and their relationships) for a certain area of interest. In the case of the design of an information system that is based on a database, the conceptual data model is, at a later stage (usually called logical design), mapped to a logical data model, such as the relational model; this in turn is mapped to a physical model during physical design. Note that sometimes, both of these phases are referred to as "physical design."

Entity–relationship Modeling

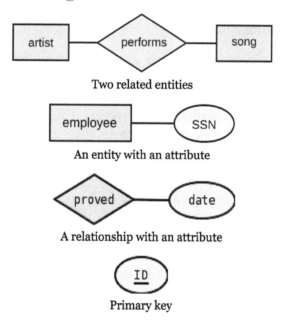

Two related entities

An entity with an attribute

A relationship with an attribute

Primary key

An entity may be defined as a thing capable of an independent existence that can be uniquely identified. An entity is an abstraction from the complexities of a domain. When we speak of an entity, we normally speak of some aspect of the real world that can be distinguished from other aspects of the real world.

An entity is a thing that exists either physically or logically. An entity may be a physical object such as a house or a car (they exist physically), an event such as a house sale or a car service, or a concept such as a customer transaction or order (they exist logically—as a concept). Although the term entity is the one most commonly used, following Chen we should really distinguish between an entity and an entity-type. An entity-type is a category. An entity, strictly speaking, is an instance of a given entity-type. There are usually many instances of an entity-type. Because the term entity-type is somewhat cumbersome, most people tend to use the term entity as a synonym for this term.

Entities can be thought of as nouns. Examples: a computer, an employee, a song, a mathematical theorem.

A relationship captures how entities are related to one another. Relationships can be thought of as verbs, linking two or more nouns. Examples: an *owns* relationship between a company and a computer, a *supervises* relationship between an employee and a department, a *performs* relationship between an artist and a song, a *proves* relationship between a mathematician and a conjecture.

The model's linguistic aspect described above is utilized in the declarative database query language ERROL, which mimics natural language constructs. ERROL's semantics and implementation are based on reshaped relational algebra (RRA), a relational algebra that is adapted to the entity–relationship model and captures its linguistic aspect.

Entities and relationships can both have attributes. Examples: an *employee* entity might have a *Social Security Number* (SSN) attribute; the *proved* relationship may have a *date* attribute.

Every entity (unless it is a weak entity) must have a minimal set of uniquely identifying attributes, which is called the entity's primary key.

Entity–relationship diagrams don't show single entities or single instances of relations. Rather, they show entity sets(all entities of the same entity type) and relationship sets(all relationships of the same relationship type). Example: a particular *song* is an entity. The collection of all songs in a database is an entity set. The *eaten* relationship between a child and her lunch is a single relationship. The set of all such child-lunch relationships in a database is a relationship set. In other words, a relationship set corresponds to a relation in mathematics, while a relationship corresponds to a member of the relation.

Certain cardinality constraints on relationship sets may be indicated as well.

Mapping Natural Language

Chen proposed the following "rules of thumb" for mapping natural language descriptions into ER diagrams: "English, Chinese and ER diagrams" by Peter Chen.

English grammar structure	ER structure
Common noun	Entity type
Proper noun	Entity
Transitive verb	Relationship type
Intransitive verb	Attribute type
Adjective	Attribute for entity
Adverb	Attribute for relationship

Physical view show how data is actually stored.

Relationships, Roles and Cardinalities

In Chen's original paper he gives an example of a relationship and its roles. He describes a relationship "marriage" and its two roles "husband" and "wife".

A person plays the role of husband in a marriage (relationship) and another person plays the role of wife in the (same) marriage. These words are nouns. That is no surprise; naming things requires a noun.

Chen's terminology has also been applied to earlier ideas. The lines, arrows and crow's-feet of some diagrams owes more to the earlier Bachman diagrams than to Chen's relationship diamonds.

Another common extension to Chen's model is to "name" relationships and roles as verbs or phrases.

Role Naming

It has also become prevalent to name roles with phrases such as *is the owner of* and *is owned by*. Correct nouns in this case are *owner* and *possession*. Thus *person plays the role of owner* and *car plays the role of possession* rather than *person plays the role of, is the owner of*, etc.

The use of nouns has direct benefit when generating physical implementations from semantic models. When a *person* has two relationships with *car* then it is possible to generate names such as *owner_person* and *driver_person*, which are immediately meaningful.

Cardinalities

Modifications to the original specification can be beneficial. Chen described look-across cardinalities. As an aside, the Barker–Ellis notation, used in Oracle Designer, uses same-side for minimum cardinality (analogous to optionality) and role, but look-across for maximum cardinality (the crows foot).

In Merise, Elmasri & Navathe and others there is a preference for same-side for roles and both minimum and maximum cardinalities. Recent researchers (Feinerer, Dullea et al.) have shown that this is more coherent when applied to n-ary relationships of order greater than 2.

In Dullea et al. one reads "A 'look across' notation such as used in the UML does not effectively represent the semantics of participation constraints imposed on relationships where the degree is higher than binary."

In Feinerer it says "Problems arise if we operate under the look-across semantics as used for UML associations. Hartmann investigates this situation and shows how and why different transformations fail." *(Although the "reduction" mentioned is spurious as the two diagrams 3.4 and 3.5 are in fact the same)* and also "As we will see on the next few pages, the look-across interpretation introduces several difficulties that prevent the extension of simple mechanisms from binary to n-ary associations."

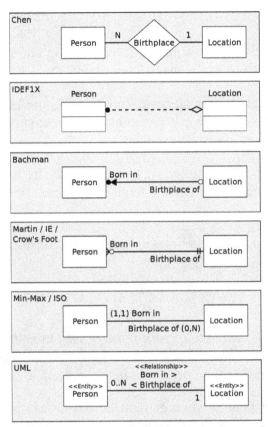

Various methods of representing the same one to many relationship. In each case, the diagram shows the relationship between a person and a place of birth: each person must have been born at one, and only one, location, but each location may have had zero or more people born at it.

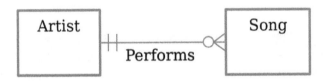

Two related entities shown using Crow's Foot notation. In this example, an optional relationship is shown between Artist and Song; the symbols closest to the song entity represents "zero, one, or many", whereas a song has "one and only one" Artist. The former is therefore read as, an Artist (can) perform(s) "zero, one, or many" song(s).

Chen's notation for entity–relationship modeling uses rectangles to represent entity sets, and diamonds to represent relationships appropriate for first-class objects: they can have attributes and relationships of their own. If an entity set participates in a relationship set, they are connected with a line.

Attributes are drawn as ovals and are connected with a line to exactly one entity or relationship set.

Cardinality constraints are expressed as follows:

- a double line indicates a *participation constraint*, totality or surjectivity: all entities in the entity set must participate in *at least one* relationship in the relationship set;

- an arrow from entity set to relationship set indicates a key constraint, i.e. injectivity: each entity of the entity set can participate in *at most one* relationship in the relationship set;

- a thick line indicates both, i.e. bijectivity: each entity in the entity set is involved in *exactly one* relationship.

- an underlined name of an attribute indicates that it is a key: two different entities or relationships with this attribute always have different values for this attribute.

Attributes are often omitted as they can clutter up a diagram; other diagram techniques often list entity attributes within the rectangles drawn for entity sets.

Related diagramming convention techniques:

- Bachman notation

- Barker's notation

- EXPRESS

- IDEF1X

- Martin notation

- (min, max)-notation of Jean-Raymond Abrial in 1974

- UML class diagrams

- Merise

- Object-role modeling

Crow's Foot Notation

Crow's foot notation is used in Barker's Notation, Structured Systems Analysis and Design Method (SSADM) and information engineering. Crow's foot diagrams represent entities as boxes, and relationships as lines between the boxes. Different shapes at the ends of these lines represent the cardinality of the relationship.

Crow's foot notation was used in the consultancy practice CACI. Many of the consultants at CACI (including Richard Barker) subsequently moved to Oracle UK, where they developed the early versions of Oracle's CASE tools, introducing the notation to a wider audience.

Modelling Issues

In modelling a database you can encounter two issues that impact the results obtained from queries, that are notorious enough to have received their own names.

The first is the 'fan trap'. It occurs when you have a (master) table linking to multiple tables in a one-to-many relationship. The issue derives its name from the way the model looks when you draw it in an entity-relationship diagram: the linked tables 'fan out' from the master table. This type of model looks similar to a star schema, a type of model used in data warehouses. When trying to calculate sums over aggregates using standard SQL over the master table, you get unexpected (and incorrect) results. The solution is to either adjust the model or the SQL. This issue occurs mostly in databases for decision support systems, and software that queries such systems sometimes includes specific methods for handling this issue.

The second issue is a 'chasm trap'. A chasm trap occurs when a model suggests the existence of a relationship between entity types, but the pathway does not exist between certain entity occurrences. For example, a Building has one-or-more Rooms, that hold zero-or-more Computers. You would expect to be able to query the model to see all the Computers in the Building. However, Computers not currently assigned to a Room (because they are under repair or somewhere else) are not shown on the list. You need another relation between Building and Computers to capture all the computers in the building. This last modelling issue is the result of a failure to capture all the relationships that exist in the real world in the model.

Entity–relationships and Semantic Modeling

Semantic Model

A semantic model is a model of concepts, it is sometimes called a "platform independent model". It is an intensional model. At the latest since Carnap, it is well known that:

> "...the full meaning of a concept is constituted by two aspects, its intension and its extension. The first part comprises the embedding of a concept in the world of concepts as a whole, i.e. the totality of all relations to other concepts. The second part establishes the referential meaning of the concept, i.e. its counterpart in the real or in a possible world".

Extension Model

An extensional model is one that maps to the elements of a particular methodology or technology, and is thus a "platform specific model". The UML specification explicitly states that associations in class models are extensional and this is in fact self-evident by considering the extensive array of additional "adornments" provided by the specification over and above those provided by any of the prior candidate "semantic modelling languages"."UML as a Data Modeling Notation, Part 2"

Entity–relationship Origins

Peter Chen, the father of ER modeling said in his seminal paper:

> "The entity-relationship model adopts the more natural view that the real world consists of entities and relationships. It incorporates some of the important semantic information about the real world."

In his original 1976 article Chen explicitly contrasts entity–relationship diagrams with record modelling techniques:

> *"The data structure diagram is a representation of the organisation of records and is not an exact representation of entities and relationships."*

Several other authors also support Chen's program:

Philosophical Alignment

Chen is in accord with philosophic and theoretical traditions from the time of the Ancient Greek philosophers: Socrates, Plato and Aristotle (428 BC) through to modern epistemology, semiotics and logic of Peirce, Frege and Russell.

Plato himself associates knowledge with the apprehension of unchanging Forms (The forms, according to Socrates, are roughly speaking archetypes or abstract representations of the many types of things, and properties) and their relationships to one another.

Limitations

- ER assume information content that can readily be represented in a relational database. They describe only a relational structure for this information.

- They are inadequate for systems in which the information cannot readily be represented in relational form, such as with semi-structured data.

- For many systems, possible changes to information contained are nontrivial and important enough to warrant explicit specification.

- Some authors have extended ER modeling with constructs to represent change, an approach supported by the original author; an example is Anchor Modeling. An alternative is to model change separately, using a process modeling technique. Additional techniques can be used for other aspects of systems. For instance, ER models roughly correspond to just 1 of the 14 different modeling techniques offered by UML.

- Even where it is suitable in principle, ER modeling is rarely used as a separate activity. One reason for this is today's abundance of tools to support diagramming and other design support directly on relational database management systems. These tools can readily extract database diagrams that are very close to ER diagrams from existing databases, and they provide alternative views on the information contained in such diagrams.

- In a survey, Brodie and Liu could not find a single instance of entity–relationship modeling inside a sample of ten Fortune 100 companies. Badia and Lemire blame this lack of use on the lack of guidance but also on the lack of benefits, such as lack of support for data integration.

- The enhanced entity–relationship model (EER modeling) introduces several concepts not in ER modeling, but are closely related to object-oriented design, like is-a relationships.

- For modelling temporal databases, numerous ER extensions have been considered. Similarly, the ER model was found unsuitable for multidimensional databases (used in OLAP applications); no dominant conceptual model has emerged in this field yet, although they generally revolve around the concept of OLAP cube (also known as *data cube* within the field).

Entity–attribute–value Model

Entity–attribute–value model (EAV) is a data model to encode, in a space-efficient manner, entities where the number of attributes (properties, parameters) that can be used to describe them is potentially vast, but the number that will actually apply to a given entity is relatively modest. Such entities correspond to the mathematical notion of a sparse matrix. EAV is also known as object–attribute–value model, vertical database model and open schema.

Structure of an EAV Table

This data representation is analogous to space-efficient methods of storing a sparse matrix, where only non-empty values are stored. In an EAV data model, each attribute-value pair is a fact describing an entity, and a row in an EAV table stores a single fact. EAV tables are often described as "long and skinny": "long" refers to the number of rows, "skinny" to the few columns.

Data is recorded as three columns:

- The *entity*: the item being described.

- The *attribute* or *parameter*: typically implemented as a foreign key into a table of attribute definitions. The attribute definitions table might contain the following columns: an attribute ID, attribute name, description, data type, and columns assisting input validation, e.g., maximum string length and regular expression, set of permissible values, etc.

- The *value* of the attribute.

Consider how one would try to represent a general-purpose clinical record in a relational database. Clearly creating a table (or a set of tables) with thousands of columns is not feasible, because the vast majority of columns would be null. To complicate things, in a longitudinal medical record that follows the patient over time, there may be multiple values of the same parameter: the height and weight of a child, for example, change as the child grows. Finally, the universe of clinical findings keeps growing: for example, diseases emerge and new lab tests are devised; this would require constant addition of columns, and constant revision of the user interface. (The situation where the list of attributes changes frequently is termed "attribute volatility" in database parlance.)

The following shows a snapshot of an EAV table for clinical findings from a visit to a doctor for a fever on the morning of 1/5/98. The entries shown within angle brackets are references to entries in other tables, shown here as text rather than as encoded foreign key values for ease of understanding. In this example, the values are all literal values, but they could also be pre-defined value lists. The latter are particularly useful when the possible values are known to be limited (i.e., enumerable).

- The *entity*. For clinical findings, the entity is the *patient event*: a foreign key into a table that contains at a minimum a patient ID and one or more time-stamps (e.g., the start and end of the examination date/time) that record when the event being described happened.

- The *attribute* or *parameter*: a foreign key into a table of attribute definitions (in this example, definitions of clinical findings). At the very least, the attribute definitions table would contain the following columns: an attribute ID, attribute name, description, data type, units of measurement, and columns assisting input validation, e.g., maximum string length and regular expression, maximum and minimum permissible values, set of permissible values, etc.

- The *value* of the attribute. This would depend on the data type, and we discuss how values are stored shortly.

The example below illustrates symptoms findings that might be seen in a patient with pneumonia.

(<patient XYZ, 1/5/98 9:30 AM>, <Temperature in degrees Fahrenheit>, "102")

(<patient XYZ, 1/5/98 9:30 AM>, <Presence of Cough>, "True")

(<patient XYZ, 1/5/98 9:30 AM>, <Type of Cough>, "With phlegm, yellowish, streaks of blood")

(<patient XYZ, 1/5/98 9:30 AM>, <Heart Rate in beats per minute>, "98")

...

EAV Databases

The term "EAV database" refers to a database design where a significant proportion of the data is modeled as EAV. However, even in a database described as "EAV-based", some tables in the system are traditional relational tables.

- As noted above, EAV modeling makes sense for categories of data, such as clinical findings, where attributes are numerous and sparse. Where these conditions do not hold, standard relational modeling (i.e., one column per attribute) is preferable; using EAV does not mean abandoning common sense or principles of good relational design. In clinical record systems, the subschemas dealing with patient demographics and billing are typically modeled conventionally. (While most vendor database schemas are proprietary, VistA, the system used throughout the United States Department of Veterans Affairs (VA) medical system, known as the Veterans Health Administration (VHA), is open-source and its schema is readily inspectable, though it uses a MUMPS database engine rather than a relational database.)

- As discussed shortly, an EAV database is essentially unmaintainable without numerous supporting tables that contain supporting metadata. The metadata tables, which typically outnumber the EAV tables by a factor of at least three or more, are typically standard relational tables. An example of a metadata table is the Attribute Definitions table mentioned above.

Physical Representation of EAV Data

EAV Versus Row Modeling

The EAV data described above is comparable to the contents of a supermarket sales receipt (which would be reflected in a Sales Line Items table in a database). The receipt lists only details of the items actually purchased, instead of listing every product in the store that the customer might have purchased but didn't. Like the clinical findings for a given patient, the sales receipt is sparse.

- The "entity" is the sale/transaction id — a foreign key into a sales transactions table. This is used to tag each line item internally, though on the receipt the information about the Sale appears at the top (store location, sale date/time) and at the bottom (total value of sale).

- The "attribute" is a foreign key into a products table, from where one looks up description, unit price, discounts and promotions, etc. (Products are just as volatile as clinical findings, possibly even more so: new products are introduced every month, while others are taken off the market if consumer acceptance is poor. No competent database designer would hard-code individual products such as Doritos or Diet Coke as columns in a table.)

- The "values" are the quantity purchased and total line item price.

Row modeling, where facts about something (in this case, a sales transaction) are recorded as multiple *rows* rather than multiple *columns*, is a standard data modeling technique. The differences between row modeling and EAV (which may be considered a *generalization* of row-modeling) are:

- A row-modeled table is *homogeneous* in the facts that it describes: a Line Items table describes only products sold. By contrast, an EAV table contains almost any type of fact.

- The data type of the value column/s in a row-modeled table is pre-determined by the nature of the facts it records. By contrast, in an EAV table, the conceptual data type of a value in a particular row depend on the attribute in that row. It follows that in production systems, allowing direct data entry into an EAV table would be a recipe for disaster, because the database engine itself would not be able to perform robust input validation. We shall see later how it is possible to build generic frameworks that perform most of the tasks of input validation, without endless coding on an attribute-by-attribute basis.

In a clinical data repository, row modeling also finds numerous uses; the laboratory test subschema is typically modeled this way, because lab test results are typically numeric, or can be encoded numerically.

The circumstances where you would need to go beyond standard row-modeling to EAV are listed below:

- The data type of individual attributes varies (as seen with clinical findings).

- The categories of data are numerous, growing or fluctuating, but the number of instances (records/rows) within each category is very small. Here, with conventional modeling, the database's entity–relationship diagram might have hundreds of tables: the tables that contain thousands/ millions of rows/instances are emphasized visually to the same extent as those with very few rows. The latter are candidates for conversion to an EAV representation.

This situation arises in ontology-modeling environments, where categories ("classes") must often be created on the fly, and some classes are often eliminated in subsequent cycles of prototyping.

- Certain ("hybrid") classes have some attributes that are non-sparse (present in all or most instances), while other attributes are highly variable and sparse. The latter are suitable for EAV modeling. For example, descriptions of products made by a conglomerate corporation depend on the product category, e.g., the attributes necessary to describe a brand of light bulb are quite different from those required to describe a medical imaging device, but both have common attributes such as packaging unit and per-item cost.

The Entity

In clinical data, the entity is typically a clinical event, as described above. In more general-purpose settings, the entity is a foreign key into an "objects" table that records common information about every "object" (thing) in the database – at the minimum, a preferred name and brief description, as well as the category/class of entity to which it belongs. Every record (object) in this table is assigned a machine-generated object ID.

The "objects table" approach was pioneered by Tom Slezak and colleagues at Lawrence Livermore Laboratories for the Chromosome 19 database, and is now standard in most large bioinformatics databases. The use of an objects table does not mandate the concurrent use of an EAV design: conventional tables can be used to store the category-specific details of each object.

The major benefit to a central objects table is that, by having a supporting table of object synonyms and keywords, one can provide a standard Google-like search mechanism across the entire system where the user can find information about any object of interest without having to first specify the category that it belongs to. (This is important in bioscience systems where a keyword like "acetylcholine" could refer either to the molecule itself, which is a neurotransmitter, or the biological receptor to which it binds.

The Attribute

In the EAV table itself, this is just an attribute ID, a foreign key into an Attribute Definitions table, as stated above. However, there are usually multiple metadata tables that contain attribute-related information, and these are discussed shortly.

The Value

Coercing all values into strings, as in the EAV data example above, results in a simple, but non-scalable, structure: constant data type inter-conversions are required if one wants to do anything with the values, and an index on the value column of an EAV table is essentially useless. Also, it is not convenient to store large binary data, such as images, in Base64 encoded form in the same table as small integers or strings. Therefore, larger systems use separate EAV tables for each data type (including binary large objects, "BLOBS"), with the metadata for a given attribute identifying the EAV table in which its data will be stored. This approach is actually quite efficient because the modest amount of attribute metadata for a given class or form that a user chooses to work with can be cached readily in memory. However, it requires moving of data from one table to another if an attribute's data type is changed. (This does not happen often, but mistakes can be made in metadata definition just as in database schema design.)

Representing Substructure: EAV With Classes and Relationships (EAV/CR)

In a simple EAV design, the values of an attribute are simple or primitive data types as far as the database engine is concerned. However, in EAV systems used for representation of highly diverse data, it is possible that a given object (class instance) may have substructure: that is, some of its attributes may represent other kinds of objects, which in turn may have substructure, to an arbitrary level of complexity. A car, for example, has an engine, a transmission, etc., and the engine has components such as cylinders. (The permissible substructure for a given class is defined within the system's attribute metadata, as discussed later. Thus, for example, the attribute "random-access-memory" could apply to the class "computer" but not to the class "engine".)

To represent substructure, one incorporates a special EAV table where the value column contains references to *other* entities in the system (i.e., foreign key values into the objects table). To get all the information on a given object requires a recursive traversal of the metadata, followed by a recursive traversal of the data that stops when every attribute retrieved is simple (atomic). Recursive traversal is necessary whether details of an individual class are represented in conventional or EAV form; such traversal is performed in standard object–relational systems, for example. In practice, the number of levels of recursion tends to be relatively modest for most classes, so the performance penalties due to recursion are modest, especially with indexing of object IDs.

EAV/CR (EAV with Classes and Relationships) refers to a framework that supports complex substructure. Its name is somewhat of a misnomer: while it was an outshoot of work on EAV systems, in practice, many or even most of the classes in such a system may be represented in standard relational form, based on whether the attributes are sparse or dense. EAV/CR is really characterized by its very detailed metadata, which is rich enough to support the automatic generation of browsing interfaces to individual classes without having to write class-by-class user-interface code. The basis of such browser interfaces is that it is possible to generate a batch of dynamic SQL queries that is independent of the class of the object, by first consulting its metadata and using metadata information to generate a sequence of queries against the data tables, and some of these queries may be arbitrarily recursive. This approach works well for object-at-a-time queries, as in Web-based browsing interfaces where clicking on the name of an object brings up all details of the object in a separate page: the metadata associated with that object's class also facilitates presentation of the object's details, because it includes captions of individual attributes, the order in which they are to be presented as well as how they are to be grouped.

One approach to EAV/CR is to allow columns to hold JSON structures, which thus provide the needed class structure. For example, Postgres, as of version 9.4, offers JSON binary column (JSONB) support, allowing JSON attributes to be queried, indexed and joined.

The Critical Role of Metadata in EAV Systems

In the words of Prof. Dr. Daniel Masys (formerly Chair of Vanderbilt University's Medical Informatics Department), the challenges of working with EAV stem from the fact that in an EAV database, the "physical schema" (the way data are stored) is radically different from the "logical schema" – the way users, and many software applications such as statistics packages, regard it, i.e., as conventional rows and columns for individual classes. (Because an EAV table conceptually mixes apples, oranges, grapefruit and chop suey, if you want to do any analysis of the data using standard off-the-shelf software, in most cases you have to convert subsets of it into columnar form. The process of doing this, called pivoting, is important enough to be discussed separately.)

Metadata helps perform the sleight of hand that lets users interact with the system in terms of the logical schema rather than the physical: the software continually consults the metadata for various operations such as data presentation, interactive validation, bulk data extraction and ad hoc query. The metadata can actually be used to customize the behavior of the system.

EAV systems trade off simplicity in the physical and logical structure of the data for complexity in their metadata, which, among other things, plays the role that database constraints and referential integrity do in standard database designs. Such a tradeoff is generally worthwhile, because in the typical mixed schema of production systems, the data in conventional relational tables can also benefit from functionality such as automatic interface generation. The structure of the metadata is complex enough that it comprises its own subschema within the database: various foreign keys in the data tables refer to tables within this subschema. This subschema is standard-relational, with features such as constraints and referential integrity being used to the hilt.

The correctness of the metadata contents, in terms of the intended system behavior, is critical and the task of ensuring correctness means that, when creating an EAV system, considerable design efforts must go into building user interfaces for metadata editing that can be used by people on the team who know the problem domain (e.g., clinical medicine) but are not necessarily programmers. (Historically, one of the main reasons why the pre-relational TMR system failed to be adopted at sites other than its home institution was that all metadata was stored in a single file with a non-intuitive structure. Customizing system behavior by altering the contents of this file, without causing the system to break, was such a delicate task that the system's authors only trusted themselves to do it.)

Where an EAV system is implemented through RDF, the RDF Schema language may conveniently be used to express such metadata. This Schema information may then be used by the EAV database engine to dynamically re-organize its internal table structure for best efficiency.

Some final caveats regarding metadata:

- Because the business logic is in the metadata rather than explicit in the database schema (i.e., one level removed, compared with traditionally designed systems), it is less apparent to one who is unfamiliar with the system. Metadata-browsing and metadata-reporting tools are therefore important in ensuring the maintainability of an EAV system. In the common scenario where metadata is implemented as a relational sub-schema, these tools are nothing more than applications built using off-the-shelf reporting or querying tools that operate on the metadata tables.

- It is easy for an insufficiently knowledgeable user to corrupt (i.e., introduce inconsistencies and errors in) metadata. Therefore, access to metadata must be restricted, and an audit trail of accesses and changes put into place to deal with situations where multiple individuals have metadata access. Using an RDBMS for metadata will simplify the process of maintaining consistency during metadata creation and editing, by leveraging RDBMS features such as support for transactions. Also, if the metadata is part of the same database as the data itself, this ensures that it will be backed up at least as frequently as the data itself, so that it can be recovered to a point in time.

- The quality of the annotation and documentation within the metadata (i.e., the narrative/explanatory text in the descriptive columns of the metadata sub-schema) must be much higher, in order to facilitate understanding by various members of the development team. Ensuring metadata quality (and keeping it current as the system evolves) takes very high priority in the long-term management and maintenance of any design that uses an EAV component. Poorly-documented or out-of-date metadata can compromise the system's long-term viability .

Information Captured in Metadata

Attribute Metadata

- Validation metadata include data type, range of permissible values or membership in a set of values, regular expression match, default value, and whether the value is permitted to be null. In EAV systems representing classes with substructure, the validation metadata will also record what class, if any, a given attribute belongs to.

- Presentation metadata: how the attribute is to be displayed to the user (e.g., as a text box or image of specified dimensions, a pull-down list or a set of radio buttons). When a compound object is composed of multiple attributes, as in the EAV/CR design, there is additional metadata on the order in which the attributes should be presented, and how these attributes should optionally be grouped (under descriptive headings).

- For attributes which happen to be laboratory parameters, *ranges of normal values*, which may vary by age, sex, physiological state and assay method, are recorded.

- Grouping metadata: Attributes are typically presented as part of a higher-order group, e.g., a specialty-specific form. Grouping metadata includes information such as the order in which attributes are presented. Certain presentation metadata, such as fonts/colors and the number of attributes displayed per row, apply to the group as a whole.

Advanced Validation Metadata

- Dependency metadata: in many user interfaces, entry of specific values into certain fields/attributes is required to either disable/hide certain other fields or enable/show other fields.

(For example, if a user chooses the response "No" to a Boolean question "Does the patient have diabetes?", then subsequent questions about the duration of diabetes, medications for diabetes, etc. must be disabled.) To effect this in a generic framework involves storing of dependencies between the controlling attributes and the controlled attributes.

- Computations and complex validation: As in a spreadsheet, the value of certain attributes can be computed, and displayed, based on values entered into fields that are presented earlier in sequence. (For example, body surface area is a function of height and width). Similarly, there may be "constraints" that must be true for the data to be valid: for example, in a differential white cell count, the sum of the counts of the individual white cell types must always equal 100, because the individual counts represent percentages. Computed formulas and complex validation are generally effected by storing expressions in the metadata that are macro-substituted with the values that the user enters and can be evaluated. In Web browsers, both JavaScript and VBScript have an Eval() function that can be leveraged for this purpose.

Validation, presentation and grouping metadata make possible the creation of code frameworks that support automatic user interface generation for both data browsing as well as interactive editing. In a production system that is delivered over the Web, the task of validation of EAV data is essentially moved from the back-end/database tier (which is powerless with respect to this task) to the middle /Web server tier. While back-end validation is always ideal, because it is impossible to subvert by attempting direct data entry into a table, middle tier validation through a generic framework is quite workable, though a significant amount of software design effort must go into building the framework first. The availability of open-source frameworks that can be studied and modified for individual needs can go a long way in avoiding wheel reinvention.

Scenarios that are Appropriate for EAV Modeling

EAV modeling, under the alternative terms "generic data modeling" or "open schema", has long been a standard tool for advanced data modelers. Like any advanced technique, it can be double-edged, and should be used judiciously.

Also, the employment of EAV does not preclude the employment of traditional relational database modeling approaches within the same database schema. In EMRs that rely on an RDBMS, such as Cerner, which use an EAV approach for their clinical-data subschema, the vast majority of tables in the schema are in fact traditionally modeled, with attributes represented as individual columns rather than as rows.

The modeling of the metadata subschema of an EAV system, in fact, is a very good fit for traditional modeling, because of the inter-relationships between the various components of the metadata. In the TrialDB system, for example, the number of metadata tables in the schema outnumber the data tables by about ten to one. Because the correctness and consistency of metadata is critical to the correct operation of an EAV system, the system designer wants to take full advantages of all of the features that RDBMSs provide, such as referential integrity and programmable constraints, rather than having to reinvent the RDBMS-engine wheel. Consequently, the numerous metadata tables that support EAV designs are typically in third-normal relational form.

Commercial Electronic Health Record Systems (EHRs) use row-modeling for classes of data such as diagnoses, surgical procedures performed on and laboratory test results, which are segregated into separate tables. In each table, the "entity" is a composite of the patient ID and the date/time the diagnosis was made (or the surgery or lab test performed); the attribute is a foreign key into a specially designated lookup table that contains a controlled vocabulary - e.g., ICD-10 for diagnoses, Current Procedural Terminology for surgical procedures, with a set of value attributes. (E.g., for laboratory-test results, one may record the value measured, whether it is in the normal, low or high range, the ID of the person responsible for performing the test, the date/time the test was performed, and so on. As stated earlier, this is not a full-fledged EAV approach because the domain of attributes for a given table is restricted, just as the domain of product IDs in a supermarket's Sales table would be restricted to the domain of Products in a Products table.

However, to capture data on parameters that are not always defined in standard vocabularies, EHRs also provide a "pure" EAV mechanism, where specially designated power-users can define new attributes, their data type, maximum and minimal permissible values (or permissible set of values/codes), and then allow others to capture data based on these attributes. In the Epic (TM) EHR, this mechanism is termed "Flowsheets", and is commonly used to capture inpatient nursing observation data.

Modeling Sparse Attributes

The typical case for using the EAV model is for highly sparse, heterogeneous attributes, such as clinical parameters in the electronic medical record (EMRs), as stated above. Even here, however, it is accurate to state that the EAV modeling principle is applied to a *sub-schema* of the database rather than for all of its contents. (Patient demographics, for example, are most naturally modeled in one-column-per-attribute, traditional relational structure.)

Consequently, the arguments about EAV vs. "relational" design reflect incomplete understanding of the problem: An EAV design should be employed only for that sub-schema of a database where sparse attributes need to be modeled: even here, they need to be supported by third normal form metadata tables. There are relatively few database-design problems where sparse attributes are encountered: this is why the circumstances where EAV design is applicable are relatively rare. Even where they are encountered, a set of EAV tables is not the only way to address sparse data: an XML-based solution (discussed below) is applicable when the maximum number of attributes per entity is relatively modest, and the total volume of sparse data is also similarly modest. An example of this situation is the problems of capturing variable attributes for different product types.

Sparse attributes may also occur in E-commerce situations where an organization is purchasing or selling a vast and highly diverse set of commodities, with the details of individual categories of commodities being highly variable. The Magento E-commerce software employs an EAV approach to address this issue.

Modeling Numerous Classes With Very Few Instances Per Class: Highly Dynamic Schemas

Another application of EAV is in modeling classes and attributes that, while not sparse, are dynamic, but where the number of data rows per class will be relatively modest – a couple of hundred rows at most, but typically a few dozen – and the system developer is also required to provide a Web-based end-user interface within a very short turnaround time. "Dynamic" means that new classes and attributes need to be continually defined and altered to represent an evolving data model. This scenario can occur in rapidly evolving scientific fields as well as in ontology develop- ment, especially during the prototyping and iterative refinement phases.

While creation of new tables and columns to represent a new category of data is not especially labor-intensive, the programming of Web-based interfaces that support browsing or basic editing with type- and range-based validation is. In such a case, a more maintainable long-term solution is to create a framework where the class and attribute definitions are stored in metadata, and the software generates a basic user interface from this metadata dynamically.

The EAV/CR framework, mentioned earlier, was created to address this very situation. Note that an EAV data model is not essential here, but the system designer may consider it an ac- ceptable alternative to creating, say, sixty or more tables containing a total of not more than two thousand rows. Here, because the number of rows per class is so few, efficiency consider- ations are less important; with the standard indexing by class ID/attribute ID, DBMS optimiz- ers can easily cache the data for a small class in memory when running a query involving that class or attribute.

In the dynamic-attribute scenario, it is worth noting that Resource Description Framework (RDF) is being employed as the underpinning of Semantic-Web-related ontology work. RDF, intended to be a general method of representing information, is a form of EAV: an RDF triple comprises an object, a property, and a value.

At the end of Jon Bentley's book "Writing Efficient Programs", the author warns that making code more efficient generally also makes it harder to understand and maintain, and so one does not rush in and tweak code unless one has first determined that there is a performance problem, and measures such as code profiling have pinpointed the exact location of the bottle- neck. Once you have done so, you modify only the specific code that needs to run faster. Sim- ilar considerations apply to EAV modeling: you apply it only to the sub-system where tradi- tional relational modeling is known *a priori* to be unwieldy (as in the clinical data domain), or is discovered, during system evolution, to pose significant maintenance challenges. Database Guru (and currently a vice-president of Core Technologies at Oracle Corporation) Tom Kyte, for example, correctly points out drawbacks of employing EAV in traditional business scenar- ios, and makes the point that mere "flexibility" is not a sufficient criterion for employing EAV. (However, he makes the sweeping claim that EAV should be avoided in *all* circumstances, even though Oracle's Health Sciences division itself employs EAV to model clinical-data attributes in its commercial systems ClinTrial and Oracle Clinical.)

Working With EAV Data

The Achilles heel of EAV is the difficulty of working with large volumes of EAV data. It is often nec- essary to transiently or permanently inter-convert between columnar and row-or EAV-modeled representations of the same data; this can be both error-prone if done manually as well as CPU-in- tensive. Generic frameworks that utilize attribute and attribute-grouping metadata address the former but not the latter limitation; their use is more or less mandated in the case of mixed schemas that contain a mixture of conventional-relational and EAV data, where the error quotient can be very significant.

The conversion operation is called pivoting. Pivoting is not required only for EAV data but also for any form or row-modeled data. (For example, implementations of the Apriori algorithm for Association Analysis, widely used to process supermarket sales data to identify other products that purchasers of a given product are also likely to buy, pivot row-modeled data as a first step.) Many database engines have proprietary SQL extensions to facilitate pivoting, and packages such as Microsoft Excel also support it. The circumstances where pivoting is necessary are considered below.

- Browsing of modest amounts of data for an individual entity, optionally followed by data editing based on inter-attribute dependencies. This operation is facilitated by caching the modest amounts of the requisite supporting metadata. Some programs, such as TrialDB, access the metadata to generate semi-static Web pages that contain embedded programming code as well as data structures holding metadata.

- Bulk extraction transforms large (but predictable) amounts of data (e.g., a clinical study's complete data) into a set of relational tables. While CPU-intensive, this task is infrequent and does not need to be done in real-time; i.e., the user can wait for a batched process to complete. The importance of bulk extraction cannot be overestimated, especially when the data is to be processed or analyzed with standard third-party tools that are completely unaware of EAV structure. Here, it is not advisable to try to reinvent entire sets of wheels through a generic framework, and it is best just to bulk-extract EAV data into relational tables and then work with it using standard tools.

- Ad hoc query interfaces to row- or EAV-modeled data, when queried from the perspective of individual attributes, (e.g., "retrieve all patients with the presence of liver disease, with signs of liver failure and no history of alcohol abuse") must typically show the results of the query with individual attributes as separate columns. For most EAV database scenarios ad hoc query performance must be tolerable, but sub-second responses are not necessary, since the queries tend to be exploratory in nature.

Relational Division

However, the structure of EAV data model is a perfect candidate for Relational Division. With a good indexing strategy it's possible to get a response time in less than a few hundred milliseconds on a billion row EAV table. Microsoft SQL Server MVP Peter Larsson has proved this on a laptop and made the solution general available.

Optimizing Pivoting Performance

- One possible optimization is the use of a separate "warehouse" or queryable schema whose contents are refreshed in batch mode from the production (transaction) schema. See data warehousing. The tables in the warehouse are heavily indexed and optimized using de-normalization, which combines multiple tables into one to minimize performance penalty due to table joins. This is the approach that Kalido uses to convert highly normalized EAV tables to standard reporting schemas.

- Certain EAV data in a warehouse may be converted into standard tables using "materialized views" but this is generally a last resort that must be used carefully, because the number of views of this kind tends to grow non-linearly with the number of attributes in a system.

- In-memory data structures: One can use hash tables and two-dimensional arrays in memory in conjunction with attribute-grouping metadata to pivot data, one group at a time. This data is written to disk as a flat delimited file, with the internal names for each attribute in the first row: this format can be readily bulk-imported into a relational table. This "in-memory" technique significantly outperforms alternative approaches by keeping the queries on EAV tables as simple as possible and minimizing the number of I/O operations. Each statement retrieves a large amount of data, and the hash tables help carry out the pivoting operation, which involves placing a value for a given attribute instance into the appropriate row and column. Random Access Memory (RAM) is sufficiently abundant and affordable in modern hardware that the complete data set for a single attribute group in even large data sets will usually fit completely into memory, though the algorithm can be made smarter by working on slices of the data if this turns out not to be the case.

Obviously, no matter what approaches you take, querying EAV will not be as fast as querying standard column-modeled relational data for certain types of query, in much the same way that access of elements in sparse matrices are not as fast as those on non-sparse matrices if the latter fit entirely into main memory. (Sparse matrices, represented using structures such as linked lists, require list traversal to access an element at a given X-Y position, while access to elements in matrices represented as 2-D arrays can be performed using fast CPU register operations.) If, however, you chose the EAV approach correctly for the problem that you were trying to solve, this is the price that you pay; in this respect, EAV modeling is an example of a space (and schema maintenance) versus CPU-time tradeoff.

Consideration for Postgres: JSONB Columns

Postgres version 9.4 includes support for JSON binary columns (JSONB), which can be queried, indexed and joined. This allows performance improvements by factors of a thousand or more over traditional EAV table designs.

Consideration for SQL Server 2008 and later: Sparse Columns

Microsoft SQL Server 2008 offers a (proprietary) alternative to EAV: columns with an atomic data type (e.g., numeric, varchar or datetime columns) can be designated as *sparse* simply by including the word SPARSE in the column definition of the CREATE TABLE statement. Sparse columns optimize the storage of NULL values (which now take up no space at all) and are useful when the majority records in a table will have NULL values for that column. Indexes on sparse columns are also optimized: only those rows with values are indexed. In addition, the contents of all sparse columns in a particular row of a table can be collectively aggregated into a single XML column (a column set), whose contents are of the form [<column-name>column contents </column-name>]*.... In fact, if a column set is defined for a table as part of a CREATE TABLE statement, all sparse columns subsequently defined are typically added to it. This has the interesting consequence that the SQL statement SELECT * from <tablename> will not return the individual sparse columns, but concatenate all of them into a single XML column whose name is that of the column set (which therefore acts as a virtual, computed column).

Sparse columns are convenient for business applications such as product information, where the applicable attributes can be highly variable depending on the product type, but where the total number of variable attributes per product type are relatively modest. Limitations include:

- The maximum number of sparse columns in a table is 30,000, which may fall short for some implementations, such as for storing clinical data, where the possible number of attributes is one order of magnitude larger. Therefore, this is not a solution for modeling *all* possible clinical attributes for a patient.

- Addition of new attributes – one of the primary reasons an EAV model might be sought – still requires a DBA, and the problem of building a user interface to such data is not addressed: only the storage mechanism is streamlined. Applications can be written to dynamically add and remove sparse columns from a table at run-time: in contrast an attempt to perform such an action in a multi-user scenario where other users/processes are still using the table would be prevented for tables without sparse columns. This capability offers power and flexibility, but can result in significant performance penalties, in part because any compiled query plans that use this table are automatically invalidated. (In addition, dynamic column addition or removal is an operation that should be audited, at the very least – column removal can cause data loss – and allowing an application to modify a table without maintaining some kind of a trail – including a justification for the action – is not good software practice. Such a feature therefore invites abuse and should be used infrequently and judiciously.)

- Another major limitation is that SQL constraints (e.g., range checks) cannot be applied to sparse columns: the only check that is applied is for correct data type. These would have to be implemented in metadata tables and middle-tier code, as is done in production EAV systems. (This consideration also applies to business applications as well.)

- SQL Server has limitations on row size if attempting to change the storage format of a column: the total contents of all atomic-datatype columns, sparse and non-sparse, in a row that contain data cannot exceed 8016 bytes if that table contains a sparse column for the data to be automatically copied over. Further, sparse columns that happen to contain data have a storage overhead of 4 bytes per column in addition to storage for the data type itself (e.g., 4 bytes for datetime columns). This impacts the amount of sparse-column data that you can associate with a given row. This size restriction is relaxed for the varchar data type, which means that, if one hits row-size limits in a production system, one has to work around it by designating sparse columns as varchar even though they may have a different intrinsic data type. Unfortunately, this approach now subverts server-side data-type checking.

EAV Vs. the Universal Data Model

Originally postulated by Maier, Ullman and Vardi, the "Universal Data Model" (UDM) seeks to create to simplify the query of a complex relational schema by naive users, by creating the illusion that everything is stored in a single giant "universal table". It does this by utilizing inter-table relationships, so that the user does not need to be concerned about what table contains what attribute. C.J. Date, however, pointed out that in circumstances where a table is multiply related to another (as in genealogy databases, where an individual's father and mother are also individuals, or in some business databases where all addresses are stored centrally, and an organization can have different office addresses and shipping addresses), there is insufficient metadata within the database schema to specify unambiguous joins. When UDM has been commercialized, as in SAP BusinessObjects, this limitation is worked around through the creation of "Universes", which are relational views with predefined joins between sets of tables: the "Universe" developer disambiguates ambiguous joins by including the multiply-related table in a view multiple times using different aliases.

Apart from the way in which data is explicitly modeled (UDM simply uses relational views to intercede between the user and the database schema), EAV differs from Universal Data Models is that it also applies to transactional systems, not only query oriented (read-only) systems as in UDM. Also, when used as the basis for clinical-data query systems, EAV implementations do not necessarily shield the user from having to specify the class of an object of interest. In the EAV-based i2b2 clinical data mart, for example, when the user searches for a term, she has the option of specifying the category of data that the user is interested in. For example, the phrase "lithium" can refer either to the medication (which is used to treat bipolar disorder), or a laboratory assay for lithium level in the patient's blood. (The blood level of lithium must be monitored carefully: too much of the drug causes severe side effects, while too little is ineffective.)

XML and JSON

An Open Schema implementation can use an XML column in a table to capture the variable/sparse information. Similar ideas can be applied to databases that support JSON-valued columns: sparse, heirarchical data can be represented as JSON. If the database has native JSON support (such as Postgres), then attributes can be queried, indexed and joined. This can offer performance improvements of over 1000x over naive EAV implementations.

Note that there are two ways in which XML or JSON data can be stored: one way is to store it as a plain string, opaque to the database server; the other way is to use a database server that can "see into" the structure. There are obviously some severe drawbacks to storing opaque strings: these cannot be queried directly, one cannot form an index based on their contents, and it is impossible to perform joins based on the content.

Building an application that has to manage data gets extremely complicated when using EAV models, because of the extent of infrastructure that has to be developed in terms of metadata tables and application-framework code. Using XML solves the problem of server-based data validation (which must be done by middle-tier and browser-based code in EAV-based frameworks), but has the following drawbacks:

- It is programmer-intensive: because XML schemas are notoriously tricky to write by hand, a recommended approach is to create them by defining relational tables, generating XML-schema code, and then dropping these tables. This is problematic in many production operations involving dynamic schemas, where new attributes are required to be defined by power-users who understand a specific knowledge domain (e.g. inventory management or biomedicine) but are not necessarily programmers. In production systems that use EAV, such users define new attributes (and the data-type and validation checks associated with each) through a GUI. (Because the validation-associated metadata is required to be stored in multiple relational tables in a normalized design, a GUI that ties these tables together and enforces the appropriate metadata-consistency checks is the only practical way to allow entry of attribute information, even for advanced developers.)

- The server-based diagnostics that result if incorrect data is attempted to be inserted (e.g., range check or regular-expression pattern violations) are not comprehensible to the end-user: to convey the error accurately, one would, at the least, need to associate a detailed and user-friendly error diagnostic with each attribute.

- The solution does not address the user-interface-generation problem.

All of the above drawbacks are remediable by creating a layer of metadata and application code, but in creating this, the original "advantage" of not having to create a framework has vanished. The fact is that modeling sparse data robustly is a hard database-application-design problem, and there are no shortcuts. Sarka's work, however, proves the viability of using an XML field instead of type-specific relational EAV tables for the data-storage layer, and in situations where the number of attributes per entity is extremely modest (e.g., variable product attributes for different product types) the XML-based solution is more compact than an EAV-table-based one. (XML itself may be regarded as a means of attribute-value data representation, though it is based on structured text rather than on tables.)

Graph Databases

An alternative approach to managing the various problems encountered with EAV-structured data is to employ a graph database. These represent entities as the nodes of a graph or hypergraph, and attributes as links or edges of that graph. The issue of table joins are addressed by providing graph-specific query languages, such as Apache TinkerPop, or the OpenCog atomspace pattern matcher.

EAV and Cloud Computing

Many cloud computing vendors offer data stores based on the EAV model, where an arbitrary number of attributes can be associated with a given entity. Roger Jennings provides an in-depth comparison of these. In Amazon's offering, SimpleDB, the data type is limited to strings, and data that is intrinsically non-string must be coerced to string (e.g., numbers must be padded with leading zeros) if you wish to perform operations such as sorting. Microsoft's offering, Windows Azure Table Storage, offers a limited set of data types: byte[], bool, DateTime, double, Guid, int, long and string . The Google App Engine offers the greatest variety of data types: in addition to dividing numeric data into int, long, or float, it also defines custom data types such as phone number, E-mail address, geocode and hyperlink. Google, but not Amazon or Microsoft, lets you define metadata that would prevent invalid attributes from being associated with a particular class of entity, by letting you create a metadata model.

Google lets you operate on the data using a subset of SQL; Microsoft offer a URL-based querying syntax that is abstracted via a LINQ provider; Amazon offer a more limited syntax. Of concern, built-in support for combining different entities through joins is currently (April '10) non-existent with all three engines. Such operations have to be performed by application code. This may not be a concern if the application servers are co-located with the data servers at the vendor's data center, but a lot of network traffic would be generated if the two were geographically separated.

An EAV approach is justified only when the attributes that are being modeled are numerous and sparse: if the data being captured does not meet this requirement, the cloud vendors' default EAV approach is often a mismatch for applications that require a true back-end database (as opposed to merely a means of persistent data storage). Retrofitting the vast majority of existing database applications, which use a traditional data-modeling approach, to an EAV-type cloud architecture, would require major surgery. Microsoft discovered, for example, that its database-application-developer base was largely reluctant to invest such effort. More recently, therefore, Microsoft has provided a premium offering – a cloud-accessible full-fledged relational engine, SQL Server Azure, which allows porting of existing database applications with modest changes.

One limitation of SQL Azure is that physical databases are limited to 500GB in size as of January 2015. Microsoft recommends that data sets larger than this be split into multiple physical databases and accessed with parallel queries.

Tree Structures and Relational Databases

There exist several other approaches for the representation of tree-structured data, be it XML, JSON or other formats, such as the nested set model, in a relational database. On the other hand, database vendors have begun to include JSON and XML support into their data structures and query features, like in IBM DB2, where XML data is stored as XML separate from the tables, using Xpath queries as part of SQL statements, or in PostgreSQL, with a JSON data type that can be indexed and queried. These developments accomplish, improve or substitute the EAV model approach.

It should be noted, however, that the uses of JSON and XML are not necessarily the same as the use of an EAV model, though they can overlap. XML is preferable to EAV for arbitrarily hierarchical data that is relatively modest in volume for a single entity: it is not intended to scale up to the multi-gigabyte level with respect to data-manipulation performance. XML is not concerned per-se with the sparse-attribute problem, and when the data model underlying the information to be represented can be decomposed straightforwardly into a relational structure, XML is better suited as a means of data interchange than as a primary storage mechanism. EAV, as stated earlier, is specifically (and only) applicable to the sparse-attribute scenario. When such a scenario holds, the use of datatype-specific attribute-value tables than can be indexed by entity, by attribute, and by value and manipulated through simple SQL statements is vastly more scaleable than the use of an XML tree structure. The Google App Engine, mentioned above, uses strongly-typed-value tables for a good reason.

History of EAV Database Systems

EAV, as a general-purpose means of knowledge representation, originated with the concept of "association lists" (attribute-value pairs). Commonly used today, these were first introduced in the language LISP. Attribute-value pairs are widely used for diverse applications, such as configuration files (using a simple syntax like *attribute = value*). An example of non-database use of EAV is in UIMA (Uniform Information Management Architecture), a standard now managed by the Apache Foundation and employed in areas such as natural language processing. Software that analyses text typically marks up ("annotates") a segment: the example provided in the UIMA tutorial is a program that performs named-entity recognition (NER) on a document, annotating the text segment "President Bush" with the annotation-attribute-value triple *(Person, Full_Name, "George W. Bush")*. Such annotations may be stored in a database table.

While EAV does not have a direct connection to AV-pairs, Stead and Hammond appear to be the first to have conceived of their use for persistent storage of arbitrarily complex data. The first medical record systems to employ EAV were the Regenstrief electronic medical record (the effort led by Clement MacDonald), William Stead and Ed Hammond's TMR (The Medical Record) system and the HELP Clinical Data Repository (CDR) created by Homer Warner's group at LDS Hospital, Salt Lake City, Utah. (The Regenstrief system actually used a Patient-Attribute-Timestamp-Value design: the use of the timestamp supported retrieval of values for a given patient/attribute in chronological order.) All these systems, developed in the 1970s, were released before commercial systems based on E.F. Codd's relational database model were available, though HELP was much later ported to a relational architecture and commercialized by the 3M corporation. (Note that while Codd's landmark paper was published in 1970, its heavily mathematical tone had the unfortunate effect of diminishing its accessibility among non-computer-science types and consequently delaying the model's acceptance in IT and software-vendor circles. The value of the subsequent contribution of Christopher J. Date, Codd's colleague at IBM, in translating these ideas into accessible language, accompanied by simple examples that illustrated their power, cannot be overestimated.)

A group at the Columbia-Presbyterian Medical Center were the first to use a relational database engine as the foundation of an EAV system.

The open-source TrialDB clinical study data management system of Nadkarni et al. was the first to use multiple EAV tables, one for each DBMS data type.

The EAV/CR framework, designed primarily by Luis Marenco and Prakash Nadkarni, overlaid the principles of object orientation onto EAV; it built on Tom Slezak's object table approach (described earlier in the "Entity" section). SenseLab, a publicly accessible neuroscience database, is built with the EAV/CR framework. Additionally, there are numerous commercial applications that use aspects of EAV internally including Oracle Designer (applied to ER modeling), Kalido (applied to data warehousing and master data management), and Lazysoft Sentences (applied to custom software development). An EAV system that does not sit on top of a tabular structure but instead directly on a B Tree is InfinityDB, which eliminates the need for one table per value data type.

References

- Funding a Revolution: Government Support for Computing Research. National Academies Press. 8 Jan 1999. ISBN 0309062780.

- Guy Harrison; Steven Feuerstein (2008). MySQL Stored Procedure Programming. O'Reilly Media. p. 49. ISBN 978-0-596-10089-6.

- Stonebraker,. Michael with Moore, Dorothy. Object-Relational DBMSs: The Next Great Wave. Morgan Kaufmann Publishers, 1996. ISBN 1-55860-397-2.

- Stonebraker, M; Rowe, LA. The POSTGRES data model (PDF). Proceedings of the 13th International Conference on Very Large Data Bases. Brighton, England: Morgan Kaufmann Publishers. pp. 83–96. ISBN 0-934613-46-X.

- Momjian, Bruce (2001). "Subqueries". PostgreSQL: Introduction and Concepts. Addison-Wesley. ISBN 0-201-70331-9. Retrieved 2010-09-25.

- Alapati, Sam R. (2004). OCP Oracle Database 10g: New Features for Administrators Exam Guide. McGraw-Hill/Osborne. pp. 18? or 287?. ISBN 0-07-225862-4.

- Bancilhon, Francois; Delobel,Claude; and Kanellakis, Paris. Building an Object-Oriented Database System: The Story of O2. Morgan Kaufmann Publishers, 1992. ISBN 1-55860-169-4.

- Jack Belzer. Encyclopedia of Computer Science and Technology - Volume 14: Very Large Data Base Systems to Zero-Memory and Markov Information Source. Marcel Dekker Inc. ISBN 0-8247-2214-0.

- Codd, E. F (1990), The Relational Model for Database Management, Addison-Wesley, pp. 371–388, ISBN 0-201-14192-2.

- Date, C.J (2006). "18. Why Three- and Four-Valued Logic Don't Work". Date on Database: Writings 2000–2006. Apress. pp. 329–41. ISBN 978-1-59059-746-0.

- A.P.G. Brown, "Modelling a Real-World System and Designing a Schema to Represent It", in Douque and Nijssen (eds.), Data Base Description, North-Holland, 1975, ISBN 0-7204-2833-5.

- RICCARDO TORLONE (2003). "Conceptual Multidimensional Models". In Maurizio Rafanelli. Multidimensional Databases: Problems and Solutions (PDF). Idea Group Inc (IGI). ISBN 978-1-59140-053-0.

Database Design: An Integrated Study

Database design is a method that is particularly used in producing data models. The model usually contains the logical and physical designs that are needed to generate a design that helps in creating a database. Some of the aspects of database design database refactoring, data structure, database engine, database server and database schema. This section will provide an integrated understanding of database design.

Database Design

Database design is the process of producing a detailed data model of database. This data model contains all the needed logical and physical design choices and physical storage parameters needed to generate a design in a data definition language, which can then be used to create a database. A fully attributed data model contains detailed attributes for each entity.

The term database design can be used to describe many different parts of the design of an overall database system. Principally, and most correctly, it can be thought of as the logical design of the base data structures used to store the data. In the relational model these are the tables and views. In an object database the entities and relationships map directly to object classes and named relationships. However, the term database design could also be used to apply to the overall process of designing, not just the base data structures, but also the forms and queries used as part of the overall database application within the database management system (DBMS).

The process of doing database design generally consists of a number of steps which will be carried out by the database designer. Usually, the designer must:

- Determine the data to be stored in the database.

- Determine the relationships between the different data elements.

- Superimpose a logical structure upon the data on the basis of these relationships.

Within the relational model the final step above can generally be broken down into two further steps, that of determining the grouping of information within the system, generally determining what are the basic objects about which information is being stored, and then determining the relationships between these groups of information, or objects. This step is not necessary with an Object database.

Determining Data to be Stored

In a majority of cases, a person who is doing the design of a database is a person with expertise in the area of database design, rather than expertise in the domain from which the data to be stored is drawn e.g. financial information, biological information etc. Therefore, the data to be stored in the database must be determined in cooperation with a person who does have expertise in that domain, and who is aware of what data must be stored within the system.

This process is one which is generally considered part of requirements analysis, and requires skill on the part of the database designer to elicit the needed information from those with the domain knowledge. This is because those with the necessary domain knowledge frequently cannot express clearly what their system requirements for the database are as they are unaccustomed to thinking in terms of the discrete data elements which must be stored. Data to be stored can be determined by Requirement Specification.

Determining Data Relationships

Once a database designer is aware of the data which is to be stored within the database, they must then determine where dependency is within the data. Sometimes when data is changed you can be changing other data that is not visible. For example, in a list of names and addresses, assuming a situation where multiple people can have the same address, but one person cannot have more than one address, the address is dependent upon the name. When provided a name and the list the address can be uniquely determined; however, the inverse does not hold - when given an address and the list, a name cannot be uniquely determined because multiple people can reside at an address. Because an address is determined by a name, an address is considered dependent on a name.

(NOTE: A common misconception is that the relational model is so called because of the stating of relationships between data elements therein. This is not true. The relational model is so named because it is based upon the mathematical structures known as relations.)

Logically Structuring Data

Once the relationships and dependencies amongst the various pieces of information have been determined, it is possible to arrange the data into a logical structure which can then be mapped into the storage objects supported by the database management system. In the case of relational databases the storage objects are tables which store data in rows and columns. In an Object database the storage objects correspond directly to the objects used by the Object-oriented programming language used to write the applications that will manage and access the data. The relationships may be defined as attributes of the object classes involved or as methods that operate on the object classes.

The way this mapping is generally performed is such that each set of related data which depends upon a single object, whether real or abstract, is placed in a table. Relationships between these dependent objects is then stored as links between the various objects.

Each table may represent an implementation of either a logical object or a relationship joining one or more instances of one or more logical objects. Relationships between tables may then be stored as links connecting child tables with parents. Since complex logical relationships are themselves tables they will probably have links to more than one parent.

ER Diagram (Entity-relationship Model)

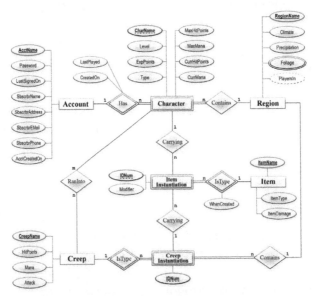

A sample Entity-relationship diagram

Database designs also include ER (entity-relationship model) diagrams. An ER diagram is a diagram that helps to design databases in an efficient way.

Attributes in ER diagrams are usually modeled as an oval with the name of the attribute, linked to the entity or relationship that contains the attribute.

A Design Process Suggestion for Microsoft Access

1. Determine the purpose of the database - This helps prepare for the remaining steps.

2. Find and organize the information required - Gather all of the types of information to record in the database, such as product name and order number.

3. Divide the information into tables - Divide information items into major entities or subjects, such as Products or Orders. Each subject then becomes a table.

4. Turn information items into columns - Decide what information needs to be stored in each table. Each item becomes a field, and is displayed as a column in the table. For example, an Employees table might include fields such as Last Name and Hire Date.

5. Specify primary keys - Choose each table's primary key. The primary key is a column, or a set of columns, that is used to uniquely identify each row. An example might be Product ID or Order ID.

6. Set up the table relationships - Look at each table and decide how the data in one table is related to the data in other tables. Add fields to tables or create new tables to clarify the relationships, as necessary.

7. Refine the design - Analyze the design for errors. Create tables and add a few records of

sample data. Check if results come from the tables as expected. Make adjustments to the design, as needed.

8. Apply the normalization rules - Apply the data normalization rules to see if tables are structured correctly. Make adjustments to the tables

Normalization

In the field of relational database design, *normalization* is a systematic way of ensuring that a database structure is suitable for general-purpose querying and free of certain undesirable characteristics—insertion, update, and deletion anomalies that could lead to loss of data integrity.

A standard piece of database design guidance is that the designer should create a fully normalized design; selective denormalization can subsequently be performed, but only for performance reasons. However, some modeling disciplines, such as the dimensional modeling approach to data warehouse design, explicitly recommend non-normalized designs, i.e. designs that in large part do not adhere to 3NF. Normalization consists of normal forms that are 1NF,2NF,3NF,BOYCE-CODD NF (3.5NF),4NF and 5NF

Conceptual Schema

Schema refinement

Schema refinement of the database specifies that the data is normalized to reduce data insufficiency and conflicts.

Physical Design

The physical design of the database specifies the physical configuration of the database on the storage media. This includes detailed specification of data elements, data types, indexing options and other parameters residing in the DBMS data dictionary. It is the detailed design of a system that includes modules & the database's hardware & software specifications of the system.

Database Refactoring

A database refactoring is a simple change to a database schema that improves its design while retaining both its behavioral and informational semantics. A database refactoring is conceptually more difficult than a code refactoring; code refactorings only need to maintain behavioral semantics while database refactorings also must maintain informational semantics.

The process of database refactoring is the act of applying database refactorings to evolve an existing database schema (database refactoring is a core practice of evolutionary database design). You refactor a database schema for one of two reasons: to develop the schema in an evolutionary manner in parallel with the evolutionary design of the rest of your system or to fix design problems with an existing legacy database schema

Database refactoring does not change the way data is interpreted or used and does not fix bugs or add new functionality. Every refactoring to a database leaves the system in a working state, thus not causing maintenance lags, provided the meaningful data exists in the production environment.

An example of database refactoring would be splitting an aggregate table into two different tables in the process of database normalization

Tools

- LiquiBase

Database Normalization

Database normalization, or simply normalization, is the process of organizing the columns (attributes) and tables (relations) of a relational database to reduce data redundancy and improve data integrity.

Normalization involves arranging attributes in tables based on dependencies between attributes, ensuring that the dependencies are properly enforced by database integrity constraints. Normalization is accomplished through applying some formal rules either by a process of synthesis or decomposition. Synthesis creates a normalized database design based on a known set of dependencies. Decomposition takes an existing (insufficiently normalized) database design and improves it based on the known set of dependencies.

Edgar F. Codd, the inventor of the relational model (RM), introduced the concept of normalization and what we now know as the First normal form (1NF) in 1970. Codd went on to define the Second normal form (2NF) and Third normal form (3NF) in 1971, and Codd and Raymond F. Boyce defined the Boyce-Codd Normal Form (BCNF) in 1974. Informally, a relational database table is often described as "normalized" if it meets Third Normal Form. Most 3NF tables are free of insertion, update, and deletion anomalies.

Objectives

A basic objective of the first normal form defined by Codd in 1970 was to permit data to be queried and manipulated using a "universal data sub-language" grounded in first-order logic. (SQL is an example of such a data sub-language, albeit one that Codd regarded as seriously flawed.)

The objectives of normalization beyond 1NF (First Normal Form) were stated as follows by Codd:

1. To free the collection of relations from undesirable insertion, update and deletion dependencies;

2. To reduce the need for restructuring the collection of relations, as new types of data are introduced, and thus increase the life span of application programs;

3. To make the relational model more informative to users;

4. To make the collection of relations neutral to the query statistics, where these statistics are liable to change as time goes by.

— *E.F. Codd, "Further Normalization of the Data Base Relational Model"*

The sections below give details of each of these objectives.

Free the Database of Modification Anomalies

Employees' Skills

Employee ID	Employee Address	Skill
426	87 Sycamore Grove	Typing
426	87 Sycamore Grove	Shorthand
519	94 Chestnut Street	Public Speaking
519	96 Walnut Avenue	Carpentry

An **update anomaly**. Employee 519 is shown as having different addresses on different records.

Faculty and Their Courses

Faculty ID	Faculty Name	Faculty Hire Date	Course Code
389	Dr. Giddens	10-Feb-1985	ENG-206
407	Dr. Saperstein	19-Apr-1999	CMP-101
407	Dr. Saperstein	19-Apr-1999	CMP-201
424	Dr. Newsome	29-Mar-2007	?

An **insertion anomaly**. Until the new faculty member, Dr. Newsome, is assigned to teach at least one course, his details cannot be recorded.

Faculty and Their Courses

Faculty ID	Faculty Name	Faculty Hire Date	Course Code
389	Dr. Giddens	10-Feb-1985	ENG-206
407	Dr. Saperstein	19-Apr-1999	CMP-101
407	Dr. Saperstein	19-Apr-1999	CMP-201

DELETE

A **deletion anomaly**. All information about Dr. Giddens is lost if he temporarily ceases to be assigned to any courses.

When an attempt is made to modify (update, insert into, or delete from) a table, undesired side-effects may arise in tables that have not been sufficiently normalized. An insufficiently normalized table might have one or more of the following characteristics:

- The same information can be expressed on multiple rows; therefore updates to the table may result in logical inconsistencies. For example, each record in an "Employees' Skills" table might contain an Employee ID, Employee Address, and Skill; thus a change of address for a particular employee will potentially need to be applied to multiple records (one for each skill). If the update is not carried through successfully—if, that is, the employee's address is updated on some records but not others—then the table is left in an inconsistent state. Specifically, the table provides conflicting answers to the question of what this particular employee's address is. This phenomenon is known as an update anomaly.

- There are circumstances in which certain facts cannot be recorded at all. For example, each record in a "Faculty and Their Courses" table might contain a Faculty ID, Faculty Name, Faculty Hire Date, and Course Code—thus we can record the details of any faculty member who teaches at least one course, but we cannot record the details of a newly hired faculty member who has not yet been assigned to teach any courses except by setting the Course Code to null. This phenomenon is known as an insertion anomaly.

- Under certain circumstances, deletion of data representing certain facts necessitates deletion of data representing completely different facts. The "Faculty and Their Courses" table described in the previous example suffers from this type of anomaly, for if a faculty member temporarily ceases to be assigned to any courses, we must delete the last of the records on which that faculty member appears, effectively also deleting the faculty member, unless we set the Course Code to null in the record itself. This phenomenon is known as a deletion anomaly.

Minimize Redesign When Extending the Database Structure

When a fully normalized database structure is extended to allow it to accommodate new types of data, the pre-existing aspects of the database structure can remain largely or entirely unchanged. As a result, applications interacting with the database are minimally affected.

Normalized tables, and the relationship between one normalized table and another, mirror real-world concepts and their interrelationships.

Example

Querying and manipulating the data within a data structure that is not normalized, such as the following non-1NF representation of customers, credit card transactions, involves more complexity than is really necessary:

Customer	Cust. ID	Transactions		
		Tr. ID	**Date**	**Amount**
Jones	1	12890	14-Oct-2003	−87
		12904	15-Oct-2003	−50
		Tr. ID	**Date**	**Amount**
Wilkins	2	12898	14-Oct-2003	−21
		Tr. ID	**Date**	**Amount**
		12907	15-Oct-2003	−18
Stevens	3	14920	20-Nov-2003	−70
		15003	27-Nov-2003	−60

To each customer corresponds a *repeating group* of transactions. The automated evaluation of any query relating to customers' transactions therefore would broadly involve two stages:

1. Unpacking one or more customers' groups of transactions allowing the individual transactions in a group to be examined, and

2. Deriving a query result based on the results of the first stage

For example, in order to find out the monetary sum of all transactions that occurred in October 2003 for all customers, the system would have to know that it must first unpack the *Transactions* group of each customer, then sum the *Amounts* of all transactions thus obtained where the *Date* of the transaction falls in October 2003.

One of Codd's important insights was that this structural complexity could always be removed completely, leading to much greater power and flexibility in the way queries could be formulated (by users and applications) and evaluated (by the DBMS). The normalized equivalent of the structure above would look like this:

Customer	Cust. ID
Jones	1
Wilkins	2
Stevens	3

Cust. ID	Tr. ID	Date	Amount
1	12890	14-Oct-2003	−87
1	12904	15-Oct-2003	−50
2	12898	14-Oct-2003	−21
3	12907	15-Oct-2003	−18
3	14920	20-Nov-2003	−70
3	15003	27-Nov-2003	−60

In the modified structure, the keys are {Customer} and {Cust. ID} in the first table, {Cust. ID, Tr ID} in the second table.

Now each row represents an individual credit card transaction, and the DBMS can obtain the answer of interest, simply by finding all rows with a Date falling in October, and summing their Amounts. The data structure places all of the values on an equal footing, exposing each to the DBMS directly, so each can potentially participate directly in queries; whereas in the previous situation some values were embedded in lower-level structures that had to be handled specially. Accordingly, the normalized design lends itself to general-purpose query processing, whereas the unnormalized design does not. The normalized version also allows the user to change the customer name in one place and guards against errors that arise if the customer name is misspelled on some records.

List of Normal Forms

- UNF - "Unnormalized Form"

- 1NF - First Normal Form

- 2NF - Second Normal Form

- 3NF - Third Normal Form

- EKNF - Elementary Key Normal Form

- BCNF - Boyce–Codd Normal Form

- 4NF - Fourth Normal Form

- ETNF - Essential Tuple Normal Form

- 5NF - Fifth Normal Form

- 6NF - Sixth Normal Form

- DKNF - Domain/Key Normal Form

Data Structure

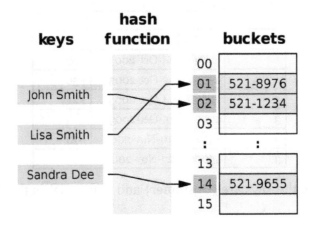

A hash table.

In computer science, a data structure is a particular way of organizing data in a computer so that it can be used efficiently. Data structures can implement one or more particular abstract data types (ADT), which specify the operations that can be performed on a data structure and the computational complexity of those operations. In comparison, a data structure is a concrete implementation of the specification provided by an ADT.

Different kinds of data structures are suited to different kinds of applications, and some are highly specialized to specific tasks. For example, relational databases commonly use B-tree indexes for data retrieval, while compiler implementations usually use hash tables to look up identifiers.

Data structures provide a means to manage large amounts of data efficiently for uses such as large databases and internet indexing services. Usually, efficient data structures are key to designing efficient algorithms. Some formal design methods and programming languages emphasize data structures, rather than algorithms, as the key organizing factor in software design. Data structures can be used to organize the storage and retrieval of information stored in both main memory and secondary memory.

Overview

Data structures are generally based on the ability of a computer to fetch and store data at any place in its memory, specified by a pointer—a bit string, representing a memory address, that can be itself stored in memory and manipulated by the program. Thus, the array and record data structures are based on computing the addresses of data items with arithmetic operations; while the linked data structures are based on storing addresses of data items within the structure itself. Many data structures use both principles, sometimes combined in non-trivial ways (as in XOR linking).

The implementation of a data structure usually requires writing a set of procedures that create and manipulate instances of that structure. The efficiency of a data structure cannot be analyzed separately from those operations. This observation motivates the theoretical concept of an abstract data type, a data structure that is defined indirectly by the operations that may be performed on it, and the mathematical properties of those operations (including their space and time cost).

Examples

There are numerous types of data structures, generally built upon simpler primitive data types:

- An *array* is a number of elements in a specific order, typically all of the same type. Elements are accessed using an integer index to specify which element is required (Depending on the language, individual elements may either all be forced to be the same type, or may be of almost any type). Typical implementations allocate contiguous memory words for the elements of arrays (but this is not always a necessity). Arrays may be fixed-length or resizable.

- A *linked list* (also just called *list*) is a linear collection of data elements of any type, called nodes, where each node has itself a value, and points to the next node in the linked list. The principal advantage of a linked list over an array, is that values can always be efficiently inserted and removed without relocating the rest of the list. Certain other operations, such as random access to a certain element, are however slower on lists than on arrays.

- A *record* (also called *tuple* or *struct*) is an aggregate data structure. A record is a value that contains other values, typically in fixed number and sequence and typically indexed by names. The elements of records are usually called *fields* or *members*.

- A *union* is a data structure that specifies which of a number of permitted primitive types may be stored in its instances, e.g. *float* or *long integer*. Contrast with a record, which could be defined to contain a float *and* an integer; whereas in a union, there is only one value at a time. Enough space is allocated to contain the widest member datatype.

- A *tagged union* (also called *variant, variant record, discriminated union,* or *disjoint union*) contains an additional field indicating its current type, for enhanced type safety.

- A *class* is a data structure that contains data fields, like a record, as well as various methods which operate on the contents of the record. In the context of object-oriented programming, records are known as plain old data structures to distinguish them from classes.

Language Support

Most assembly languages and some low-level languages, such as BCPL (Basic Combined Programming Language), lack built-in support for data structures. On the other hand, many high-level programming languages and some higher-level assembly languages, such as MASM, have special syntax or other built-in support for certain data structures, such as records and arrays. For example, the C and Pascal languages support structs and records, respectively, in addition to vectors (one-dimensional arrays) and multi-dimensional arrays.

Most programming languages feature some sort of library mechanism that allows data structure implementations to be reused by different programs. Modern languages usually come with standard libraries that implement the most common data structures. Examples are the C++ Standard Template Library, the Java Collections Framework, and Microsoft's .NET Framework.

Modern languages also generally support modular programming, the separation between the interface of a library module and its implementation. Some provide opaque data types that allow clients to hide implementation details. Object-oriented programming languages, such as C++, Java and Smalltalk may use classes for this purpose.

Many known data structures have concurrent versions that allow multiple computing threads to access the data structure simultaneously.

Database Engine

A database engine (or storage engine) is the underlying software component that a database management system (DBMS) uses to create, read, update and delete (CRUD) data from a database. Most database management systems include their own application programming interface (API) that allows the user to interact with their underlying engine without going through the user interface of the DBMS.

The term "database engine" is frequently used interchangeably with "database server" or "database management system". A 'database instance' refers to the processes and memory structures of the running database engine.

Storage Engines

Many of the modern DBMS support multiple storage engines within the same database. For example, MySQL supports InnoDB as well as MyISAM.

Some storage engines are transactional.

Name	License	Transactional
Aria	GPL	No
BlitzDB	GPL	No
Falcon	GPL	Yes
InnoDB	GPL	Yes
MyISAM	GPL	No
InfiniDB	CPL	No
TokuDB	GPL	Yes
WiredTiger	GPL	Yes
XtraDB	GPL	Yes

Additional engine types include:

- Embedded database engines

- In-memory database engines

Design Considerations

Database bits are laid out in storage in data structures and groupings that can take advantage of both known effective algorithms to retrieve and manipulate them and the storage own properties. Typically the storage itself is designed to meet requirements of various areas that extensively utilize storage, including databases. A DBMS in operation always simultaneously utilizes several storage types (e.g., memory, and external storage), with respective layout methods.

In principle the database storage can be viewed as a linear address space, where every bit of data has its unique address in this address space. In practice, only a very small percentage of addresses are kept as initial reference points (which also requires storage); most data is accessed by indirection using displacement calculations (distance in bits from the reference points) and data structures which define access paths (using pointers) to all needed data in an effective manner, optimized for the needed data access operations.

Database Storage Hierarchy

A database, while in operation, resides simultaneously in several types of storage, forming a storage hierarchy. By the nature of contemporary computers most of the database part inside a computer that hosts the DBMS resides (partially replicated) in volatile storage. Data (pieces of the database) that are being processed/manipulated reside inside a processor, possibly in processor's caches. These data are being read from/written to memory, typically through a computer bus (so far typically volatile storage components). Computer memory is communicating data (transferred to/from) external storage, typically through standard storage interfaces or networks (e.g., fibre channel, iSCSI). A storage array, a common external storage unit, typically has storage hierarchy of its own, from a fast cache, typically consisting of (volatile and fast) DRAM, which is connected (again via standard interfaces) to drives, possibly with different speeds, like flash drives and magnetic disk drives (non-volatile). The drives may be connected to magnetic tapes, on which typically the least active parts of a large database may reside, or database backup generations.

Typically a correlation exists currently between storage speed and price, while the faster storage is typically volatile.

Data Structures

A data structure is an abstract construct that embeds data in a well defined manner. An efficient data structure allows to manipulate the data in efficient ways. The data manipulation may include data insertion, deletion, updating and retrieval in various modes. A certain data structure type may be very effective in certain operations, and very ineffective in others. A data structure type is selected upon DBMS development to best meet the operations needed for the types of data it contains. Type of data structure selected for a certain task typically also takes into consideration the type of storage it resides in (e.g., speed of access, minimal size of storage chunk accessed, etc.). In some DBMSs database administrators have the flexibility to select among options of data structures to contain user data for performance reasons. Sometimes the data structures have selectable parameters to tune the database performance.

Databases may store data in many data structure types. Common examples are the following:

- ordered/unordered flat files

- hash tables

- B+ trees

- ISAM

- heaps

Data Orientation and Clustering

In contrast to conventional row-orientation, relational databases can also be column-oriented or correlational in the way they store data in any particular structure.

In general, substantial performance improvement is gained if different types of database objects that are usually utilized together are laid in storage in proximity, being "clustered". This usually allows to retrieve needed related objects from storage in minimum number of input operations (each sometimes substantially time consuming). Even for in-memory databases clustering provides performance advantage due to common utilization of large caches for input-output operations in memory, with similar resulting behavior.

For example, it may be beneficial to cluster a record of an "item" in stock with all its respective "order" records. The decision of whether to cluster certain objects or not depends on the objects' utilization statistics, object sizes, caches sizes, storage types, etc.

Database Indexing

Indexing is a technique some storage engines use for improving database performance. The many types of indexes share the common property that they reduce the need to examine every entry when running a query. In large databases, this can reduce query time/cost by orders of magnitude. The simplest form of index is a sorted list of values that can be searched using a binary search with an adjacent reference to the location of the entry, analogous to the index in the back of a book. The same data can have multiple indexes (an employee database could be indexed by last name and hire date).

Indexes affect performance, but not results. Database designers can add or remove indexes without changing application logic, reducing maintenance costs as the database grows and database usage evolves. Indexes can speed up data access, but they consume space in the database, and must be updated each time the data is altered. Indexes therefore can speed data access but slow data maintenance. These two properties determine whether a given index is worth the cost.

Database Server

A database server is a computer program that provides database services to other computer programs or computers, as defined by the client–server model. The term may also refer to a computer dedicated to running such a program. Database management systems frequently provide database server functionality, and some DBMSs (e.g., MySQL) rely exclusively on the client–server model for database access.

Such a server is accessed either through a "front end" running on the user's computer which displays requested data or the "back end" which runs on the server and handles tasks such as data analysis and storage.

In a master-slave model, database master servers are central and primary locations of data while database slave servers are synchronized backups of the master acting as proxies.

Most of the Database servers works with the base of Query language. Each Database understands its query language and converts it to Server readable form and executes it to retrieve the results.

Some examples of proprietary database servers are Oracle, DB2, Informix, and Microsoft SQL Server. Examples of GNU General Public Licence database servers are Ingres and MySQL. Every server uses its own query logic and structure. The SQL query language is more or less the same in all relational database servers. DB-Engines lists over 200 DBMSs in its ranking.

History

The foundations for modeling large sets of data were first introduced by Charles Bachman in 1969. Bachman introduced Data Structure Diagrams (DSDs) as a means to graphically represent data. DSDs provided a means to represent the relationships between different data entities. In 1970, Codd introduced the concept that users of a database should be ignorant of the "inner workings" of the database. Codd proposed the "relational view" of data which later evolved into the Relational Model which most databases use today. In 1971, the Database Task Report Group of CODASYL (the driving force behind the development of the programming language COBOL) first proposed a "data description language for describing a database, a data description language for describing that part of the data base known to a program, and a data manipulation language." Most of the research and development of databases focused on the relational model during the 1970s.

In 1975 Bachman demonstrated how the relational model and the data structure set were similar and "congruent" ways of structuring data while working for the Honeywell. The Entity-relationship model was first proposed in its current form by Peter Chen in 1976 while he was conducting research at MIT. This model became the most frequently used model to describe relational databases. Chen was able to propose a model that was superior to the navigational model and was more applicable to the "real world" than the relational model proposed by Codd.

Database Schema

A database schema of a database system is its structure described in a formal language supported by the database management system (DBMS). The term "schema" refers to the organization of data as a blueprint of how the database is constructed (divided into database tables in the case of relational databases). The formal definition of a database schema is a set of formulas (sentences) called integrity constraints imposed on a database. These integrity constraints ensure compatibility between parts of the schema. All constraints are expressible in the same language. A database can be considered a structure in realization of the database language. The states of a created conceptual schema are transformed into an explicit mapping, the database schema. This describes how real-world entities are modeled in the database.

"A database schema specifies, based on the database administrator's knowledge of possible applications, the facts that can enter the database, or those of interest to the possible end-users." The notion of a database schema plays the same role as the notion of theory in predicate calculus. A model of this "theory" closely corresponds to a database, which can be seen at any instant of time as a mathematical object. Thus a schema can contain formulas representing integrity constraints specifically for an application and the constraints specifically for a type of database, all expressed in the same database language. In a relational database, the schema defines the tables, fields, relationships, views, indexes, packages, procedures, functions, queues, triggers, types, sequences, materialized views, synonyms, database links, directories, XML schemas, and other elements.

A database generally stores its schema in a data dictionary. Although a schema is defined in text database language, the term is often used to refer to a graphical depiction of the database structure. In other words, schema is the structure of the database that defines the objects in the database.

In an Oracle Database system, the term "schema" has a slightly different connotation.

Ideal Requirements for Schema Integration

The requirements listed below influence the detailed structure of schemas that are produced. Certain applications will not require that all of these conditions are met, but these four requirements are the most ideal.

Overlap preservation

> Each of the overlapping elements specified in the input mapping is also in a database schema relation.

Extended overlap preservation

> Source-specific elements that are associated with a source's overlapping elements are passed through to the database schema.

Normalization

> Independent entities and relationships in the source data should not be grouped together in the same relation in the database schema. In particular, source specific schema elements should not be grouped with overlapping schema elements, if the grouping co-locates independent entities or relationships.

Minimality

> If any elements of the database schema are dropped then the database schema is not ideal.

Example of two Schema Integrations

Suppose we want a mediated (database) schema to integrate two travel databases, Go-travel and Ok-travel.

Go-travel has two relations:

Go-flight(f-num, time, meal(yes/no))

Go-price(f-num, date, price)

(f-num being the flight number)

Ok-travel has just one relation:

Ok-flight(f-num, date, time, price, nonstop(yes/no))

The overlapping information in Ok-travel's and Go-travel's schemas could be represented in a mediated schema:

Flight(f-num, date, time, price)

Oracle Database Specificity

In the context of Oracle databases, a schema object is a logical data storage structure.

An Oracle database associates a separate schema with each database user. A schema comprises a collection of schema objects. Examples of schema objects include:

- tables
- views

- sequences

- synonyms

- indexes

- clusters

- database links

- snapshots

- procedures

- functions

- packages

On the other hand, non-schema objects may include:

- users

- roles

- contexts

- directory objects

Schema objects do not have a one-to-one correspondence to physical files on disk that store their information. However, Oracle databases store schema objects logically within a tablespace of the database. The data of each object is physically contained in one or more of the tablespace's datafiles. For some objects (such as tables, indexes, and clusters) a database administrator can specify how much disk space the Oracle RDBMS allocates for the object within the tablespace's datafiles.

There is no necessary relationship between schemas and tablespaces: a tablespace can contain objects from different schemas, and the objects for a single schema can reside in different tablespaces.

Reversible Changes in Database Schema

Schema Migration

In software engineering, schema migration (also database migration, database change management) refers to the management of incremental, reversible changes to relational database schemas. A schema migration is performed on a database whenever it is necessary to update or revert that database's schema to some newer or older version.

Migrations are performed programmatically by using a *schema migration tool*. When invoked with a specified desired schema version, the tool automates the successive application or reversal of an appropriate sequence of schema changes until it is brought to the desired state.

Most schema migration tools aim to minimise the impact of schema changes on any existing data in the database. Despite this, preservation of data in general is not guaranteed because schema changes such as the deletion of a database column can destroy data (i.e. all values stored under that column for all rows in that table are deleted). Instead, the tools help to preserve the meaning of the data or to reorganize existing data to meet new requirements. Since meaning of the data often cannot be encoded, the configuration of the tools usually needs manual intervention.

Risks and Benefits

Schema migration allows for fixing mistakes and adapting the data as requirements change. They are an essential part of software evolution, especially in agile environments.

Applying a schema migration to a production database is always a risk. Development and test databases tend to be smaller and cleaner. The data in them is better understood or, if everything else fails, the amount of data is small enough for a human to process. Production databases are usually huge, old and full of surprises. The surprises can come from many sources:

- Corrupt data that was written by old versions of the software and not cleaned properly

- Implied dependencies in the data which no one knows about anymore

- People directly changing the database without using the designated tools

- Bugs in the schema migration tools

- Mistakes in assumptions how data should be migrated

For these reasons, the migration process needs a high level of discipline, thorough testing and a sound backup strategy.

Schema Migration in Agile Software Development

When developing software applications backed by a database, developers typically develop the application source code in tandem with an evolving database schema. The code typically has rigid expectations of what columns, tables and constraints are present in the database schema whenever it needs to interact with one, so only the version of database schema against which the code was developed is considered fully compatible with that version of source code.

In software testing, while developers may mock the presence of a compatible database system for unit testing, any level of testing higher than this (e.g. integration testing or system testing) it is common for developers to test their application against a local or remote test database schematically compatible with the version of source code under test. In advanced applications, the migration itself can be subject to migration testing.

With schema migration technology, data models no longer need to be fully designed up-front, and are more capable of being adapted with changing project requirements throughout the software development lifecycle.

Relation to Revision Control Systems

Teams of software developers usually use version control systems to manage and collaborate on changes made to versions of source code. Different developers can develop on divergent, relatively older or newer branches of the same source code to make changes and additions during development.

Supposing that the software under development interacts with a database, every version of the source code can be associated with at least one database schema with which it is compatible.

Under good software testing practise, schema migrations can be performed on test databases to ensure that their schema is compatible to the source code. To streamline this process, a schema migration tool is usually invoked as a part of an automated software build as a prerequisite of the automated testing phase.

Schema migration tools can be said to solve versioning problems for database schemas just as version control systems solve versioning problems for source code. In practice, many schema migration tools actually rely on a textual representation of schema changes (such as files containing SQL statements) such that the version history of schema changes can effectively be stored alongside program source code within VCS. This approach ensures that the information necessary to recover a compatible database schema for a particular code branch is recoverable from the source tree itself. Another benefit of this approach is the handling of concurrent conflicting schema changes; developers may simply use their usual text-based conflict resolution tools to reconcile differences.

Relation to Schema Evolution

Schema migration tooling could be seen as a facility to track the history of an evolving schema.

Advantages

Developers no longer need to remove the entire test database in order to create a new test database from scratch (e.g. using schema creation scripts from DDL generation tools). Further, if generation of test data costs a lot of time, developers can avoid regenerating test data for small, non-destructive changes to the schema.

Available Tools

- ESF Database Migration Toolkit A toolkit migrate data between various database formats. Supports Oracle, MS-SQL, MySQL, PostgreSQL, DB2, MS-Access, SQLite and so on.

- Flyway - database migration tool (for Windows, OSX, Linux, Android and the JVM) where migrations are written in SQL or Java

- LiquiBase - cross platform tool where migrations are written in XML, YAML, JSON or SQL.

- Datical - Enterprise commercial version of Liquibase.

- Redgate SQL Compare - a schema comparison and deployment tool for SQL Server and Oracle.

- ReadyRoll - a migrations-based Visual Studio extension for SQL Server development and deployment.

- Active Record (Migrations) - schema migration tool for Ruby on Rails projects based on Active Record.

- Ruckusing-migrations - schema migration tool for PHP projects.

- Phinx - another framework-independent PHP migration tool.

- MyBatis Migrations - seeks to be the best migration tool of its kind.

- Ragtime - a SQL database schema migration library written in Clojure

- Lobos - a SQL database schema manipulation and migration library written in Clojure.

- Alembic - a lightweight database migration tool for usage with the SQLAlchemy Database Toolkit for Python.

- RoundhousE - a SQL database versioning and change management tool written in C#.

- XMigra - a SQL database evolution management tool written in Ruby that generates scripts without communicating with the database.

- DBmaestro - a database version control and schema migration solution for SQL Server and Oracle.

- DB Change Manager - Commercial Change Management Software by Embarcadero.

- Sqitch - Sqitch by Theory.

- Goose - database migration tool where migrations are written in SQL or Go

- knexjs - schema and data migration tool built on top of a query builder tool written in javascript

Flyway (Software)

Flyway is an open source database migration tool. It strongly favors simplicity and convention over configuration.

It is based around 6 basic commands: Migrate, Clean, Info, Validate, Baseline and Repair.

Migrations can be written in SQL (database-specific syntax (such as PL/SQL, T-SQL, ...) is supported) or Java (for advanced data transformations or dealing with LOBs).

It has a Command-line client, a Java API (also works on Android) for migrating the database on application startup, a Maven plugin, Gradle plugin, SBT plugin and Ant tasks.

Plugins are available for Spring Boot, Dropwizard, Grails, Play, Griffon, Grunt, Ninja and more.

Supported databases are Oracle, SQL Server, SQL Azure, DB2, DB2 z/OS, MySQL (including Amazon RDS), MariaDB, Google Cloud SQL, PostgreSQL (including Amazon RDS and Heroku), Redshift, Vertica, H2, Hsql, Derby, SQLite, SAP HANA, solidDB, Sybase ASE and Phoenix.

Adoption

Flyway has been widely adopted in the industry, with over 850,000 downloads in 2015 alone.

In January 2015, Flyway was placed in the "Adopt" section of the Thoughtworks Technology Radar.

Liquibase

Liquibase is an open source database-independent library for tracking, managing and applying database schema changes. It was started in 2006 to allow easier tracking of database changes, especially in an agile software development environment.

Overview

All changes to the database are stored in text files (XML, YAML, JSON or SQL) and identified by a combination of an "id" and "author" tag as well as the name of the file itself. A list of all applied changes is stored in each database which is consulted on all database updates to determine what new changes need to be applied. As a result, there is no database version number but this approach allows it to work in environments with multiple developers and code branches.

Automatically creates DatabaseChangeLog Table and DatabaseChangeLogLock Table when you first execute a changeLog File.

Major Functionality

- Over 30 built-in database refactorings
- Extensibility to create custom changes
- Update database to current version
- Rollback last X changes to database
- Rollback database changes to particular date/time
- Rollback database to "tag"
- SQL for Database Updates and Rollbacks can be saved for manual review
- Stand-alone IDE and Eclipse plug-in
- "Contexts" for including/excluding change sets to execute
- Database diff report
- Database diff changelog generation

- Ability to create changelog to generate an existing database

- Database change documentation generation

- DBMS Check, user check, and SQL check preconditions

- Ability to split change log into multiple files for easier management

- Executable via command line, Apache Ant, Apache Maven, servlet container, or Spring Framework.

- Support for 10 database systems

Commercial Version

Datical is both the largest contributor to the Liquibase project and the developer of Datical DB – a commercial product which provides the core Liquibase functionality plus additional features to remove complexity, simplify deployment and bridge the gap between development and operations. Datical DB was created to satisfy the Application Schema management requirements of large enterprises as they move from Continuous Integration to Continuous Delivery.

- Change Forecasting: Forecast upcoming changes to be executed before they are run to determine how those changes will impact your data.

- Rules Engine to enforce Corporate Standards and Policies.

- Supports database Stored Logic: functions, stored procedures, packages, table spaces, triggers, sequences, user defined types, synonyms, etc.

- Compare Databases enables you to compare two database schemas to identify change and easily move it to your change log.

- Change Set Wizard to easily define and capture database changes in a database neutral manner.

- Deployment Plan Wizard for modeling and managing your logical deployment workflow

- Plug-ins to Jenkins, Bamboo, UrbanCode, CA Release Automation (Nolio), Serena Release Automation, BMC Bladelogic, Puppet, Chef, as well all popular source control systems like SVN, Git, TFS, CVS, etc.

Datical DB is used by DBAs, Release Managers, DevOps teams, Application Owners, Architects, and Developers involved in the Application Release process. It manages Database Schema changes together with application code in a programmatic fashion that eliminates errors and delays and enables rapid Agile releases. Datical DB builds upon the Liquibase Data Model Approach for managing data structure specific content across application versions as they advance from Development to Test to Production environments. Datical previews the impact of Schema changes in any environment before deployment thus mitigating risk and resulting in smoother and faster application changes.

Liquibase developer, Nathan Voxland, is an executive at Datical.

Sample Liquibase ChangeLog file

```xml
<?xml version="1.0" encoding="UTF-8"?>


<databaseChangeLog
    xmlns="http://www.liquibase.org/xml/ns/dbchangelog/1.3"
    xmlns:xsi="http://www.w3.org/2001/XMLSchema-instance"
    xsi:schemaLocation="http://www.liquibase.org/xml/ns/dbchangelog/1.3
    http://www.liquibase.org/xml/ns/dbchangelog/dbchangelog-1.3.xsd">
    <preConditions>
        <dbms type="oracle"/>
    </preConditions>


    <changeSet id="1" author="alice">
      <createTable tableName="news">
        <column name="id" type="int">
          <constraints primaryKey="true" nullable="false"/>
        </column>
        <column name="title" type="varchar(50)"/>
      </createTable>
    </changeSet>


    <changeSet id="12" author="bob">
      <createSequence sequenceName="seq_news"/>
    </changeSet>


    <changeSet id="2" author="cpa" context="test">
      <insert tableName="news">
        <column name="id" value="1"/>
```

```
        <column name="title" value="Liquibase 0.8 Released"/>

    </insert>

    <insert tableName="news">

        <column name="id" value="2"/>

        <column name="title" value="Liquibase 0.9 Released"/>

    </insert>

  </changeSet>

</databaseChangeLog>
```

References

- Teorey, T.; Lightstone, S. and Nadeau, T.(2005) Database Modeling & Design: Logical Design, 4th edition, Morgan Kaufmann Press. ISBN 0-12-685352-5

- Gavin Powell (2006). "Chapter 8: Building Fast-Performing Database Models". Beginning Database Design ISBN 978-0-7645-7490-0. Wrox Publishing.

Tools and Techniques of Database Management

The tools and techniques of database management are ACID, null, candidate key, unique key, surrogate key and NoSQL. ACID is a collection of properties of database transactions whereas null is particularly used to indicate the existence of a data value in a database. The topics discussed in the chapter are of great importance to broaden the existing knowledge on database management.

ACID

In computer science, ACID (*Atomicity, Consistency, Isolation, Durability*) is a set of properties of database transactions. In the context of databases, a single logical operation on the data is called a transaction. For example, a transfer of funds from one bank account to another, even involving multiple changes such as debiting one account and crediting another, is a single transaction.

Jim Gray defined these properties of a reliable transaction system in the late 1970s and developed technologies to achieve them automatically.

In 1983, Andreas Reuter and Theo Härder coined the acronym *ACID* to describe them.

Characteristics

The characteristics of these four properties as defined by Reuter and Härder:

Atomicity

Atomicity requires that each transaction be "all or nothing": if one part of the transaction fails, then the entire transaction fails, and the database state is left unchanged. An atomic system must guarantee atomicity in each and every situation, including power failures, errors, and crashes. To the outside world, a committed transaction appears (by its effects on the database) to be indivisible ("atomic"), and an aborted transaction does not happen.

Consistency

The consistency property ensures that any transaction will bring the database from one valid state to another. Any data written to the database must be valid according to all defined rules, including constraints, cascades, triggers, and any combination thereof. This does not guarantee correctness of the transaction in all ways the application programmer might have wanted (that is the responsibility of application-level code) but merely that any programming errors cannot result in the violation of any defined rules.

Isolation

The isolation property ensures that the concurrent execution of transactions results in a system state that would be obtained if transactions were executed serially, i.e., one after the other. Providing isolation is the main goal of concurrency control. Depending on the concurrency control method (i.e., if it uses strict - as opposed to relaxed - serializability), the effects of an incomplete transaction might not even be visible to another transaction.

Durability

The durability property ensures that once a transaction has been committed, it will remain so, even in the event of power loss, crashes, or errors. In a relational database, for instance, once a group of SQL statements execute, the results need to be stored permanently (even if the database crashes immediately thereafter). To defend against power loss, transactions (or their effects) must be recorded in a non-volatile memory.

Examples

The following examples further illustrate the ACID properties. In these examples, the database table has two columns, A and B. An integrity constraint requires that the value in A and the value in B must sum to 100. The following SQL code creates a table as described above:

CREATE TABLE acidtest (A INTEGER, B INTEGER, CHECK (A + B = 100));

Atomicity Failure

In database systems, atomicity (or atomicness; from Greek a-tomos, undividable) is one of the ACID transaction properties. In an atomic transaction, a series of database operations either all occur, or nothing occurs. The series of operations cannot be divided apart and executed partially from each other, which makes the series of operations "indivisible", hence the name. A guarantee of atomicity prevents updates to the database occurring only partially, which can cause greater problems than rejecting the whole series outright. In other words, atomicity means indivisibility and irreducibility.

Consistency Failure

Consistency is a very general term, which demands that the data must meet all validation rules. In the previous example, the validation is a requirement that A + B = 100. Also, it may be inferred that both A and B must be integers. A valid range for A and B may also be inferred. All validation rules must be checked to ensure consistency. Assume that a transaction attempts to subtract 10 from A without altering B. Because consistency is checked after each transaction, it is known that A + B = 100 before the transaction begins. If the transaction removes 10 from A successfully, atomicity will be achieved. However, a validation check will show that A + B = 90, which is inconsistent with the rules of the database. The entire transaction must be cancelled and the affected rows rolled back to their pre-transaction state. If there had been other constraints, triggers, or cascades, every single change operation would have been checked in the same way as above before the transaction was committed.

Isolation Failure

To demonstrate isolation, we assume two transactions execute at the same time, each attempting to modify the same data. One of the two must wait until the other completes in order to maintain isolation.

Consider two transactions. T_1 transfers 10 from A to B. T_2 transfers 10 from B to A. Combined, there are four actions:

- T_1 subtracts 10 from A.

- T_1 adds 10 to B.

- T_2 subtracts 10 from B.

- T_2 adds 10 to A.

If these operations are performed in order, isolation is maintained, although T_2 must wait. Consider what happens if T_1 fails halfway through. The database eliminates T_1's effects, and T_2 sees only valid data.

By interleaving the transactions, the actual order of actions might be:

- T_1 subtracts 10 from A.

- T_2 subtracts 10 from B.

- T_2 adds 10 to A.

- T_1 adds 10 to B.

Again, consider what happens if T_1 fails halfway through. By the time T_1 fails, T_2 has already modified A; it cannot be restored to the value it had before T_1 without leaving an invalid database. This is known as a write-write failure, because two transactions attempted to write to the same data field. In a typical system, the problem would be resolved by reverting to the last known good state, canceling the failed transaction T_1, and restarting the interrupted transaction T_2 from the good state.

Durability Failure

Consider a transaction that transfers 10 from A to B. First it removes 10 from A, then it adds 10 to B. At this point, the user is told the transaction was a success, however the changes are still queued in the disk buffer waiting to be committed to disk. Power fails and the changes are lost. The user assumes (understandably) that the changes have been persisted.

Implementation

Processing a transaction often requires a sequence of operations that is subject to failure for a number of reasons. For instance, the system may have no room left on its disk drives, or it may have used up its allocated CPU time. There are two popular families of techniques: write-ahead logging and shadow paging. In both cases, locks must be acquired on all information to be updated, and depending on the level of isolation, possibly on all data that be read as well. In write ahead logging, atomicity is guaranteed by copying the original (unchanged) data to a log before changing the database. That allows the database to return to a consistent state in the event of a crash. In shadowing, updates are applied to a partial copy of the database, and the new copy is activated when the transaction commits.

Locking Vs Multiversioning

Many databases rely upon locking to provide ACID capabilities. Locking means that the transaction marks the data that it accesses so that the DBMS knows not to allow other transactions to modify it until the first transaction succeeds or fails. The lock must always be acquired before processing data, including data that is read but not modified. Non-trivial transactions typically require a large number of locks, resulting in substantial overhead as well as blocking other transactions. For example, if user A is running a transaction that has to read a row of data that user B wants to modify, user B must wait until user A's transaction completes. Two phase locking is often applied to guarantee full isolation.

An alternative to locking is multiversion concurrency control, in which the database provides each reading transaction the prior, unmodified version of data that is being modified by another active transaction. This allows readers to operate without acquiring locks, i.e. writing transactions do not block reading transactions, and readers do not block writers. Going back to the example, when user A's transaction requests data that user B is modifying, the database provides A with the version of that data that existed when user B started his transaction. User A gets a consistent view of the database even if other users are changing data. One implementation, namely snapshot isolation, relaxes the isolation property.

Distributed Transactions

Guaranteeing ACID properties in a distributed transaction across a distributed database, where no single node is responsible for all data affecting a transaction, presents additional complications. Network connections might fail, or one node might successfully complete its part of the transaction and then be required to roll back its changes because of a failure on another node. The two-phase commit protocol provides atomicity for distributed transactions to ensure that each participant in the transaction agrees on whether the transaction should be committed or not. Briefly, in the first phase, one node (the coordinator) interrogates the other nodes (the participants) and only when all reply that they are prepared does the coordinator, in the second phase, formalize the transaction.

Create, Read, Update and Delete

In computer programming, create, read, update and delete (as an acronym CRUD) are the four basic functions of persistent storage. Alternate words are sometimes used when defining the four basic functions of *CRUD*, *retrieve* instead of *read*, *modify* instead of *update*, or *destroy* instead of *delete*. *CRUD* is also sometimes used to describe user interface conventions that facilitate viewing, searching, and changing information; often using computer-based forms and reports. The term was likely first popularized by James Martin in his 1983 book *Managing the Data-base Environment*. The acronym may be extended to CRUDL to cover *listing* of large data sets which bring additional complexity such as pagination when the data sets are too large to hold easily in memory.

Another variation of CRUD is BREAD, an acronym for "Browse, Read, Edit, Add, Delete".This extension is mostly used in context with data protection concepts, when it is legally not allowed to delete data directly. Locking the data prevents the access for users without destroying still needed data. Yet another variation, used before CRUD became more common, is MADS, an acronym for "Modify, Add, Delete, Show."

Database Applications

The acronym CRUD refers to all of the major functions that are implemented in relational database applications. Each letter in the acronym can map to a standard SQL statement, HTTP method (this is typically used to build RESTful APIs) or DDS operation:

Operation	SQL	HTTP	DDS
Create	INSERT	PUT / POST	write
Read (Retrieve)	SELECT	GET	read / take
Update (Modify)	UPDATE	POST / PUT / PATCH	write
Delete (Destroy)	DELETE	DELETE	dispose

The comparison of the database oriented CRUD operations to HTTP methods has some flaws. Strictly speaking, both PUT and POST can create resources; the key difference is that POST leaves it for the server to decide at what URI to make the new resource available, whilst PUT dictates what URI to use; URIs are of course a concept that doesn't really line up with CRUD. The significant point about PUT is that it will replace whatever resource the URI was previously referring to with a brand new version, hence the PUT method being listed for Update as well. PUT is a 'replace' operation, which one could argue is not 'update'.

Although a relational database provides a common persistence layer in software applications, numerous other persistence layers exist. CRUD functionality can be implemented with an object database, an XML database, flat text files, custom file formats, tape, or card, for example.

User Interface

CRUD is also relevant at the user interface level of most applications. For example, in address book software, the basic storage unit is an individual *contact entry*. As a bare minimum, the software must allow the user to

- Create or add new entries

- Read, retrieve, search, or view existing entries

- Update or edit existing entries

- Delete/deactivate/remove existing entries

Without at least these four operations, the software cannot be considered complete. Because these operations are so fundamental, they are often documented and described under one comprehensive heading, such as "contact management", "content management" or "contact maintenance" (or "document management" in general, depending on the basic storage unit for the particular application).

Null (SQL)

The Greek lowercase omega (ω) character is used to represent Null in database theory.

Null (or NULL) is a special marker used in Structured Query Language (SQL) to indicate that a data value does not exist in the database. Introduced by the creator of the relational database model, E. F. Codd, SQL Null serves to fulfil the requirement that all *true relational database management systems (RDBMS)* support a representation of "missing information and inapplicable information". Codd also introduced the use of the lowercase Greek omega (ω) symbol to represent Null in database theory. In SQL, NULL is a reserved word used to identify this marker.

This should not be confused with a value of 0. A null value indicates a lack of a value - a lack of a value is not the same thing as a value of zero in the same way that a lack of an answer is not the same thing as an answer of "no". For example, consider the question "How many books does Juan own?" The answer may be "zero" (we *know* that he owns *none*) or "null" (we *do not know* how many he owns). In a database table, the column reporting this answer would start out with no value (marked by Null), and it would not be updated with the value "zero" until we have ascertained that Juan owns no books.

SQL null is a state, not a value. This usage is quite different from most programming languages, where null means not assigned to a particular instance.

History

E. F. Codd mentioned nulls as a method of representing missing data in the relational model in a 1975 paper in the *FDT Bulletin of ACM-SIGMOD*. Codd's paper that is most commonly cited in relation with the semantics of Null (as adopted in SQL) is his 1979 paper in the *ACM Transactions on Database Systems*, in which he also introduced his Relational Model/Tasmania, although much of the other proposals from the latter paper have remained obscure. Section 2.3 of his 1979 paper details the semantics of Null propagation in arithmetic operations as well as comparisons employing a ternary (three-valued) logic when comparing to nulls; it also details the treatment of Nulls on other set operations (the latter issue still controversial today). In database theory circles, the original proposal of Codd (1975, 1979) is now referred to as "Krokk tables". Codd later reinforced his requirement that all RDBMSs support Null to indicate missing data in a 1985 two-part article published in *ComputerWorld* magazine.

The 1986 SQL standard basically adopted Codd's proposal after an implementation prototype in IBM System R. Although Don Chamberlin recognized nulls (alongside duplicate rows) as one of the most controversial features of SQL, he defended the design of Nulls in SQL invoking the pragmatic arguments that it was the least expensive form of system support for missing information, saving the programmer from many duplicative application-level checks while at the same time providing the database designer with the option not to use Nulls if he so desires; for example, in order to avoid well known anomalies. Chamberlin also argued that besides providing some missing-value functionality, practical experience with Nulls also led to other language features which rely on Nulls, like certain grouping constructs and outer joins. Finally, he argued that in practice Nulls also end up being used as a quick way to patch an existing schema when it needs to evolve beyond its original intent, coding not for missing but rather for inapplicable information; for example, a database that quickly needs to support electric cars while having a miles-per-gallon column.

Codd indicated in his 1990 book *The Relational Model for Database Management, Version 2* that the single Null mandated by the SQL standard was inadequate, and should be replaced by two separate Null-type markers to indicate the reason why data is missing. In Codd's book, these two Null-type markers are referred to as 'A-Values' and 'I-Values', representing 'Missing But Applicable' and 'Missing But Inapplicable', respectively. Codd's recommendation would have required SQL's logic system be expanded to accommodate a four-valued logic system. Because of this additional complexity, the idea of multiple Nulls with different definitions has not gained widespread acceptance in the database practitioners' domain. It remains an active field of research though, with numerous papers still being published.

Challenges

Null has been the focus of controversy and a source of debate because of its associated three-valued logic (3VL), special requirements for its use in SQL joins, and the special handling required by aggregate functions and SQL grouping operators. Computer science professor Ron van der Meyden summarized the various issues as: "The inconsistencies in the SQL standard mean that it is not possible to ascribe any intuitive logical semantics to the treatment of nulls in SQL." Although various proposals have been made for resolving these issues, the complexity of the alternatives has prevented their widespread adoption.

Null Propagation

Arithmetic Operations

Because Null is not a data value, but a marker for an absent value, using mathematical operators on Null gives an unknown result, which is represented by Null. In the following example, multiplying 10 by Null results in Null:

```
10 * NULL      -- Result is NULL
```

This can lead to unanticipated results. For instance, when an attempt is made to divide Null by zero, platforms may return Null instead of throwing an expected "data exception - division by zero". Though this behavior is not defined by the ISO SQL standard many DBMS vendors treat this operation similarly. For instance, the Oracle, PostgreSQL, MySQL Server, and Microsoft SQL Server platforms all return a Null result for the following:

NULL / 0

String Concatenation

String concatenation operations, which are common in SQL, also result in Null when one of the operands is Null. The following example demonstrates the Null result returned by using Null with the SQL || string concatenation operator.

'Fish ' || NULL || 'Chips' -- Result is NULL

This is not true for all database implementations. In an Oracle RDBMS for example NULL and the empty string are considered the same thing and therefore 'Fish ' || NULL || 'Chips' results in 'Fish Chips'.

Comparisons With NULL and the three-valued Logic (3VL)

Since Null is not a member of any data domain, it is not considered a "value", but rather a marker (or placeholder) indicating the absence of value. Because of this, comparisons with Null can never result in either True or False, but always in a third logical result, Unknown. The logical result of the expression below, which compares the value 10 to Null, is Unknown:

SELECT 10 = NULL   -- Results in Unknown

However, certain operations on Null can return values if the absent value is not relevant to the outcome of the operation. Consider the following example:

SELECT NULL OR TRUE   -- Results in True

In this case, the fact that the value on the left of OR is unknowable is irrelevant, because the outcome of the OR operation would be True regardless of the value on the left.

SQL implements three logical results, so SQL implementations must provide for a specialized three-valued logic (3VL). The rules governing SQL three-valued logic are shown in the tables below (p and q represent logical states)" The truth tables SQL uses for AND, OR, and NOT correspond to a common fragment of the Kleene and Łukasiewicz three-valued logic (which differ in their definition of implication, however SQL defines no such operation).

p	q	p OR q	p AND q	$p = q$
True	True	True	True	True
True	False	True	False	False
True	Unknown	True	Unknown	Unknown
False	True	True	False	False

False	False	False	False	True
False	Unknown	Unknown	False	Unknown
Unknown	True	True	Unknown	Unknown
Unknown	False	Unknown	False	Unknown
Unknown	Unknown	Unknown	Unknown	Unknown

p	NOT *p*
True	False
False	True
Unknown	Unknown

Effect of Unknown in WHERE Clauses

SQL three-valued logic is encountered in Data Manipulation Language (DML) in comparison predicates of DML statements and queries. The WHERE clause causes the DML statement to act on only those rows for which the predicate evaluates to True. Rows for which the predicate evaluates to either False or Unknown are not acted on by INSERT, UPDATE, or DELETE DML statements, and are discarded by SELECT queries. Interpreting Unknown and False as the same logical result is a common error encountered while dealing with Nulls. The following simple example demonstrates this fallacy:

SELECT *

FROM t

WHERE i = NULL;

The example query above logically always returns zero rows because the comparison of the *i* column with Null always returns Unknown, even for those rows where *i* is Null. The Unknown result causes the SELECT statement to summarily discard each and every row. (However, in practice, some SQL tools will retrieve rows using a comparison with Null.)

Null-specific and 3VL-specific Comparison Predicates

Basic SQL comparison operators always return Unknown when comparing anything with Null, so the SQL standard provides for two special Null-specific comparison predicates. The IS NULL and IS NOT NULL predicates (which use a postfix syntax) test whether data is, or is not, Null.

The SQL standard contains an extension F571 "Truth value tests" that introduces three additional logical unary operators (six in fact, if we count their negation, which is part of their syntax), also using postfix notation. They have the following truth tables:

p	true	false	unknown
p IS TRUE	true	false	false
p IS NOT TRUE	false	true	true
p IS FALSE	false	true	false
p IS NOT FALSE	true	false	true

p IS UNKNOWN	false	false	true
p IS NOT UNKNOWN	true	true	false

The F571 extension is orthogonal to the presence of the boolean datatype in SQL and, despite syntactic similarities, F571 does not introduce boolean or three-valued literals in the language. The F571 extension was actually present in SQL92, well before the boolean datatype was introduced to the standard in 1999. The F571 extension is implemented by few systems however; PostgreSQL is one of those implementing it.

The addition of IS UNKNOWN to the other operators of SQL's three-valued logic makes the SQL three-valued logic functionally complete, meaning its logical operators can express (in combination) any conceivable three-valued logical function.

On systems which don't support the F571 extension, it is possible to emulate IS UNKNOWN p by going over every argument that could make the expression p Unknown and test those arguments with IS NULL or other NULL-specific functions, although this may be more cumbersome.

Law of the Excluded Fourth (in WHERE Clauses)

In SQL's three-valued logic the law of the excluded middle, p OR NOT p, no longer evaluates to true for all p. More precisely, in SQL's three-valued logic p OR NOT p is unknown precisely when p is unknown and true otherwise. Because direct comparisons with Null result in the unknown logical value, the following query

SELECT * FROM stuff WHERE (x = 10) OR NOT (x = 10);

is not equivalent in SQL with

SELECT * FROM stuff;

if the column x contains any Nulls; in that case the second query would return some rows the first one does not return, namely all those in which x is Null. In classical two-valued logic, the law of the excluded middle would allow the simplification of the WHERE clause predicate, in fact its elimination. Attempting to apply the law of the excluded middle to SQL's 3VL is effectively a false dichotomy. The second query is actually equivalent with:

SELECT * FROM stuff;

-- is (because of 3VL) equivalent to:

SELECT * FROM stuff WHERE (x = 10) OR NOT (x = 10) OR x IS NULL;

Thus, to correctly simplify the first statement in SQL requires that we return all rows in which x is not null.

SELECT * FROM stuff WHERE x IS NOT NULL;

In view of the above, observe that for SQL's WHERE clause a tautology similar to the law of excluded middle can be written. Assuming the IS UNKNOWN operator is present, p OR (NOT p) OR (p IS UNKNOWN) is true for every predicate p. Among logicians, this is called law of excluded fourth.

There are some SQL expressions in which it is less obvious where the false dilemma occurs, for example:

SELECT 'ok' WHERE 1 NOT IN (SELECT CAST (NULL AS INTEGER))

UNION

SELECT 'ok' WHERE 1 IN (SELECT CAST (NULL AS INTEGER));

produces no rows because IN is translates to an iterated version of equality over the argument set and 1<>NULL is Unknown, just as a 1=NULL is Unknown. (The CAST in this example is needed only in some SQL implementations like PostgreSQL, which would reject it with a type checking error otherwise. In many systems plain SELECT NULL works in the subquery.) The missing case above is of course:

SELECT 'ok' WHERE (1 IN (SELECT CAST (NULL AS INTEGER))) IS UNKNOWN;

Effect of Null and Unknown in Other Constructs

Joins

Joins evaluate using the same comparison rules as for WHERE clauses. Therefore, care must be taken when using nullable columns in SQL join criteria. In particular a table containing any nulls is *not equal* with a natural self-join of itself, meaning that whereas $R \setminus R = R$ is true for any relation R in relational algebra, a SQL self-join will exclude all rows having a Null anywhere. An example of this behavior is given in the section analyzing the missing-value semantics of Nulls.

The SQL COALESCE function or CASE expressions can be used to "simulate" Null equality in join criteria, and the IS NULL and IS NOT NULL predicates can be used in the join criteria as well. The following predicate tests for equality of the values A and B and treats Nulls as being equal.

(A = B) OR (A IS NULL AND B IS NULL)

CASE Expressions

SQL provides two flavours of conditional expressions. One is called "simple CASE" and operates like a switch statement. The other is called a "searched CASE" in the standard, and operates like an if...elseif.

The simple CASE expressions use implicit equality comparisons which operate under the same rules as the DML WHERE clause rules for Null. Thus, a *simple CASE expression* cannot check for the existence of Null directly. A check for Null in a simple CASE expression always results in Unknown, as in the following:

SELECT CASE i WHEN NULL THEN 'Is Null' -- This will never be returned

    WHEN   0 THEN 'Is Zero' -- This will be returned when i = 0

    WHEN   1 THEN 'Is One' -- This will be returned when i = 1

    END

FROM t;

Because the expression i = NULL evaluates to Unknown no matter what value column *i* contains (even if it contains Null), the string 'Is Null' will never be returned.

On the other hand, a "searched" CASE expression can use predicates like IS NULL and IS NOT NULL in its conditions. The following example shows how to use a searched CASE expression to properly check for Null:

SELECT CASE WHEN i IS NULL THEN 'Null Result' -- This will be returned when i is NULL

      WHEN   i = 0 THEN 'Zero'   -- This will be returned when i = 0

      WHEN   i = 1 THEN 'One'   -- This will be returned when i = 1

      END

FROM t;

In the searched CASE expression, the string 'Null Result' is returned for all rows in which *i* is Null.

Oracle's dialect of SQL provides a built-in function DECODE which can be used instead of the simple CASE expressions and considers two nulls equal.

SELECT DECODE(i, NULL, 'Null Result', 0, 'Zero', 1, 'One') FROM t;

Finally, all these constructs return a NULL if no match is found; they have a default ELSE NULL clause.

IF Statements in Procedural Extensions

SQL/PSM (SQL Persistent Stored Modules) defines procedural extensions for SQL, such as the IF statement. However, the major SQL vendors have historically included their own proprietary procedural extensions. Procedural extensions for looping and comparisons operate under Null comparison rules similar to those for DML statements and queries. The following code fragment, in ISO SQL standard format, demonstrates the use of Null 3VL in an IF statement.

IF i = NULL THEN

    SELECT 'Result is True'

ELSEIF NOT(i = NULL) THEN

    SELECT 'Result is False'

ELSE

    SELECT 'Result is Unknown';

The IF statement performs actions only for those comparisons that evaluate to True. For statements that evaluate to False or Unknown, the IF statement passes control to the ELSEIF clause, and finally to the ELSE clause. The result of the code above will always be the message 'Result is Unknown' since the comparisons with Null always evaluate to Unknown.

Analysis of SQL Null Missing-value Semantics

The groundbreaking work of T. Imielinski and W. Lipski (1984) provided a framework in which to evaluate the intended semantics of various proposals to implement missing-value semantics. This section roughly follows chapter 19 the "Alice" textbook. A similar presentation appears in the review of Ron van der Meyden, §10.4.

In Selections and Projections: Weak Representation

Constructs representing missing information, such as Codd tables, are actually intended to represent a set of relations, one for each possible instantiation of their parameters; in the case of Codd tables, this means replacement of Nulls with some concrete value. For example,

This Codd table	may represent	this relation	or equally well	this relation

Emp	
Name	**Age**
George	43
Harriet	NULL
Charles	56

EmpH22	
Name	**Age**
George	43
Harriet	22
Charles	56

EmpH37	
Name	**Age**
George	43
Harriet	37
Charles	56

A construct (such as a Codd table) is said to be a *strong representation* system (of missing information) if any answer to a query made on the construct can be particularized to obtain an answer for *any* corresponding query on the relations it represents, which are seen as models of the construct. More precisely, if q is a query formula in the relational algebra (of "pure" relations) and if $\bar{q}$ is its lifting to a construct intended to represent missing information, a strong representation has the property that for any query q and (table) construct T, $\bar{q}$ lifts *all* the answers to the construct, i.e.:

$$\text{Models}(\bar{q}(T)) = \{q(R)|\ R \in \text{Models}(T)\}$$

(The above has to hold for queries taking any number of tables as arguments, but the restriction to one table suffices for this discussion.) Clearly Codd tables do not have this strong property if selections and projections are considered as part of the query language. For example, *all* the answers to

SELECT * FROM Emp WHERE Age = 22;

should include the possibility that a relation like EmpH22 may exist. However Codd tables cannot represent the disjunction "result with possibly 0 or 1 rows". A device, mostly of theoretical interest, called conditional table (or c-table) can however represent such an answer:

Result		
Name	**Age**	**condition**
Harriet	ω_1	$\omega_1 = 22$

where the condition column is interpreted as the row doesn't exist if the condition is false. It turns out that because the formulas in the condition column of a c-table can be arbitrary propositional logic formulas, an algorithm for the problem whether a c-table represents some concrete relation has a co-NP-complete complexity, thus is of little practical worth.

A weaker notion of representation is therefore desirable. Imielinski and Lipski introduced the notion of *weak representation*, which essentially allows (lifted) queries over a construct to return a representation only for *sure* information, i.e. if it's valid for all "possible world" instantiations (models) of the construct. Concretely, a construct is a weak representation system if

$$\bigcap \text{Models}(\overline{q}(T)) = \bigcap \{q(R) | R \in \text{Models}(T)\}$$

The right-hand side of the above equation is the *sure* information, i.e. information which can be certainly extracted from the database regardless of what values are used to replace Nulls in the database. In the example we considered above, it's easy to see that the intersection of all possible models (i.e. the sure information) of the query selecting WHERE Age = 22 is actually empty because, for instance, the (unlifted) query returns no rows for the relation EmpH37. More generally, it was shown by Imielinski and Lipski that Codd tables are a weak representation system if the query language is restricted to projections, selections (and renaming of columns). However, as soon as we add either joins or unions to the query language, even this weak property is lost, as evidenced in the next section.

If Joins or Unions are Considered: Not Even Weak Representation

Let us consider the following query over the same Codd table Emp from the previous section:

SELECT Name FROM Emp WHERE Age = 22

UNION

SELECT Name FROM Emp WHERE Age <> 22;

Whatever concrete value one would choose for the NULL age of Harriet, the above query will return the full column of names of any model of Emp, but when the (lifted) query is run on Emp itself, Harriet will always be missing, i.e. we have:

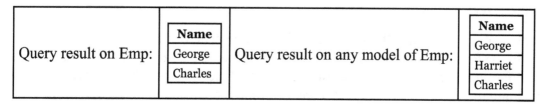

Query result on Emp:	Name
	George
	Charles

Query result on any model of Emp:	Name
	George
	Harriet
	Charles

Thus when unions are added to the query language, Codd tables are not even a weak representation system of missing information, meaning that queries over them don't even report all *sure* information. It's important to note here that semantics of UNION on Nulls, which are discussed in a later section, did not even come into play in this query. The "forgetful" nature of the two sub-queries was all that it took to guarantee that some sure information went unreported when the above query was run on the Codd table Emp.

For natural joins, the example needed to show that sure information may be unreported by some query is slightly more complicated. Consider the table

J

F1	F2	F3
11	NULL	13
21	NULL	23
31	32	33

and the query

SELECT F1, F3 FROM

(SELECT F1, F2 FROM J) AS F12

NATURAL JOIN

(SELECT F2, F3 FROM J) AS F23;

Query result on J:		Query result on any model of J:	

F1	F3
31	33

F1	F3
11	13
21	23
31	33

The intuition for what happens above is that the Codd tables representing the projections in the subqueries lose track of the fact that the Nulls in the columns F12.F2 and F23.F2 are actually copies of the originals in the table J. This observation suggests that a relatively simple improvement of Codd tables (which works correctly for this example) would be to use *Skolem constants* (meaning Skolem functions which are also constant functions), say ω_{12} and ω_{22} instead of a single NULL symbol. Such an approach, called v-tables or Naive tables, is computationally less expensive that the c-tables discussed above. However it is still not a complete solution for incomplete information in the sense that v-tables are only a weak representation for queries not using any negations in selection (and not using any set difference either). The first example considered in this section is using a negative selection clause, WHERE Age <> 22, so it is also an example where v-tables queries would not report sure information.

Check Constraints and Foreign Keys

The primary place in which SQL three-valued logic intersects with SQL Data Definition Language (DDL) is in the form of check constraints. A check constraint placed on a column operates under a slightly different set of rules than those for the DML WHERE clause. While a DML WHERE clause must evaluate to True for a row, a check constraint must not evaluate to False. (From a logic perspective, the designated values are True and Unknown.) This means that a check constraint will succeed if the result of the check is either True or Unknown. The following example table with a check constraint will prohibit any integer values from being inserted into column *i*, but will allow Null to be inserted since the result of the check will always evaluate to Unknown for Nulls.

CREATE TABLE t (

i INTEGER,

CONSTRAINT ck_i CHECK (i < 0 AND i = 0 AND i > 0));

Because of the change in designated values relative to the WHERE clause, from a logic perspective the law of excluded middle is a tautology for CHECK constraints, meaning CHECK (p OR NOT p) always succeeds. Furthermore, assuming Nulls are to be interpreted as existing but unknown values, some pathological CHECKs like the one above allow insertion of Nulls that could never be replaced by any non-null value.

In order to constrain a column to reject Nulls, the NOT NULL constraint can be applied, as shown in the example below. The NOT NULL constraint is semantically equivalent to a check constraint with an IS NOT NULL predicate.

CREATE TABLE t (i INTEGER NOT NULL);

By default check constraints against foreign keys succeed if any of the fields in such keys are Null. For example, the table

CREATE TABLE Books

(title VARCHAR(100),

  author_last VARCHAR(20),

  author_first VARCHAR(20),

FOREIGN KEY (author_last, author_first)

  REFERENCES Authors(last_name, first_name));

would allow insertion of rows where author_last or author_first are NULL irrespective of how the table Authors is defined or what it contains. More precisely, a null in any of these fields would allow any value in the other one, even on that is not found in Authors table. For example, if Authors contained only ('Doe', 'John'), then ('Smith', NULL) would satisfy the foreign key constraint. SQL-92 added two extra options for narrowing down the matches in such cases. If MATCH PARTIAL is added after the REFERENCES declaration then any non-null must match the foreign key, e. g. ('Doe', NULL) would still match, but ('Smith', NULL) would not. Finally, if MATCH FULL is added then ('Smith', NULL) would not match the constraint either, but (NULL, NULL) would still match it.

Outer Joins

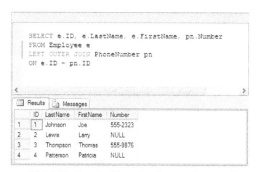

Example SQL outer join query with Null placeholders in the result set. The Null markers are represented by the word NULL in place of data in the results. Results are from Microsoft SQL Server, as shown in SQL Server Management Studio.

SQL outer joins, including left outer joins, right outer joins, and full outer joins, automatically produce Nulls as placeholders for missing values in related tables. For left outer joins, for instance, Nulls are produced in place of rows missing from the table appearing on the right-hand side of the LEFT OUTER JOIN operator. The following simple example uses two tables to demonstrate Null placeholder production in a left outer join.

The first table (Employee) contains employee ID numbers and names, while the second table (PhoneNumber) contains related employee ID numbers and phone numbers, as shown below.

Employee		
ID	**LastName**	**FirstName**
1	Johnson	Joe
2	Lewis	Larry
3	Thompson	Thomas
4	Patterson	Patricia

PhoneNumber	
ID	**Number**
1	555-2323
3	555-9876

The following sample SQL query performs a left outer join on these two tables.

SELECT e.ID, e.LastName, e.FirstName, pn.Number

FROM Employee e

LEFT OUTER JOIN PhoneNumber pn

ON e.ID = pn.ID;

The result set generated by this query demonstrates how SQL uses Null as a placeholder for values missing from the right-hand (PhoneNumber) table, as shown below.

Query result			
ID	**LastName**	**FirstName**	**Number**
1	Johnson	Joe	555-2323
2	Lewis	Larry	**NULL**
3	Thompson	Thomas	555-9876
4	Patterson	Patricia	**NULL**

Aggregate Functions

SQL defines aggregate functions to simplify server-side aggregate calculations on data. Except for the COUNT(*) function, all aggregate functions perform a Null-elimination step, so that Nulls are not included in the final result of the calculation.

Note that the elimination of Null is not equivalent to replacing Null with zero. For example, in the following table, AVG(i) (the average of the values of i) will give a different result from that of AVG(j):

Table	
i	**j**
150	150
200	200
250	250
NULL	0

Here AVG(i) is 200 (the average of 150, 200, and 250), while AVG(j) is 150 (the average of 150, 200, 250, and 0). A well-known side effect of this is that in SQL AVG(z) is not equivalent with SUM(z)/COUNT(*).

When two Nulls are Equal: Grouping, Sorting, and Some Set Operations

Because SQL:2003 defines all Null markers as being unequal to one another, a special definition was required in order to group Nulls together when performing certain operations. SQL defines "any two values that are equal to one another, or any two Nulls", as "not distinct". This definition of *not distinct* allows SQL to group and sort Nulls when the GROUP BY clause (and other keywords that perform grouping) are used.

Other SQL operations, clauses, and keywords use "not distinct" in their treatment of Nulls. These include the following:

- PARTITION BY clause of ranking and windowing functions like ROW_NUMBER

- UNION, INTERSECT, and EXCEPT operator, which treat NULLs as the same for row comparison/elimination purposes

- DISTINCT keyword used in SELECT queries

The principle that Nulls aren't equal to each other (but rather that the result is Unknown) is effectively violated in the SQL specification for the UNION operator, which does identify nulls with each other. Consequently, some set operations in SQL, like union or difference, may produce results not representing sure information, unlike operations involving explicit comparisons with NULL (e.g. those in a WHERE clause discussed above). In Codd's 1979 proposal (which was basically adopted by SQL92) this semantic inconsistency is rationalized by arguing that removal of duplicates in set operations happens "at a lower level of detail than equality testing in the evaluation of retrieval operations."

The SQL standard does not explicitly define a default sort order for Nulls. Instead, on conforming systems, Nulls can be sorted before or after all data values by using the NULLS FIRST or NULLS LAST clauses of the ORDER BY list, respectively. Not all DBMS vendors implement this functionality, however. Vendors who do not implement this functionality may specify different treatments for Null sorting in the DBMS.

Effect on Index Operation

Some SQL products do not index keys containing NULLs. For instance, PostgreSQL versions prior to 8.3 did not, with the documentation for a B-tree index stating that

B-trees can handle equality and range queries on data that can be sorted into some ordering. In particular, the PostgreSQL query planner will consider using a B-tree index whenever an indexed column is involved in a comparison using one of these operators: $<$ $\leq$ $=$ $\geq$ $>$

Constructs equivalent to combinations of these operators, such as BETWEEN and IN, can also be implemented with a B-tree index search. (But note that IS NULL is not equivalent to = and is not indexable.)

In cases where the index enforces uniqueness, NULLs are excluded from the index and uniqueness is not enforced between NULLs. Again, quoting from the PostgreSQL documentation:

When an index is declared unique, multiple table rows with equal indexed values will not be allowed. Nulls are not considered equal. A multicolumn unique index will only reject cases where all of the indexed columns are equal in two rows.

This is consistent with the SQL:2003-defined behavior of scalar Null comparisons.

Another method of indexing Nulls involves handling them as *not distinct* in accordance with the SQL:2003-defined behavior. For example, Microsoft SQL Server documentation states the following:

For indexing purposes, NULLs compare as equal. Therefore, a unique index, or UNIQUE constraint, cannot be created if the keys are NULL in more than one row. Select columns that are defined as NOT NULL when columns for a unique index or unique constraint are chosen.

Both of these indexing strategies are consistent with the SQL:2003-defined behavior of Nulls. Because indexing methodologies are not explicitly defined by the SQL:2003 standard, indexing strategies for Nulls are left entirely to the vendors to design and implement.

Null-handling Functions

SQL defines two functions to explicitly handle Nulls: NULLIF and COALESCE. Both functions are abbreviations for searched CASE expressions.

NULLIF

The NULLIF function accepts two parameters. If the first parameter is equal to the second parameter, NULLIF returns Null. Otherwise, the value of the first parameter is returned.

NULLIF(value1, value2)

Thus, NULLIF is an abbreviation for the following CASE expression:

CASE WHEN value1 = value2 THEN NULL ELSE value1 END

COALESCE

The COALESCE function accepts a list of parameters, returning the first non-Null value from the list:

COALESCE(value1, value2, value3, ...)

COALESCE is defined as shorthand for the following SQL CASE expression:

CASE WHEN value1 IS NOT NULL THEN value1

    WHEN value2 IS NOT NULL THEN value2

    WHEN value3 IS NOT NULL THEN value3

    ...

    END

Some SQL DBMSs implement vendor-specific functions similar to COALESCE. Some systems (e.g. Transact-SQL) implement an ISNULL function, or other similar functions that are functionally similar to COALESCE.

NVL

The Oracle NVL function accepts two parameters. It returns the first non-NULL parameter or NULL if all parameters are NULL.

A COALESCE expression can be converted into an equivalent NVL expression thus:

COALESCE (val1, ... , val{n})

turns into:

NVL(val1 , NVL(val2 , NVL(val3 , ... , NVL (val{n-1} , val{n}) ...)))

A use case of this function is to replace in an expression a NULL by a value like in NVL(SALARY, 0) which says, 'if SALARY is NULL, replace it with the value 0'.

There is, however, one notable exception. In most implementations, COALESCE evaluates its parameters until it reaches the first non-NULL one, while NVL evaluates all of its parameters. This is important for several reasons. A parameter *after* the first non-NULL parameter could be a function, which could either be computationally expensive, invalid, or could create unexpected side effects.

Data Typing of Null and Unknown

The NULL literal is untyped in SQL, meaning that it is not designated as an integer, character, or any other specific data type. Because of this, it is sometimes mandatory (or desirable) to explicitly convert Nulls to a specific data type. For instance, if overloaded functions are supported by the RDBMS, SQL might not be able to automatically resolve to the correct function without knowing the data types of all parameters, including those for which Null is passed.

Conversion from the NULL literal to a Null of a specific type is possible using the CAST introduced in SQL-92. For example:

CAST (NULL AS INTEGER)

represents an absent value of type INTEGER.

The actual typing of Unknown (distinct or not from NULL itself) varies between SQL implementations. For example, the following

SELECT 'ok' WHERE (NULL <> 1) IS NULL;

parses and executes successfully in some environments (e.g. SQLite or PostgreSQL) which unify a NULL boolean with Unknown but fails to parse in others (e.g. in SQL Server Compact). MySQL behaves similarly to PostgreSQL in this regard (with the minor exception that MySQL regards TRUE and FALSE as no different from the ordinary integers 1 and 0). PostgreSQL additionally implements a IS UNKNOWN predicate, which can be used to test whether a three-value logical outcome is Unknown, although this is merely syntactic sugar.

BOOLEAN Data Type

The ISO SQL:1999 standard introduced the BOOLEAN data type to SQL, however it's still just an optional, non-core feature, coded T031.

When restricted by a NOT NULL constraint, the SQL BOOLEAN works like the Boolean type from other languages. Unrestricted however, the BOOLEAN datatype, despite its name, can hold the truth values TRUE, FALSE, and UNKNOWN, all of which are defined as boolean literals according to the standard. The standard also asserts that NULL and UNKNOWN "may be used interchangeably to mean exactly the same thing".

The Boolean type has been subject of criticism, particularly because of the mandated behavior of the UNKNOWN literal, which is never equal to itself because of the identification with NULL.

As discussed above, in the PostgreSQL implementation of SQL, Null is used to represent all UNKNOWN results, including the UNKNOWN BOOLEAN. PostgreSQL does not implement the UNKNOWN literal (although it does implement the IS UNKNOWN operator, which is an orthogonal feature.) Most other major vendors do not support the Boolean type (as defined in T031) as of 2012. The procedural part of Oracle's PL/SQL supports BOOLEAN however variables; these can also be assigned NULL and the value is considered the same as UNKNOWN.

Controversy

Common Mistakes

Misunderstanding of how Null works is the cause of a great number of errors in SQL code, both in ISO standard SQL statements and in the specific SQL dialects supported by real-world database management systems. These mistakes are usually the result of confusion between Null and either 0 (zero) or an empty string (a string value with a length of zero, represented in SQL as ''). Null is defined by the ISO SQL standard as different from both an empty string and the numerical value 0, however. While Null indicates the absence of any value, the empty string and numerical zero both represent actual values.

A classic error is attempting to use the equality operator to find NULLs. Most SQL implementations will execute the following query as syntactically correct (therefore give no error message) but it never returns any rows, regardless of whether NULLs do exist in the table.

SELECT *

FROM sometable

WHERE num = NULL; -- Should be "WHERE num IS NULL"

In a related, but more subtle example, a WHERE clause or conditional statement might compare a column's value with a constant. It is often incorrectly assumed that a missing value would be "less than" or "not equal to" a constant if that field contains Null, but, in fact, such expressions return Unknown. An example is below:

SELECT *

FROM sometable

WHERE num <> 1; -- Rows where num is NULL will not be returned,

       -- contrary to many users' expectations.

Similarly, Nulls are often confused with empty strings. Consider the LENGTH function, which returns the number of characters in a string. When a Null is passed into this function, the function returns Null. This can lead to unexpected results, if users are not well versed in 3-value logic. An example is below:

SELECT *

FROM sometable

WHERE LENGTH(string) < 20; -- Rows where string is NULL will not be returned.

This is complicated by the fact that in some database interface programs (or even database implementations like Oracle's), NULL is reported as an empty string, and empty strings may be incorrectly stored as NULL.

Criticisms

The ISO SQL implementation of Null is the subject of criticism, debate and calls for change. In *The Relational Model for Database Management: Version 2*, Codd suggested that the SQL implementation of Null was flawed and should be replaced by two distinct Null-type markers. The markers he proposed were to stand for *"Missing but Applicable"* and *"Missing but Inapplicable"*, known as *A-values* and *I-values*, respectively. Codd's recommendation, if accepted, would have required the implementation of a four-valued logic in SQL. Others have suggested adding additional Null-type markers to Codd's recommendation to indicate even more reasons that a data value might be

"Missing", increasing the complexity of SQL's logic system. At various times, proposals have also been put forth to implement multiple user-defined Null markers in SQL. Because of the complexity of the Null-handling and logic systems required to support multiple Null markers, none of these proposals have gained widespread acceptance.

Chris Date and Hugh Darwen, authors of *The Third Manifesto*, have suggested that the SQL Null implementation is inherently flawed and should be eliminated altogether, pointing to inconsistencies and flaws in the implementation of SQL Null-handling (particularly in aggregate functions) as proof that the entire concept of Null is flawed and should be removed from the relational model. Others, like author Fabian Pascal, have stated a belief that "how the function calculation should treat missing values is not governed by the relational model."

Closed World Assumption

Another point of conflict concerning Nulls is that they violate the closed world assumption model of relational databases by introducing an open world assumption into it. The closed world assumption, as it pertains to databases, states that "Everything stated by the database, either explicitly or implicitly, is true; everything else is false." This view assumes that the knowledge of the world stored within a database is complete. Nulls, however, operate under the open world assumption, in which some items stored in the database are considered unknown, making the database's stored knowledge of the world incomplete.

Candidate Key

In the relational model of databases, a candidate key of a relation is a minimal superkey for that relation; that is, a set of attributes such that:

1. the relation does not have two distinct tuples (i.e. rows or records in common database language) with the same values for these attributes (which means that the set of attributes is a superkey)

2. there is no proper subset of these attributes for which (1) holds (which means that the set is minimal).

The constituent attributes are called prime attributes. Conversely, an attribute that does not occur in ANY candidate key is called a non-prime attribute.

Since a relation contains no duplicate tuples, the set of all its attributes is a superkey if NULL values are not used. It follows that every relation will have at least one candidate key.

The candidate keys of a relation tell us all the possible ways we can identify its tuples. As such they are an important concept for the design of database schema.

Example

The definition of candidate keys can be illustrated with the following (abstract) example. Consider a relation variable (relvar) R with attributes (A, B, C, D) that has only the following two legal values $r1$ and $r2$:

r1			
A	**B**	**C**	**D**
a1	b1	c1	d1
a1	b2	c2	d1
a2	b1	c2	d1

r2			
A	**B**	**C**	**D**
a1	b1	c1	d1
a1	b2	c2	d1
a1	b1	c2	d2

Here $r2$ differs from $r1$ only in the A and D values of the last tuple.

For $r1$ the following sets have the uniqueness property, i.e., there are no two distinct tuples in the instance with the same values for the attributes in the set:

{A,B}, {A,C}, {B,C}, {A,B,C}, {A,B,D}, {A,C,D}, {B,C,D}, {A,B,C,D}

For $r2$ the uniqueness property holds for the following sets;

{B,C}, {B,D}, {C,D}, {A,B,C}, {A,B,D}, {A,C,D}, {B,C,D}, {A,B,C,D}

Since superkeys of a relvar are those sets of attributes that have the uniqueness property for *all* legal values of that relvar and because we assume that $r1$ and $r2$ are all the legal values that R can take, we can determine the set of superkeys of R by taking the intersection of the two lists:

{B,C}, {A,B,C}, {A,B,D}, {A,C,D}, {B,C,D}, {A,B,C,D}

Finally we need to select those sets for which there is no proper subset in the list, which are in this case:

{B,C}, {A,B,D}, {A,C,D}

These are indeed the candidate keys of relvar R.

We have to consider *all* the relations that might be assigned to a relvar to determine whether a certain set of attributes is a candidate key. For example, if we had considered only $r1$ then we would have concluded that {A,B} is a candidate key, which is incorrect. However, we *might* be able to conclude from such a relation that a certain set is *not* a candidate key, because that set does not have the uniqueness property (example {A,D} for $r1$). Note that the existence of a proper subset of a set that has the uniqueness property *cannot* in general be used as evidence that the superset is not a candidate key. In particular, note that in the case of an empty relation, every subset of the heading has the uniqueness property, including the empty set.

Determining Candidate Keys

The set of all candidate keys can be computed e.g. from the set of functional dependencies. To this end we need to define the attribute closure for an attribute set . The set contains all attributes that are functionally implied by .

It is quite simple to find a single candidate key. We start with a set of attributes and try to remove successively each attribute. If after removing an attribute the attribute closure stays the same, then this attribute is not necessary and we can remove it permanently. We call the result . If is the set of all attributes, then is a candidate key.

Actually we can detect every candidate key with this procedure by simply trying every possible order of removing attributes. However there are many more permutations of attributes than subsets. That is, many attribute orders will lead to the same candidate key.

There is a fundamental difficulty for efficient algorithms for candidate key computation: Certain sets of functional dependencies lead to exponentially many candidate keys. Consider the functional dependencies which yields candidate keys: . That is, the best we can expect is an algorithm that is efficient with respect to the number of candidate keys.

The following algorithm actually runs in polynomial time in the number of candidate keys and functional dependencies:

function find_candidate_keys(A, F)

  /* A is the set of all attributes and F is the set of functional dependencies */

  K := minimize(A);

  n := 1; /* Number of Keys known so far */

  i := 0; /* Currently processed key */

  while i < n do

    foreach $\alpha \rightarrow \beta \in F$ do

      /* Build a new potential key from the previous known key and the current FD */

      S := $\alpha \cup (K[i] - \beta)$;

      /* Search whether the new potential key is part of the already known keys */

      found := false;

      for j := 0 to n-1 do

        if K[j] ⊆ S then found := true;

      /* If not, add if

      if not found then

K[n] := minimize(S);

n := n + 1;

i := i + 1

return K

The idea behind the algorithm is that given a candidate key and a functional dependency , the reverse application of the functional dependency yields the set , which is a key, too. It may however be covered by other already known candidate keys. (The algorithm checks this case using the 'found' variable.) If not, then minimizing the new key yields a new candidate key. The key insight is that all candidate keys can be created this way.

Foreign Key

In the context of relational databases, a foreign key is a field (or collection of fields) in one table that uniquely identifies a row of another table or the same table. In simpler words, the foreign key is defined in a second table, but it refers to the primary key in the first table. For example, a table called Employee has a primary key called employee_id. Another table called Employee Details has a foreign key which references employee_id in order to uniquely identify the relationship between both the tables.

The table containing the foreign key is called the child table, and the table containing the candidate key is called the referenced or parent table. In database relational modeling and implementation, a unique key is a set of zero or more attributes, the value(s) of which are guaranteed to be unique for each tuple (row) in a relation. The value or combination of values of unique key attributes for any tuple cannot be duplicated for any other tuple in that relation.

When more than one column is combined to form a unique key, their combined value is used to access each row and maintain uniqueness. Values are not combined, they are compared using their data types.

Since the purpose of the foreign key is to identify a particular row of the referenced table, it is generally required that the foreign key is equal to the candidate key in some row of the primary table, or else have no value (the NULL value.). This rule is called a referential integrity constraint between the two tables. Because violations of these constraints can be the source of many database problems, most database management systems provide mechanisms to ensure that every non-null foreign key corresponds to a row of the referenced table.

For example, consider a database with two tables: a CUSTOMER table that includes all customer data and an ORDER table that includes all customer orders. Suppose the business requires that each order must refer to a single customer. To reflect this in the database, a foreign key column is added to the ORDER table (e.g., CUSTOMERID), which references the primary key of CUSTOMER (e.g. ID). Because the primary key of a table must be unique, and because CUSTOMERID only contains values from that primary key field, we may assume that, when it has a value, CUSTOME-

RID will identify the particular customer which placed the order. However, this can no longer be assumed if the ORDER table is not kept up to date when rows of the CUSTOMER table are deleted or the ID column altered, and working with these tables may become more difficult. Many real world databases work around this problem by 'inactivating' rather than physically deleting master table foreign keys, or by complex update programs that modify all references to a foreign key when a change is needed.

Foreign keys play an essential role in database design. One important part of database design is making sure that relationships between real-world entities are reflected in the database by references, using foreign keys to refer from one table to another. Another important part of database design is database normalization, in which tables are broken apart and foreign keys make it possible for them to be reconstructed.

Multiple rows in the referencing (or child) table may refer to the same row in the referenced (or parent) table. In this case, the relationship between the two tables is called a one to many relationship between the referenced table and the referencing table.

In addition, the child and parent table may, in fact, be the same table, i.e. the foreign key refers back to the same table. Such a foreign key is known in SQL:2003 as a self-referencing or recursive foreign key. In database management systems, this is often accomplished by linking a first and second reference to the same table.

A table may have multiple foreign keys, and each foreign key can have a different parent table. Each foreign key is enforced independently by the database system. Therefore, cascading relationships between tables can be established using foreign keys.

Defining Foreign Keys

Foreign keys are defined in the ISO SQL Standard, through a FOREIGN KEY constraint. The syntax to add such a constraint to an existing table is defined in SQL:2003 as shown below. Omitting the column list in the REFERENCES clause implies that the foreign key shall reference the primary key of the referenced table.

ALTER TABLE <table identifier>

  ADD [CONSTRAINT <constraint identifier>]

    FOREIGN KEY (<column expression> {, <column expression>}...)

    REFERENCES <table identifier> [(<column expression> {, <column expression>}...)]

    [ON UPDATE <referential action>]

    [ON DELETE <referential action>]

Likewise, foreign keys can be defined as part of the CREATE TABLE SQL statement.

CREATE TABLE table_name (

  id   INTEGER PRIMARY KEY,

col2 CHARACTER VARYING(20),

col3 INTEGER,

...

FOREIGN KEY(col3)

  REFERENCES other_table(key_col) ON DELETE CASCADE,

...)

If the foreign key is a single column only, the column can be marked as such using the following syntax:

CREATE TABLE table_name (

  id   INTEGER PRIMARY KEY,

  col2 CHARACTER VARYING(20),

  col3 INTEGER REFERENCES other_table(column_name),

  ...)

Foreign keys can be defined with a stored procedure statement.

sp_foreignkey tabname, pktabname, col1 [, col2] ... [, col8]

- tabname: the name of the table or view that contains the foreign key to be defined.

- pktabname: the name of the table or view that has the primary key to which the foreign key applies. The primary key must already be defined.

- col1: the name of the first column that makes up the foreign key. The foreign key must have at least one column and can have a maximum of eight columns.

Referential Actions

Because the database management system enforces referential constraints, it must ensure data integrity if rows in a referenced table are to be deleted (or updated). If dependent rows in referencing tables still exist, those references have to be considered. SQL:2003 specifies 5 different referential actions that shall take place in such occurrences:

- CASCADE

- RESTRICT

- NO ACTION

- SET NULL

- SET DEFAULT

CASCADE

Whenever rows in the master (referenced) table are deleted (or updated), the respective rows of the child (referencing) table with a matching foreign key column will be deleted (or updated) as well. This is called a cascade delete (or update).

RESTRICT

A value cannot be updated or deleted when a row exists in a referencing or child table that references the value in the referenced table.

Similarly, a row cannot be deleted as long as there is a reference to it from a referencing or child table.

To understand RESTRICT (and CASCADE) better, it may be helpful to notice the following difference, which might not be immediately clear. The referential action CASCADE modifies the "behavior" of the (child) table itself where the word CASCADE is used. For example, ON DELETE CASCADE effectively says "When the referenced row is deleted from the other table (master table), then delete *also from me*". However, the referential action RESTRICT modifies the "behavior" of the master table, *not* the child table, although the word RESTRICT appears in the child table and not in the master table! So, ON DELETE RESTRICT effectively says: "When someone tries to delete the row from the other table (master table), prevent deletion *from that other table* (and of course, also don't delete from me, but that's not the main point here)."

RESTRICT is not supported by Microsoft SQL 2012 and earlier.

NO ACTION

NO ACTION and RESTRICT are very much alike. The main difference between NO ACTION and RESTRICT is that with NO ACTION the referential integrity check is done after trying to alter the table. RESTRICT does the check before trying to execute the UPDATE or DELETE statement. Both referential actions act the same if the referential integrity check fails: the UPDATE or DELETE statement will result in an error.

In other words, when an UPDATE or DELETE statement is executed on the referenced table using the referential action NO ACTION, the DBMS verifies at the end of the statement execution that none of the referential relationships are violated. This is different from RESTRICT, which assumes at the outset that the operation will violate the constraint. Using NO ACTION, the triggers or the semantics of the statement itself may yield an end state in which no foreign key relationships are violated by the time the constraint is finally checked, thus allowing the statement to complete successfully.

SET DEFAULT , SET NULL

In general, the action taken by the DBMS for SET NULL or SET DEFAULT is the same for both ON DELETE or ON UPDATE: The value of the affected referencing attributes is changed to NULL for SET NULL, and to the specified default value for SET DEFAULT.

Triggers

Referential actions are generally implemented as implied triggers (i.e. triggers with system-generated names, often hidden.) As such, they are subject to the same limitations as user-defined triggers, and their order of execution relative to other triggers may need to be considered; in some cases it may become necessary to replace the referential action with its equivalent user-defined trigger to ensure proper execution order, or to work around mutating-table limitations.

Another important limitation appears with transaction isolation: your changes to a row may not be able to fully cascade because the row is referenced by data your transaction cannot "see", and therefore cannot cascade onto. An example: while your transaction is attempting to renumber a customer account, a simultaneous transaction is attempting to create a new invoice for that same customer; while a CASCADE rule may fix all the invoice rows your transaction can see to keep them consistent with the renumbered customer row, it won't reach into another transaction to fix the data there; because the database cannot guarantee consistent data when the two transactions commit, one of them will be forced to roll back (often on a first-come-first-served basis.)

CREATE TABLE account (acct_num INT, amount DECIMAL(10,2));

CREATE TRIGGER ins_sum BEFORE INSERT ON account

   FOR EACH ROW SET @sum = @sum + NEW.amount;

Example

As a first example to illustrate foreign keys, suppose an accounts database has a table with invoices and each invoice is associated with a particular supplier. Supplier details (such as name and address) are kept in a separate table; each supplier is given a 'supplier number' to identify it. Each invoice record has an attribute containing the supplier number for that invoice. Then, the 'supplier number' is the primary key in the Supplier table. The foreign key in the Invoices table points to that primary key. The relational schema is the following. Primary keys are marked in bold, and foreign keys are marked in italics.

Supplier (SupplierNumber, Name, Address, Type)

Invoices (InvoiceNumber, *SupplierNumber*, Text)

The corresponding Data Definition Language statement is as follows.

CREATE TABLE Supplier (

   SupplierNumber INTEGER NOT NULL,

   Name   VARCHAR(20) NOT NULL,

   Address   VARCHAR(50) NOT NULL,

   Type   VARCHAR(10),

```
    CONSTRAINT supplier_pk PRIMARY KEY(SupplierNumber),

    CONSTRAINT number_value CHECK (SupplierNumber > 0) )

CREATE TABLE Invoices (

  InvoiceNumber   INTEGER NOT NULL,

  SupplierNumber  INTEGER NOT NULL,

  Text            VARCHAR(4096),

  CONSTRAINT invoice_pk PRIMARY KEY(InvoiceNumber),

  CONSTRAINT inumber_value CHECK (InvoiceNumber > 0),

  CONSTRAINT supplier_fk FOREIGN KEY(SupplierNumber)

    REFERENCES Supplier(SupplierNumber)

    ON UPDATE CASCADE ON DELETE RESTRICT )
```

Unique Key

In database relational modeling and implementation, a unique key is a superkey--that is, in the relational model of database organization, a set of attributes of a relation variable for which it holds that in all relations assigned to that variable, there are no two distinct tuples (rows) that have the same values for the attributes in this set.

When more than one column is combined to form a unique key, their combined value is used to access each row and maintain uniqueness. These keys are referred to as aggregate or compound keys. Values are not combined, they are compared using their data types.

When a column or set of columns is defined as unique to the database management system, the system verifies that each set of values is unique before assigning the constraint. After the column(s) is(are) defined as unique, an error will occur if an insertion is attempted with values that already exist. Some systems will not allow key values to be updated, all systems will not allow duplicates. This ensures that uniqueness is maintained in both the primary table and any relations that are later bound to it.

Summary

Keys provide the means for database users and application software to identify, access and update information in a database table. There may be several keys in any given table. For example, two distinct keys in a table of employees might be employee number and login name. The enforcement of a key constraint (i.e. a uniqueness constraint) in a table is also a data integrity feature of the database. The DBMS prevents updates that would cause duplicate key values and thereby ensures that tables always comply with the desired rules for uniqueness.

Proper selection of keys when designing a database is therefore an important aspect of database integrity.

A relational database table may have one or more available keys (formally called candidate keys). One of those keys per table may be designated the "primary" key, alternatively another key ("surrogate key") may be used. Any remaining keys are called alternate, or secondary, keys. Although mainly used today in the relational database context, the terms primary key and secondary key pre-date the relational model and are also used in other database models.

In relational database terms, a primary key need not differ in form or function from a key that isn't primary and in practice various different motivations may determine the choice of any one key as primary over another. The designation of a primary key may indicate the "preferred" identifier for data in the table, or that the primary key is to be used for foreign key references from other tables or it may indicate some other technical rather than semantic feature of the table. Some languages and software have special syntax features that can be used to identify a primary key as such (e.g. the PRIMARY KEY constraint in SQL).

Any key may consist of one or more attributes. For example, a Social Security Number might be a single attribute key for an employee; a combination of flight number and date might be a key consisting of two attributes for a scheduled flight.

There are several types of unique keys used in database modeling and implementations.

Key Name	Definition
Simple	A key made from only one attribute.
Concatenated	A key made from more than one attribute joined together as a single key, such as part or whole name with a system generated number appended as often used for E-mail addresses.
Compound	A key made from at least two attributes or simple keys, only simple keys exist in a compound key.
Composite	A key containing at least one compound key with at least one other attribute or simple key (this is an extension of a compound key).
Natural	A key made from data that exists outside the current database. In other words, the data is not system generated, such as a social security number imported from another system.
Surrogate	An artificial key made from data that is system assigned or generated when another candidate key exists. Surrogate keys are usually numeric ID values and often used for performance reasons.
Candidate	A key that may become the primary key.
Primary	The key that is selected as the primary key. Only one key within an entity is selected to be the primary key. This is the key that is allowed to migrate to other entities to define the relationships that exist among the entities. When the data model is instantiated into a physical database, it is the key that the system uses the most when accessing the table, or joining the tables together when selecting data.
Alternate	A non-primary key that can be used to identify only one row in a table. Alternate keys may be used like a primary key in a single-table select.
Foreign	A unique key that has migrated to another entity.

At the most basic definition, "a key is a unique identifier", so *unique* key is a pleonasm. Keys that are within their originating entity are unique within that entity. Keys that migrate to another entity may or may not be unique, depending on the design and how they are used in the other table. Foreign keys may be the primary key in another table; for example a PersonID may become the EmployeeID in the Employee table. In this case, the EmployeeID is both a foreign key and the unique primary key, meaning that the tables have a 1:1 relationship. In the case where the person entity contained the biological father ID, the father ID would not be expected to be unique because a father may have more than one child.

Here is an example of a primary key becoming a foreign key on a related table. ID migrates from the Author table to the Book table.

Author Table Schema:

Author(ID, Name, Address, Born)

Book Table Schema:

Book(ISBN, AuthorID, Title, Publisher, Price)

Here ID serves as the primary key in the table 'Author', but also as AuthorID serves as a Foreign Key in the table 'Book'. The Foreign Key serves as the link, and therefore the connection, between the two related tables in this sample database.

In a relational database, a candidate key uniquely identifies each row of data values in a database table. A candidate key comprises a single column or a set of columns in a single database table. No two distinct rows or data records in a database table can have the same data value (or combination of data values) in those candidate key columns since NULL values are not used. Depending on its design, a database table may have many candidate keys but at most one candidate key may be distinguished as the primary key.

A key constraint applies to the set of tuples in a table at any given point in time. A key is not necessarily a unique identifier across the population of all *possible* instances of tuples that could be stored in a table but it does imply a data integrity rule that duplicates should not be allowed in the database table. Some possible examples of unique keys are Social Security Numbers, ISBNs, vehicle registration numbers or user login names.

The relational model, as expressed through relational calculus and relational algebra, does not distinguish between primary keys and other kinds of keys. Primary keys were added to the SQL standard mainly as a convenience to the application programmer.

Unique keys as well as primary keys may be logically referenced by foreign keys, but most RDBMS only allow a foreign key constraint against a primary key.

Defining Primary Keys in SQL

Primary keys are defined in the ANSI SQL Standard, through the PRIMARY KEY constraint. The syntax to add such a constraint to an existing table is defined in SQL:2003 like this:

ALTER TABLE <table identifier>

  ADD [CONSTRAINT <constraint identifier>]

  PRIMARY KEY (<column expression> {, <column expression>}...)

The primary key can also be specified directly during table creation. In the SQL Standard, primary keys may consist of one or multiple columns. Each column participating in the primary key is implicitly defined as NOT NULL. Note that some RDBMS require explicitly marking primary key columns as NOT NULL.

CREATE TABLE table_name (

  ...

)

If the primary key consists only of a single column, the column can be marked as such using the following syntax:

CREATE TABLE table_name (

  id_col INT PRIMARY KEY,

  col2   CHARACTER VARYING(20),

  ...

)

Differences between Primary Key Constraint and Unique Constraint:

Primary Key constraint

1. A primary key *cannot* allow null (a primary key cannot be defined on columns that allow nulls).
2. Each table cannot have more than one primary key.
3. On some RDBMS a primary key generates a clustered index by default.

Unique constraint

1. A unique constraint can be defined on columns that allow nulls.
2. Each table can have multiple unique keys.
3. On some RDBMS a unique key generates a nonclustered index by default.

Defining Other Keys in SQL

The definition of other unique keys is syntactically very similar to primary keys.

ALTER TABLE <table identifier>

  ADD [CONSTRAINT <constraint identifier>]

  UNIQUE (<column expression> {, <column expression>}...)

Likewise, unique keys can be defined as part of the CREATE TABLE SQL statement.

CREATE TABLE table_name (

  id_col INT,

  col2   CHARACTER VARYING(20),

  key_col SMALLINT NOT NULL,

  ...

  CONSTRAINT key_unique UNIQUE(key_col),

  ...

)

CREATE TABLE table_name (

  id_col INT PRIMARY KEY,

  col2   CHARACTER VARYING(20),

  ...

  key_col SMALLINT NOT NULL UNIQUE,

  ...

)

Note that unlike the PRIMARY KEY constraint a UNIQUE constraint does not imply NOT NULL for the columns participating in the constraint. NOT NULL must be specified to make the column(s) a key. It is possible to put UNIQUE constraints on nullable columns but the SQL standard states that the constraint does not guarantee uniqueness of nullable columns (uniqueness is not enforced for rows where any of the columns contains a null).

According to the SQL standard a unique constraint does not enforce uniqueness in the presence of nulls and can therefore contain several rows with identical combinations of nulls and non-null values — however not all RDBMS implement this feature according to the SQL standard.

Surrogate Keys

In some circumstances the natural key that uniquely identifies a tuple in a relation may be cumbersome to use for software development. For example, it may involve multiple columns or large text fields. In such cases, a surrogate key can be used instead as the primary key. In other situations there may be more than one candidate key for a relation, and no candidate key is obviously preferred. A surrogate key may be used as the primary key to avoid giving one candidate key artificial primacy over the others.

Since primary keys exist primarily as a convenience to the programmer, surrogate primary keys are often used, in many cases exclusively, in database application design.

Due to the popularity of surrogate primary keys, many developers and in some cases even theoreticians have come to regard surrogate primary keys as an inalienable part of the relational data model. This is largely due to a migration of principles from the Object-Oriented Programming model to the relational model, creating the hybrid object-relational model. In the ORM, these additional restrictions are placed on primary keys:

- Primary keys should be immutable, that is, never changed or re-used; they should be deleted along with the associated record.

- Primary keys should be anonymous integer or numeric identifiers.

However, neither of these restrictions is part of the relational model or any SQL standard. Due diligence should be applied when deciding on the immutability of primary key values during database and application design. Some database systems even imply that values in primary key columns cannot be changed using the UPDATE SQL statement.

Alternate Key

Typically, one candidate key is chosen as the primary key. Other candidate keys become alternate keys, each of which may have a unique index assigned to it in order to prevent duplicates (a duplicate entry is not valid in a unique column).

Alternate keys may be used like the primary key when doing a single-table select or when filtering in a *where* clause, but are not typically used to join multiple tables.

Surrogate Key

A surrogate key (or synthetic key, entity identifier, system-generated key, database sequence number, factless key, technical key, or arbitrary unique identifier) in a database is a unique identifier for either an *entity* in the modeled world or an *object* in the database. The surrogate key is *not* derived from application data, unlike a *natural* (or *business*) key which is derived from application data.

Definition

There are at least two definitions of a surrogate:

Surrogate (1) – Hall, Owlett and Todd (1976)

> A surrogate represents an *entity* in the outside world. The surrogate is internally generated by the system but is nevertheless visible to the user or application.

Surrogate (2) – Wieringa and De Jonge (1991)

> A surrogate represents an *object* in the database itself. The surrogate is internally generated by the system and is invisible to the user or application.

The *Surrogate (1)* definition relates to a data model rather than a storage model and is used throughout this article.

An important distinction between a surrogate and a primary key depends on whether the database is a current database or a temporal database. Since a *current database* stores only *currently* valid data, there is a one-to-one correspondence between a surrogate in the modeled world and the primary key of the database. In this case the surrogate may be used as a primary key, resulting in the term *surrogate key*. In a temporal database, however, there is a many-to-one relationship between primary keys and the surrogate. Since there may be several objects in the database corresponding to a single surrogate, we cannot use the surrogate as a primary key; another attribute is required, in addition to the surrogate, to uniquely identify each object.

Although Hall *et al.* (1976) say nothing about this, others have argued that a surrogate should have the following characteristics:

- the value is unique system-wide, hence never reused
- the value is system generated
- the value is not manipulable by the user or application
- the value contains no semantic meaning
- the value is not visible to the user or application
- the value is not composed of several values from different domains.

Surrogates in Practice

In a current database, the surrogate key can be the primary key, generated by the database management system and *not* derived from any application data in the database. The only significance of the surrogate key is to act as the primary key. It is also possible that the surrogate key exists in addition to the database-generated UUID (for example, an HR number for each employee other than the UUID of each employee).

A surrogate key is frequently a sequential number (e.g. a Sybase or SQL Server "identity column", a PostgreSQL or Informix serial, an Oracle or SQL Server SEQUENCE or a column defined with AUTO_INCREMENT in MySQL). Some databases provide UUID/GUID as a possible data type for surrogate keys (e.g. PostgreSQL UUID or SQL Server UNIQUEIDENTIFIER).

Having the key independent of all other columns insulates the database relationships from changes in data values or database design (making the database more agile) and guarantees uniqueness.

In a temporal database, it is necessary to distinguish between the surrogate key and the business key. Every row would have both a business key and a surrogate key. The surrogate key identifies one unique row in the database, the business key identifies one unique entity of the modeled world. One table row represents a slice of time holding all the entity's attributes for a defined timespan. Those slices depict the whole lifespan of one business entity. For example, a table *EmployeeContracts* may hold temporal information to keep track of contracted working hours. The business key for one contract will be identical (non-unique) in both rows however the surrogate key for each row is unique.

Surrogate-Key	Business-Key	EmployeeName	WorkingHour-sPerWeek	RowValidFrom	RowValidTo
1	BOS0120	John Smith	40	2000-01-01	2000-12-31
56	P0000123	Bob Brown	25	1999-01-01	2011-12-31
234	BOS0120	John Smith	35	2001-01-01	2009-12-31

Some database designers use surrogate keys systematically regardless of the suitability of other candidate keys, while others will use a key already present in the data, if there is one.

Some of the alternate names ("system-generated key") describe the way of *generating* new surrogate values rather than the *nature* of the surrogate concept.

Approaches to generating surrogates include:

- Universally Unique Identifiers (UUIDs)
- Globally Unique Identifiers (GUIDs)
- Object Identifiers (OIDs)
- Sybase or SQL Server identity column IDENTITY OR IDENTITY(n,n)
- Oracle SEQUENCE, or GENERATED AS IDENTITY (starting from version 12.1)
- SQL Server SEQUENCE (starting from SQL Server 2012)
- PostgreSQL or IBM Informix serial
- MySQL AUTO_INCREMENT
- SQLite AUTOINCREMENT
- AutoNumber data type in Microsoft Access
- AS IDENTITY GENERATED BY DEFAULT in IBM DB2

- Identity column (implemented in DDL) in Teradata

- Table Sequence when the sequence is calculated by a procedure and a sequence table with fields: id, sequenceName, sequenceValue and incrementValue

Advantages

Immutability

Surrogate keys do not change while the row exists. This has the following advantages:

- Applications cannot lose their reference to a row in the database (since the identifier never changes).

- The primary or natural key data can always be modified, even with databases that do not support cascading updates across related foreign keys.

Requirement Changes

Attributes that uniquely identify an entity might change, which might invalidate the suitability of natural keys. Consider the following example:

> An employee's network user name is chosen as a natural key. Upon merging with another company, new employees must be inserted. Some of the new network user names create conflicts because their user names were generated independently (when the companies were separate).

In these cases, generally a new attribute must be added to the natural key (for example, an *original_company* column). With a surrogate key, only the table that defines the surrogate key must be changed. With natural keys, all tables (and possibly other, related software) that use the natural key will have to change.

Some problem domains do not clearly identify a suitable natural key. Surrogate keys avoid choosing a natural key that might be incorrect.

Performance

Surrogate keys tend to be a compact data type, such as a four-byte integer. This allows the database to query the single key column faster than it could multiple columns. Furthermore, a non-redundant distribution of keys causes the resulting b-tree index to be completely balanced. Surrogate keys are also less expensive to join (fewer columns to compare) than compound keys.

Compatibility

While using several database application development systems, drivers, and object-relational mapping systems, such as Ruby on Rails or Hibernate, it is much easier to use an integer or GUID surrogate keys for every table instead of natural keys in order to support database-system-agnostic operations and object-to-row mapping.

Uniformity

When every table has a uniform surrogate key, some tasks can be easily automated by writing the code in a table-independent way.

Validation

It is possible to design key-values that follow a well-known pattern or structure which can be automatically verified. For instance, the keys that are intended to be used in some column of some table might be designed to "look differently from" those that are intended to be used in another column or table, thereby simplifying the detection of application errors in which the keys have been misplaced. However, this characteristic of the surrogate keys should never be used to drive any of the logic of the applications themselves, as this would violate the principles of Database normalization.

Disadvantages

Disassociation

The values of generated surrogate keys have no relationship to the real-world *meaning* of the data held in a row. When inspecting a row holding a foreign key reference to another table using a surrogate key, the meaning of the surrogate key's row cannot be discerned from the key itself. Every foreign key must be joined to see the related data item. This can also make auditing more difficult, as incorrect data is not obvious.

Surrogate keys are unnatural for data that is exported and shared. A particular difficulty is that tables from two otherwise identical schemas (for example, a test schema and a development schema) can hold records that are equivalent in a business sense, but have different keys. This can be mitigated by not exporting surrogate keys, except as transient data (most obviously, in executing applications that have a "live" connection to the database).

Query Optimization

Relational databases assume a unique index is applied to a table's primary key. The unique index serves two purposes: (i) to enforce entity integrity, since primary key data must be unique across rows and (ii) to quickly search for rows when queried. Since surrogate keys replace a table's identifying attributes—the natural key—and since the identifying attributes are likely to be those queried, then the query optimizer is forced to perform a full table scan when fulfilling likely queries. The remedy to the full table scan is to apply indexes on the identifying attributes, or sets of them. Where such sets are themselves a candidate key, the index can be a unique index.

These additional indexes, however, will take up disk space and slow down inserts and deletes.

Normalization

Surrogate keys can result in duplicate values in any natural keys. It is part of the implementation to ensure that such duplicates should not be possible.

Business Process Modeling

Because surrogate keys are unnatural, flaws can appear when modeling the business requirements. Business requirements, relying on the natural key, then need to be translated to the surrogate key. A strategy is to draw a clear distinction between the logical model (in which surrogate keys do not appear) and the physical implementation of that model, to ensure that the logical model is correct and reasonably well normalised, and to ensure that the physical model is a correct implementation of the logical model.

Inadvertent Disclosure

Proprietary information can be leaked if sequential key generators are used. By subtracting a previously generated sequential key from a recently generated sequential key, one could learn the number of rows inserted during that time period. This could expose, for example, the number of transactions or new accounts per period. There are a few ways to overcome this problem:

- Increase the sequential number by a random amount.

- Generate a random key such as a uuid

Inadvertent Assumptions

Sequentially generated surrogate keys can imply that events with a higher key value occurred after events with a lower value. This is not necessarily true, because such values do not guarantee time sequence as it is possible for inserts to fail and leave gaps which may be filled at a later time. If chronology is important then date and time must be separately recorded.

NoSQL

A NoSQL (originally referring to "non SQL", "non relational" or "not only SQL") database provides a mechanism for storage and retrieval of data which is modeled in means other than the tabular relations used in relational databases. Such databases have existed since the late 1960s, but did not obtain the "NoSQL" moniker until a surge of popularity in the early twenty-first century, triggered by the needs of Web 2.0 companies such as Facebook, Google, and Amazon.com. NoSQL databases are increasingly used in big data and real-time web applications. NoSQL systems are also sometimes called "Not only SQL" to emphasize that they may support SQL-like query languages.

Motivations for this approach include: simplicity of design, simpler "horizontal" scaling to clusters of machines (which is a problem for relational databases), and finer control over availability. The data structures used by NoSQL databases (e.g. key-value, wide column, graph, or document) are different from those used by default in relational databases, making some operations faster in NoSQL. The particular suitability of a given NoSQL database depends on the problem it must solve. Sometimes the data structures used by NoSQL databases are also viewed as "more flexible" than relational database tables.

Many NoSQL stores compromise consistency (in the sense of the CAP theorem) in favor of availability, partition tolerance, and speed. Barriers to the greater adoption of NoSQL stores include the use of low-level query languages (instead of SQL, for instance the lack of ability to perform ad-hoc JOINs across tables), lack of standardized interfaces, and huge previous investments in existing relational databases. Most NoSQL stores lack true ACID transactions, although a few databases, such as MarkLogic, Aerospike, FairCom c-treeACE, Google Spanner (though technically a NewSQL database), Symas LMDB, and OrientDB have made them central to their designs.

Instead, most NoSQL databases offer a concept of "eventual consistency" in which database changes are propagated to all nodes "eventually" (typically within milliseconds) so queries for data might not return updated data immediately or might result in reading data that is not accurate, a problem known as stale reads. Additionally, some NoSQL systems may exhibit lost writes and other forms of data loss. Fortunately, some NoSQL systems provide concepts such as write-ahead logging to avoid data loss. For distributed transaction processing across multiple databases, data consistency is an even bigger challenge that is difficult for both NoSQL and relational databases. Even current relational databases "do not allow referential integrity constraints to span databases." There are few systems that maintain both ACID transactions and X/Open XA standards for distributed transaction processing.

History

The term *NoSQL* was used by Carlo Strozzi in 1998 to name his lightweight, Strozzi NoSQL open-source relational database that did not expose the standard Structured Query Language (SQL) interface, but was still relational. His NoSQL RDBMS is distinct from the circa-2009 general concept of NoSQL databases. Strozzi suggests that, because the current NoSQL movement "departs from the relational model altogether, it should therefore have been called more appropriately 'NoREL'", referring to 'No Relational'.

Johan Oskarsson of Last.fm reintroduced the term *NoSQL* in early 2009 when he organized an event to discuss "open source distributed, non relational databases". The name attempted to label the emergence of an increasing number of non-relational, distributed data stores, including open source clones of Google's BigTable/MapReduce and Amazon's Dynamo. Most of the early NoSQL systems did not attempt to provide atomicity, consistency, isolation and durability guarantees, contrary to the prevailing practice among relational database systems.

Based on 2014 revenue, the NoSQL market leaders are MarkLogic, MongoDB, and Datastax. Based on 2015 popularity rankings, the most popular NoSQL databases are MongoDB, Apache Cassandra, and Redis.

Types and Examples of NoSQL Databases

There have been various approaches to classify NoSQL databases, each with different categories and subcategories, some of which overlap. What follows is a basic classification by data model, with examples:

- Column: Accumulo, Cassandra, Druid, HBase, Vertica

- Document: Apache CouchDB, Clusterpoint, Couchbase, DocumentDB, HyperDex, IBM Domino, MarkLogic, MongoDB, OrientDB, Qizx, RethinkDB

- Key-value: Aerospike, Couchbase, Dynamo, FairCom c-treeACE, FoundationDB, Hyper-Dex, MemcacheDB, MUMPS, Oracle NoSQL Database, OrientDB, Redis, Riak, Berkeley DB

- Graph: AllegroGraph, ArangoDB, InfiniteGraph, Apache Giraph, MarkLogic, Neo4J, OrientDB, Virtuoso, Stardog

- Multi-model: Alchemy Database, ArangoDB, CortexDB, Couchbase, FoundationDB, MarkLogic, OrientDB

A more detailed classification is the following, based on one from Stephen Yen:

Type	Examples of this type
Key-Value Cache	Coherence, eXtreme Scale, GigaSpaces, GemFire, Hazelcast, Infinispan, JBoss Cache, Memcached, Repcached, Terracotta, Velocity
Key-Value Store	Flare, Keyspace, RAMCloud, SchemaFree, Hyperdex, Aerospike
Key-Value Store (Eventually-Consistent)	DovetailDB, Oracle NoSQL Database, Dynamo, Riak, Dynomite, MotionDb, Voldemort, SubRecord
Key-Value Store (Ordered)	Actord, FoundationDB, Lightcloud, LMDB, Luxio, MemcacheDB, NMDB, Scalaris, TokyoTyrant
Data-Structures Server	Redis
Tuple Store	Apache River, Coord, GigaSpaces
Object Database	DB4O, Objectivity/DB, Perst, Shoal, ZopeDB
Document Store	Clusterpoint, Couchbase, CouchDB, DocumentDB, IBM Domino, MarkLogic, MongoDB, Qizx, RethinkDB, XML-databases
Wide Column Store	BigTable, Cassandra, Druid, HBase, Hypertable, KAI, KDI, OpenNeptune, Qbase

Correlation databases are model-independent, and instead of row-based or column-based storage, use value-based storage.

Key-value Store

Key-value (KV) stores use the associative array (also known as a map or dictionary) as their fundamental data model. In this model, data is represented as a collection of key-value pairs, such that each possible key appears at most once in the collection.

The key-value model is one of the simplest non-trivial data models, and richer data models are often implemented as an extension of it. The key-value model can be extended to a discretely ordered model that maintains keys in lexicographic order. This extension is computationally powerful, in that it can efficiently retrieve selective key *ranges*.

Key-value stores can use consistency models ranging from eventual consistency to serializability. Some databases support ordering of keys. There are various hardware implementations, and some users maintain data in memory (RAM), while others employ solid-state drives or rotating disks.

Examples include Oracle NoSQL Database, Redis, and dbm.

Document Store

The central concept of a document store is the notion of a "document". While each document-oriented database implementation differs on the details of this definition, in general, they all assume that documents encapsulate and encode data (or information) in some standard formats or encodings. Encodings in use include XML, YAML, and JSON as well as binary forms like BSON. Documents are addressed in the database via a unique *key* that represents that document. One of the other defining characteristics of a document-oriented database is that in addition to the key lookup performed by a key-value store, the database offers an API or query language that retrieves documents based on their contents.

Different implementations offer different ways of organizing and/or grouping documents:

- Collections

- Tags

- Non-visible metadata

- Directory hierarchies

Compared to relational databases, for example, collections could be considered analogous to tables and documents analogous to records. But they are different: every record in a table has the same sequence of fields, while documents in a collection may have fields that are completely different.

Graph

This kind of database is designed for data whose relations are well represented as a graph consisting of elements interconnected with a finite number of relations between them. The type of data could be social relations, public transport links, road maps or network topologies.

Graph databases and their query language

Name	Language(s)	Notes
AllegroGraph	SPARQL	RDF triple store
DEX/Sparksee	C++, Java, .NET, Python	Graph database
FlockDB	Scala	Graph database
IBM DB2	SPARQL	RDF triple store added in DB2 10
InfiniteGraph	Java	Graph database
MarkLogic	Java, JavaScript, SPARQL, XQuery	Multi-model document database and RDF triple store
Neo4j	Cypher	Graph database
OWLIM	Java, SPARQL 1.1	RDF triple store
Oracle	SPARQL 1.1	RDF triple store added in 11g
OrientDB	Java	Multi-model document and graph database

Sqrrl Enterprise	Java	Graph database
OpenLink Virtuoso	C++, C#, Java, SPARQL	Middleware and database engine hybrid
Stardog	Java, SPARQL	Graph database

Object Database

- db4o
- GemStone/S
- InterSystems Caché
- JADE
- ObjectDatabase++
- ObjectDB
- Objectivity/DB
- ObjectStore
- ODABA
- Perst
- OpenLink Virtuoso
- Versant Object Database
- ZODB

Tabular

- Apache Accumulo
- BigTable
- Apache Hbase
- Hypertable
- Mnesia
- OpenLink Virtuoso

Tuple Store

- Apache River
- GigaSpaces

- Tarantool
- TIBCO ActiveSpaces
- OpenLink Virtuoso

Triple/quad Store (RDF) Database

- AllegroGraph
- Apache JENA (It is a framework, not a database)
- MarkLogic
- Ontotext-OWLIM
- Oracle NoSQL database
- Virtuoso Universal Server
- Stardog

Hosted

- Amazon DynamoDB
- Amazon SimpleDB
- Datastore on Google Appengine
- Clusterpoint database
- Cloudant Data Layer (CouchDB)
- Freebase
- Microsoft Azure Tables
- Microsoft Azure DocumentDB
- OpenLink Virtuoso

Multivalue Databases

- D3 Pick database
- Extensible Storage Engine (ESE/NT)
- InfinityDB
- InterSystems Caché
- jBASE Pick database

- Northgate Information Solutions Reality, the original Pick/MV Database

- OpenQM

- Revelation Software's OpenInsight

- Rocket U2

Multimodel Database

- Couchbase

- FoundationDB

- MarkLogic

- OrientDB

Performance

Ben Scofield rated different categories of NoSQL databases as follows:

Data Model	Performance	Scalability	Flexibility	Complexity	Functionality
Key–Value Store	high	high	high	none	variable (none)
Column-Oriented Store	high	high	moderate	low	minimal
Document-Oriented Store	high	variable (high)	high	low	variable (low)
Graph Database	variable	variable	high	high	graph theory
Relational Database	variable	variable	low	moderate	relational algebra

Performance and scalability comparisons are sometimes done with the YCSB benchmark.

Handling Relational Data

Since most NoSQL databases lack ability for joins in queries, the database schema generally needs to be designed differently. There are three main techniques for handling relational data in a NoSQL database.

Multiple Queries

Instead of retrieving all the data with one query, it's common to do several queries to get the desired data. NoSQL queries are often faster than traditional SQL queries so the cost of having to do additional queries may be acceptable. If an excessive number of queries would be necessary, one of the other two approaches is more appropriate.

Caching/Replication/Non-normalized Data

Instead of only storing foreign keys, it's common to store actual foreign values along with the model's data. For example, each blog comment might include the username in addition to a user id, thus providing easy access to the username without requiring another lookup. When a username changes however, this will now need to be changed in many places in the database. Thus this approach works better when reads are much more common than writes.

Nesting Data

With document databases like MongoDB it's common to put more data in a smaller number of collections. For example, in a blogging application, one might choose to store comments within the blog post document so that with a single retrieval one gets all the comments. Thus in this approach a single document contains all the data you need for a specific task.

ACID and JOIN Support

If a database is marked as supporting ACID or joins, then the documentation for the database makes that claim. The degree to which the capability is fully supported in a manner similar to most SQL databases or the degree to which it meets the needs of a specific application is left up to the reader to assess.

Database	ACID	Joins
Aerospike	Yes	No
ArangoDB	Yes	Yes
CouchDB	Yes	Yes
c-treeACE	Yes	Yes
HyperDex	Yes	Yes
InfinityDB	Yes	No
LMDB	Yes	No
MarkLogic	Yes	Yes[nb 2]
OrientDB	Yes	Yes

1. HyperDex currently offers ACID support via its Warp extension, which is a commercial add-on.

2. Joins do not necessarily apply to document databases, but MarkLogic can do joins using semantics.

References

- Gray, Jim & Andreas Reuter. Distributed Transaction Processing: Concepts and Techniques. Morgan Kaufmann, 1993; ISBN 1-55860-190-2.

- Martin, James (1983). Managing the Data-base Environment. Englewood Cliffs, New Jersey: Prentice-Hall. p. 381. ISBN 0-135-50582-8.

- Don Chamberlin (1998). A Complete Guide to DB2 Universal Database. Morgan Kaufmann. pp. 28–32. ISBN 978-1-55860-482-7.

- Codd, E.F. (1990). The Relational Model for Database Management (Version 2 ed.). Addison Wesley Publishing Company. ISBN 0-201-14192-2.

- Jim Melton; Jim Melton Alan R. Simon (1993). Understanding The New SQL: A Complete Guide. Morgan Kaufmann. pp. 145–147. ISBN 978-1-55860-245-8.

- Jim Melton; Alan R. Simon (2002). SQL:1999: Understanding Relational Language Components. Morgan Kaufmann. p. 53. ISBN 978-1-55860-456-8.

- C. Date (2011). SQL and Relational Theory: How to Write Accurate SQL Code. O'Reilly Media, Inc. p. 83. ISBN 978-1-4493-1640-2.

- Martyn Prigmore (2007). Introduction to Databases With Web Applications. Pearson Education Canada. p. 197. ISBN 978-0-321-26359-9.

- Steven Feuerstein; Bill Pribyl (2009). Oracle PL/SQL Programming. O'Reilly Media, Inc. pp. 74, 91. ISBN 978-0-596-51446-4.

- Date, Christopher (2003). "5: Integrity". An Introduction to Database Systems. Addison-Wesley. pp. 268–276. ISBN 978-0-321-18956-1.

- Coronel, Carlos (2010). Database Systems: Design, Implementation, and Management. Independence KY: South-Western/Cengage Learning. p. 65. ISBN 978-0-538-74884-1.

- MySQL AB (2006). MySQL Administrator's Guide and Language Reference. Sams Publishing. p. 40. ISBN 0-672-32870-4.

- Grolinger, K.; Higashino, W. A.; Tiwari, A.; Capretz, M. A. M. (2013). "Data management in cloud environments: NoSQL and NewSQL data stores" (PDF). Aira, Springer. Retrieved 8 Jan 2014.

- "RDBMS dominate the database market, but NoSQL systems are catching up". DB-Engines.com. 21 Nov 2013. Retrieved 24 Nov 2013.

Computer Languages used in Database Management

The computer languages used in database management are data definition language, data manipulation language and query language. Database definition language is a syntax that is very similar to programming languages and helps in defining data structures. The major components of database management are discussed in the following section.

Data Definition Language

A data definition language or data description language (DDL) is a syntax similar to a computer programming language for defining data structures, especially database schemas.

History

The concept of the data definition language and its name was first introduced in relation to the Codasyl database model, where the schema of the database was written in a language syntax describing the records, fields, and sets of the user data model. Later it was used to refer to a subset of Structured Query Language (SQL) for creating tables and constraints. SQL-92 introduced a schema manipulation language and schema information tables to query schemas. These information tables were specified as SQL/Schemata in SQL:2003. The term DDL is also used in a generic sense to refer to any formal language for describing data or information structures.

Structured Query Language

Many data description languages use a declarative syntax to define columns and data types. Structured query language (e.g., SQL), however, uses a collection of imperative verbs whose effect is to modify the schema of the database by adding, changing, or deleting definitions of tables or other elements. These statements can be freely mixed with other SQL statements, making the DDL not a separate language.

CREATE Statement

The *CREATE* command is used to establish a new database, table, index, or stored procedure.

The *CREATE* statement in SQL creates a component in a relational database management system (RDBMS). In the SQL 1992 specification, the types of components that can be created are schemas, tables, views, domains, character sets, collations, translations, and assertions. Many implementations extend the syntax to allow creation of additional elements, such as indexes and user profiles. Some systems, such as PostgreSQL and SQL Server, allow *CREATE*, and other DDL commands, inside a database transaction and thus they may be rolled back.

CREATE TABLE Statement

A commonly used *CREATE* command is the *CREATE TABLE* command. The typical usage is:

CREATE TABLE *[table name]* (*[column definitions]*) *[table parameters]*

The column definitions are:

- A comma-separated list consisting of any of the following

- Column definition: *[column name] [data type] {NULL | NOT NULL} {column options}*

- Primary key definition: *PRIMARY KEY ([comma separated column list])*

- Constraints: *{CONSTRAINT} [constraint definition]*

- RDBMS specific functionality

An example statement to create a table named *employees* with a few columns is:

CREATE TABLE employees (

   id   INTEGER   PRIMARY KEY,

   first_name   VARCHAR(50) not null,

   last_name   VARCHAR(75) not null,

   fname   VARCHAR(50) not null,

   dateofbirth DATE   not null

);

Some forms of *CREATE TABLE DDL* may incorporate DML (data manipulation language)-like constructs, such as the *CREATE TABLE AS SELECT* (CTAS) syntax of SQL.

DROP Statement

The *DROP* statement destroys an existing database, table, index, or view.

A *DROP* statement in SQL removes a component from a relational database management system (RDBMS). The types of objects that can be dropped depends on which RDBMS is being used, but most support the dropping of tables, users, and databases. Some systems (such as PostgreSQL) allow DROP and other DDL commands to occur inside of a transaction and thus be rolled back. The typical usage is simply:

DROP *objecttype objectname.*

For example, the command to drop a table named employees is:

DROP TABLE employees;

The *DROP* statement is distinct from the *DELETE* and *TRUNCATE* statements, in that *DELETE* and *TRUNCATE* do not remove the table itself. For example, a *DELETE* statement might delete some (or all) data from a table while leaving the table itself in the database, whereas a *DROP* statement removes the entire table from the database.

ALTER Statement

The *ALTER* statement modifies an existing database object.

An *ALTER* statement in SQL changes the properties of an object inside of a relational database management system (RDBMS). The types of objects that can be altered depends on which RDBMS is being used. The typical usage is:

ALTER *objecttype objectname parameters.*

For example, the command to add (then remove) a column named bubbles for an existing table named sink is:

ALTER TABLE sink ADD bubbles INTEGER;

ALTER TABLE sink DROP COLUMN bubbles;

RENAME Statement

The *RENAME* statement is used to rename a database table.

RENAME TABLE old_name TO new_name;

TRUNCATE Statement

The *TRUNCATE* statement is used to delete all data from a table. It's much faster than *DELETE*.

TRUNCATE TABLE table_name;

Referential Integrity Statements

Another type of DDL sentence in SQL is used to define referential integrity relationships, usually implemented as primary key and foreign key tags in some columns of the tables. These two statements can be included in a *CREATE TABLE* or an *ALTER TABLE* sentence.

Other Languages

- XML Schema is an example of a DDL for XML.

Data Manipulation Language

A data manipulation language (DML) is a family of syntax elements similar to a computer programming language used for selecting, inserting, deleting and updating data in a database. Performing read-only queries of data is sometimes also considered a component of DML.

A popular data manipulation language is that of Structured Query Language (SQL), which is used to retrieve and manipulate data in a relational database. Other forms of DML are those used by IMS/DLI, CODASYL databases, such as IDMS and others.

Data manipulation language comprises the SQL data change statements, which modify stored data but not the schema or database objects. Manipulation of persistent database objects, e.g., tables or stored procedures, via the SQL schema statements, rather than the data stored within them, is considered to be part of a separate data definition language. In SQL these two categories are similar in their detailed syntax, data types, expressions etc., but distinct in their overall function.

Data manipulation languages have their functional capability organized by the initial word in a statement, which is almost always a verb. In the case of SQL, these verbs are:

- *SELECT ... FROM ... WHERE ...*

- *INSERT INTO ... VALUES ...*

- *UPDATE ... SET ... WHERE ...*

- *DELETE FROM ... WHERE ...*

The *SELECT* query statement is classed with the *SQL-data* statements and so is considered by the standard to be outside of DML. The *SELECT ... INTO* form is considered to be DML because it manipulates (i.e. modifies) data. In common practice though, this distinction is not made and *SELECT* is widely considered to be part of DML.

Most SQL database implementations extend their SQL capabilities by providing imperative, i.e. procedural languages. Examples of these are Oracle's PL/SQL and DB2's SQL_PL.

Data manipulation languages tend to have many different flavors and capabilities between database vendors. There have been a number of standards established for SQL by ANSI, but vendors still provide their own extensions to the standard while not implementing the entire standard.

Data manipulation languages are divided into two types, procedural programming and declarative programming.

Data manipulation languages were initially only used within computer programs, but with the advent of SQL have come to be used interactively by database administrators.

For example, the command to insert a row into table employees:

INSERT INTO employees(first_name, last_name, fname) VALUES ('John', 'Capita', 'xcapitoo');

Query Language

Query languages are computer languages used to make queries in databases and information systems.

Types

Broadly, query languages can be classified according to whether they are database query languages or information retrieval query languages. The difference is that a database query language attempts to give factual answers to factual questions, while an information retrieval query language attempts to find documents containing information that is relevant to an area of inquiry.

Examples

Examples include:

- .QL is a proprietary object-oriented query language for querying relational databases; successor of Datalog;

- Contextual Query Language (CQL) a formal language for representing queries to information retrieval systems such as web indexes or bibliographic catalogues.

- CQLF (CODYASYL Query Language, Flat) is a query language for CODASYL-type databases;

- Concept-Oriented Query Language (COQL) is used in the concept-oriented model (COM). It is based on a novel data modeling construct, concept, and uses such operations as projection and de-projection for multi-dimensional analysis, analytical operations and inference;

- Cypher is a query language for the Neo4j graph database;

- DMX is a query language for Data Mining models;

- Datalog is a query language for deductive databases;

- F-logic is a declarative object-oriented language for deductive databases and knowledge representation.

- FQL enables you to use a SQL-style interface to query the data exposed by the Graph API. It provides advanced features not available in the Graph API.

- Gellish English is a language that can be used for queries in Gellish English Databases, for dialogues (requests and responses) as well as for information modeling and knowledge modeling;

- Gremlin is an Apache Software Foundation graph traversal language for OLTP and OLAP graph systems.

- HTSQL is a query language that translates HTTP queries to SQL;

- ISBL is a query language for PRTV, one of the earliest relational database management systems;

- LINQ query-expressions is a way to query various data sources from .NET languages

- LDAP is an application protocol for querying and modifying directory services running over TCP/IP;

- LogiQL is a variant of Datalog and is the query language for the LogicBlox system.

- MQL is a cheminformatics query language for a substructure search allowing beside nominal properties also numerical properties;

- MDX is a query language for OLAP databases;

- N1QL is a Couchbase's query language finding data in Couchbase Servers;

- OQL is Object Query Language;

- OCL (Object Constraint Language). Despite its name, OCL is also an object query language and an OMG standard;

- OPath, intended for use in querying WinFS *Stores*;

- OttoQL, intended for querying tables, XML, and databases;

- Poliqarp Query Language is a special query language designed to analyze annotated text. Used in the Poliqarp search engine;

- PQL is a special-purpose programming language for managing process models based on information about scenarios that these models describe;

- QUEL is a relational database access language, similar in most ways to SQL;

- RDQL is a RDF query language;

- ReQL is a query language used in RethinkDB;

- SMARTS is the cheminformatics standard for a substructure search;

- SPARQL is a query language for RDF graphs;

- SPL is a search language for machine-generated big data, based upon Unix Piping and SQL.

- SCL is the Software Control Language to query and manipulate Endevor objects

- SQL is a well known query language and Data Manipulation Language for relational databases;

- SuprTool is a proprietary query language for SuprTool, a database access program used for accessing data in *Image/SQL* (formerly TurboIMAGE) and Oracle databases;

- TMQL Topic Map Query Language is a query language for Topic Maps;

- TQL is a language used to query topology for HP products
- Tutorial D is a query language for truly relational database management systems (TRDBMS);
- XQuery is a query language for XML data sources;
- XPath is a declarative language for navigating XML documents;
- XSPARQL is an integrated query language combining XQuery with SPARQL to query both XML and RDF data sources at once;
- YQL is an SQL-like query language created by Yahoo!
- Search engine query languages, e.g., as used by Google or Bing

Database Security: A Comprehensive Study

Database security is a process that is used to protect a database. The types of information security control are access control, auditing, authentication, encryption, backups and application security. The topics discussed in the chapter are of great importance the existing knowledge on database security.

Database Security

Database security concerns the use of a broad range of information security controls to protect databases (potentially including the data, the database applications or stored functions, the database systems, the database servers and the associated network links) against compromises of their confidentiality, integrity and availability. It involves various types or categories of controls, such as technical, procedural/administrative and physical. *Database security* is a specialist topic within the broader realms of computer security, information security and risk management.

Security risks to database systems include, for example:

- Unauthorized or unintended activity or misuse by authorized database users, database administrators, or network/systems managers, or by unauthorized users or hackers (e.g. inappropriate access to sensitive data, metadata or functions within databases, or inappropriate changes to the database programs, structures or security configurations);

- Malware infections causing incidents such as unauthorized access, leakage or disclosure of personal or proprietary data, deletion of or damage to the data or programs, interruption or denial of authorized access to the database, attacks on other systems and the unanticipated failure of database services;

- Overloads, performance constraints and capacity issues resulting in the inability of authorized users to use databases as intended;

- Physical damage to database servers caused by computer room fires or floods, overheating, lightning, accidental liquid spills, static discharge, electronic breakdowns/equipment failures and obsolescence;

- Design flaws and programming bugs in databases and the associated programs and systems, creating various security vulnerabilities (e.g. unauthorized privilege escalation), data loss/corruption, performance degradation etc.;

- Data corruption and/or loss caused by the entry of invalid data or commands, mistakes in database or system administration processes, sabotage/criminal damage etc.

Ross J. Anderson has often said that by their nature large databases will never be free of abuse by breaches of security; if a large system is designed for ease of access it becomes insecure; if made watertight it becomes impossible to use. This is sometimes known as Anderson's Rule.

Many layers and types of information security control are appropriate to databases, including:

- Access control

- Auditing

- Authentication

- Encryption

- Integrity controls

- Backups

- Application security

- Database Security applying Statistical Method

Databases have been largely secured against hackers through network security measures such as firewalls, and network-based intrusion detection systems. While network security controls remain valuable in this regard, securing the database systems themselves, and the programs/functions and data within them, has arguably become more critical as networks are increasingly opened to wider access, in particular access from the Internet. Furthermore, system, program, function and data access controls, along with the associated user identification, authentication and rights management functions, have always been important to limit and in some cases log the activities of authorized users and administrators. In other words, these are complementary approaches to database security, working from both the outside-in and the inside-out as it were.

Many organizations develop their own "baseline" security standards and designs detailing basic security control measures for their database systems. These may reflect general information security requirements or obligations imposed by corporate information security policies and applicable laws and regulations (e.g. concerning privacy, financial management and reporting systems), along with generally accepted good database security practices (such as appropriate hardening of the underlying systems) and perhaps security recommendations from the relevant database system and software vendors. The security designs for specific database systems typically specify further security administration and management functions (such as administration and reporting of user access rights, log management and analysis, database replication/synchronization and backups) along with various business-driven information security controls within the database programs and functions (e.g. data entry validation and audit trails). Furthermore, various security-related activities (manual controls) are normally incorporated into the procedures, guidelines etc. relating to the design, development, configuration, use, management and maintenance of databases.

Privileges

Two types of privileges are important relating to database security within the database environment: system privileges and object privileges.

System Privileges

System privileges allow a user to perform administrative actions in a database. These include privileges (as found in SQL Server) such as: create database, create procedure, create view, backup database, create table, create trigger, and execute.

Object Privileges

Object privileges allow for the use of certain operations on database objects as authorized by another user. Examples include: usage, select, insert, update, and references. –

The Principal of least Privilege, and Separation of Duties:

Databases fall under internal controls, that is, data used for public reporting, annual reports, etc.) are subject to the separation of duties, meaning there must be segregation of tasks between development, and production. Each task has to be validated (via code walk-through/fresh eyes) by a third person who is not writing the actual code. The database developer should not be able to execute anything in production without an independent review of the documentation/code for the work that is being performed. Typically, the role of the developer is to pass code to a DBA; however, given the cutbacks that have resulted from the economic downturn, a DBA might not be readily available. If a DBA is not involved, it is important, at minimum, for a peer to conduct a code review. This ensures that the role of the developer is clearly separate.

Another point of internal control is adherence to the principle of providing the least amount of privileges, especially in production. To allow developers more access to get their work done, it is much safer to use impersonation for exceptions that require elevated privileges (e.g. *EXECUTE AS* or sudo to do that temporarily). Often developers may dismiss this as "overhead" while on their path to coding glory. Please be aware, however, that DBAs must do all that is considered responsible because they are the *de facto* data stewards of the organization and must comply with regulations and the law.

Vulnerability Assessments to Manage Risk and Compliance

One technique for evaluating database security involves performing vulnerability assessments or penetration tests against the database. Testers attempt to find security vulnerabilities that could be used to defeat or bypass security controls, break into the database, compromise the system etc. Database administrators or information security administrators may for example use automated vulnerability scans to search out misconfiguration of controls (often referred to as 'drift') within the layers mentioned above along with known vulnerabilities within the database software. The results of such scans are used to harden the database (improve security) and close off the specific vulnerabilities identified, but other vulnerabilities often remain unrecognized and unaddressed.

In database environments where security is critical, continual monitoring for compliance with standards improves security. Security compliance requires, amongst other procedures, patch management and the review and management of permissions (especially public) granted to objects within the database. Database objects may include table or other objects listed in the Table link. The permissions granted for SQL language commands on objects are considered in this process. Compliance monitoring is similar to vulnerability assessment, except that the results of vulnerability assessments generally drive the security standards that lead to the continuous monitoring program. Essentially, vulnerability assessment is a preliminary procedure to determine risk where a compliance program is the process of on-going risk assessment.

The compliance program should take into consideration any dependencies at the application software level as changes at the database level may have effects on the application software or the application server.

Abstraction

Application level authentication and authorization mechanisms may be effective means of providing abstraction from the database layer. The primary benefit of abstraction is that of a single sign-on capability across multiple databases and platforms. A single sign-on system stores the database user's credentials and authenticates to the database on behalf of the user.

Database Activity Monitoring (DAM)

Another security layer of a more sophisticated nature includes real-time database activity monitoring, either by analyzing protocol traffic (SQL) over the network, or by observing local database activity on each server using software agents, or both. Use of agents or native logging is required to capture activities executed on the database server, which typically include the activities of the database administrator. Agents allow this information to be captured in a fashion that can not be disabled by the database administrator, who has the ability to disable or modify native audit logs.

Analysis can be performed to identify known exploits or policy breaches, or baselines can be captured over time to build a normal pattern used for detection of anomalous activity that could be indicative of intrusion. These systems can provide a comprehensive database audit trail in addition to the intrusion detection mechanisms, and some systems can also provide protection by terminating user sessions and/or quarantining users demonstrating suspicious behavior. Some systems are designed to support separation of duties (SOD), which is a typical requirement of auditors. SOD requires that the database administrators who are typically monitored as part of the DAM, not be able to disable or alter the DAM functionality. This requires the DAM audit trail to be securely stored in a separate system not administered by the database administration group.

Native Audit

In addition to using external tools for monitoring or auditing, native database audit capabilities are also available for many database platforms. The native audit trails are extracted on a regular basis and transferred to a designated security system where the database administrators do/ should not have access. This ensures a certain level of segregation of duties that may provide evidence the native audit trails were not modified by authenticated administrators, and should be conducted by a security-oriented senior DBA group with read rights into production. Turning on native impacts the performance of the server. Generally, the native audit trails of databases do not provide sufficient controls to enforce separation of duties; therefore, the network and/or kernel module level host based monitoring capabilities provides a higher degree of confidence for forensics and preservation of evidence.

Process and Procedures

A good database security program includes the regular review of privileges granted to user accounts and accounts used by automated processes. For individual accounts a two-factor authentication system improves security but adds complexity and cost. Accounts used by automated processes require appropriate controls around password storage such as sufficient encryption and access controls to reduce the risk of compromise.

In conjunction with a sound database security program, an appropriate disaster recovery program can ensure that service is not interrupted during a security incident, or any incident that results in an outage of the primary database environment. An example is that of replication for the primary databases to sites located in different geographical regions.

After an incident occurs, database forensics can be employed to determine the scope of the breach, and to identify appropriate changes to systems and processes.

Database Activity Monitoring

Database activity monitoring (DAM) is a database security technology for monitoring and analyzing database activity that operates independently of the database management system (DBMS) and does not rely on any form of native (DBMS-resident) auditing or native logs such as trace or transaction logs. DAM is typically performed continuously and in real-time.

Database activity monitoring and prevention (DAMP) is an extension to DAM that goes beyond monitoring and alerting to also block unauthorized activities.

DAM helps businesses address regulatory compliance mandates like the Payment Card Industry Data Security Standard (PCI DSS), the Health Insurance Portability and Accountability Act (HIPAA), the Sarbanes-Oxley Act (SOX), U.S. government regulations such as NIST 800-53, and EU regulations.

DAM is also an important technology for protecting sensitive databases from external attacks by cybercriminals. According to the 2009 Verizon Business' Data Breach Investigations Report—based on data analyzed from Verizon Business' caseload of 90 confirmed breaches involving 285 million compromised records during 2008—75 percent of all breached records came from compromised database servers.

According to Gartner, "DAM provides privileged user and application access monitoring that is independent of native database logging and audit functions. It can function as a compensating control for privileged user separation-of-duties issues by monitoring administrator activity. The technology also improves database security by detecting unusual database read and update activity from the application layer. Database event aggregation, correlation and reporting provide a database audit capability without the need to enable native database audit functions (which become resource-intensive as the level of auditing is increased)."

According to a survey by the Independent Oracle User Group (IOUG), "Most organizations do not have mechanisms in place to prevent database administrators and other privileged database users from reading or tampering with sensitive information in financial, HR, or other business applications. Most are still unable to even detect such breaches or incidents."

Forrester refers to this category as "database auditing and real-time protection".

Common Use Cases for DAM

Privileged User Monitoring: Monitoring privileged users (or superusers), such as database administrators (DBAs), systems administrators (or sysadmins), developers, help desk, and outsourced personnel – who typically have unfettered access to corporate databases – is essential for protecting against both external and internal threats. Privileged user monitoring includes auditing all activities and transactions; identifying anomalous activities (such as viewing sensitive data, or creating new accounts with superuser privileges); and reconciling observed activities (such as adding or deleting tables) with authorized change requests.

Since most organizations are already protected at the perimeter level, indeed a major concern lies with the need to monitor and protect from privileged users. There is a high correlation therefore between Database Security and the need to protect from the insider threat. This is a complex task as most privileged users are capable of using sophisticated techniques to attack the database - stored procedures, triggers, views and obfuscated traffic - attacks that may be difficult to detect using traditional methods.

In addition, since targeted attacks frequently result in attackers gaining privileged user credentials, monitoring of privileged activities is also an effective way to identify compromised systems.

As a result, auditors are now demanding monitoring of privileged users for security best practices as well as a wide range of regulations. Privileged user monitoring helps ensure:

• Data privacy, so that only authorized applications and users are viewing sensitive data.
• Data governance, so that critical database structures and values are not being changed outside of corporate change control procedures.

Application Activity Monitoring: The primary purpose of application activity monitoring is to provide a greater level of end-user accountability and detect fraud (and other abuses of legitimate access) that occurs via enterprise applications, rather than via direct access to the database.

Multi-tier enterprise applications such as Oracle EBS, PeopleSoft, JD Edwards, SAP, Siebel Systems, Business Intelligence, and custom applications built on standard middle-tier servers such as IBM WebSphere and Oracle WebLogic Server mask the identity of end-users at the database transaction level. This is done with an optimization mechanism known as "connection pooling." Using pooled connections, the application aggregates all user traffic within a few database connections that are identified only by a generic service account name. Application activity monitoring allows organizations to associate specific database transactions with particular application end-users, in order to identify unauthorized or suspicious activities.

End-user accountability is often required for data governance requirements such as the Sarbanes–Oxley Act. New auditor guidance from the Public Company Accounting Oversight Board for SOX compliance has also increased the emphasis on anti-fraud controls.

Cyberattack Protection: SQL injection is a type of attack used to exploit bad coding practices in applications that use relational databases. The attacker uses the application to send a SQL statement that is composed from an application statement concatenated with an additional statement that the attacker introduces.

Many application developers compose SQL statements by concatenating strings and do not use prepared statement; in this case the application is susceptible to a SQL injection attack. The technique transforms an application SQL statement from an innocent SQL call to a malicious call that can cause unauthorized access, deletion of data, or theft of information.

One way that DAM can prevent SQL injection is by monitoring the application activity, generating a baseline of "normal behavior", and identifying an attack based on a divergence from normal SQL structures and normal sequences. Alternative approaches monitor the memory of the database, where both the database execution plan and the context of the SQL statements are visible, and based on policy can provide granular protection at the object level.

Core Features of DAM

As defined by Gartner, "DAM tools use several data collection mechanisms (such as server-based agent software and in-line or out-of-band network collectors), aggregate the data in a central location for analysis, and report based on behaviors that violate the security policies and/or signatures or indicate behavioral anomalies. DAM demand is driven primarily by the need for privileged user monitoring to address compliance-related audit findings, and by threat-management requirements to monitor database access. Enterprise DAM requirements are beginning to broaden, extending beyond basic functions, such as the capability to detect malicious activity or inappropriate or unapproved database administrator (DBA) access."

More advanced DAM functions include:

- The ability to monitor intra-database attacks and back-doors in real time (such as stored procedures, triggers, views, etc.)

- A solution which is agnostic to most IT infrastructure variables - such as encryption or network topology

- Blocking and prevention, without being in-line to the transactions

- Active discovery of at-risk data

- Improved visibility into application traffic

- The ability to offer database activity monitoring in virtualized environments, or even in the cloud, where there is no well-defined or consistent network topology

Some enterprises are also seeking other functions, including:

- Configuration auditing to comply with audits required by the U.S. Sarbanes-Oxley Act

- DLP capabilities that address security concerns, as well as the data identification and protection requirements of the Payment Card Industry (PCI) and other data-centric regulatory frameworks

- Database user rights attestation reporting, required by a broad range of regulations

- The ability to offer database activity monitoring in virtualized environments, or even in the cloud, where there is no well-defined or consistent network topology

- Better integration with vulnerability scanning products

Common DAM Architectures

Interception-based: Most modern DAM systems collect what the database is doing by being able to "see" the communications between the database client and the database server. What DAM systems do is find places where they can view the communication stream and get the requests and responses without requiring participation from the database. The interception itself can be done at multiple points such as the database memory (e.g. the SGA), at the network (using a network TAP or a SPAN port if the communication is not encrypted), at the operating system level, or at the level of the database libraries.

If there is unencrypted network traffic, then packet sniffing can be used. The advantage is that no processing is done on the host, however the main disadvantage is that both local traffic and sophisticated intra-database attacks will not be detected. To capture local access some network based vendors deploy a probe that runs on the host. This probe intercepts all local access and can also intercept all networked access in case you do not want to use network gear or in case the database communications are encrypted. However, since the agent does not do all the processing — instead it relays the data to the DAM appliance where all the processing occurs — it may impact network performance with all of the local traffic and real-time session termination may be too slow to interrupt unauthorized queries.

Memory-based: Some DAM systems have a lightweight sensor that attaches to the protected databases and continuously polls the system global area (SGA) to collect SQL statements as they are being performed. A similar architecture was previously used by performance optimization products that also used the SGA and other shared data structures.

In the latest versions of this technology a lightweight sensor runs on the host and attaches to the process at the OS level to inspect private data structures. The advantages of this approach are significant:

- Complete coverage of all database transactions — the sensor covers traffic coming from the network, from the host, as well as from back-doors (stored procedures, triggers, views)

- A solution that is agnostic to most IT infrastructure variables - no need to re-architect the network, to open span ports or to worry about key management if the network is encrypted, and this model can also be used to protect databases deployed in virtualized environments or in the cloud

Log-based: Some DAM systems analyze and extract the information from the transaction logs (e.g., the redo logs). These systems use the fact that much of the data is stored within the redo logs and they scrape these logs. Unfortunately, not all of the information that is required is in the redo logs. For example, SELECT statements are not and so these systems will augment the data that they gather from the redo logs with data that they collect from the native audit trails as shown in

Figure 3. These systems are a hybrid between a true DAM system (that is fully independent from the DBMS) and a SIEM which relies on data generated by the database. These architectures usually imply more overhead on the database server.

Other Names for DAM

Enterprise database auditing and real-time protection

HP Atalla

HP Atalla is a security vendor, with experience in data security and cryptography. Atalla is required to meet government standards while providing end-to-end network security.

On September 7, 2016, HPE CEO Meg Whitman announced that the software assets of Hewlett Packard Enterprise, including Atalla, would be spun out and then merged with Micro Focus to create an independent company of which HP Enterprise shareholders would retain majority ownership. Micro Focus CEO Kevin Loosemore called the transaction "entirely consistent with our established acquisition strategy and our focus on efficient management of mature infrastructure products" and indicated that Micro Focus intended to "bring the core earnings margin for the mature assets in the deal - about 80 percent of the total - from 21 percent today to Micro Focus's existing 46 percent level within three years."

Product Overview

Atalla is a multi-chip embedded cryptographic module, which consists of a hardware platform, a firmware secure loader, and firmware. The purpose of the module is to load Approved application programs, also referred to as personalities, securely. The firmware monitors the physical security of the cryptographic module. Verification that the module is approved can be observed.

The Atalla security policy addresses the hardware and the firmware secure loader. This approach creates a security platform able to load secure code. Once control passes from the loader, the module is no longer operating in FIPS mode. Note: that no personality will have access to the module's secret keys. The cryptographic boundary of the ACS for the FIPS 140-2 Level 3 validation is the outer perimeter of the secure metal enclosure that encompasses all critical security components.

Data Breach

A data breach is the intentional or unintentional release of secure or private/confidential information to an untrusted environment. Other terms for this phenomenon include unintentional information disclosure, data leak and also data spill. Incidents range from concerted attack by black hats associated with organized crime, political activist or national governments to careless disposal of used computer equipment or data storage media.

Definition: "A data breach is a security incident in which sensitive, protected or confidential data is copied, transmitted, viewed, stolen or used by an individual unauthorized to do so." Data breaches may involve financial information such as credit card or bank details, personal health information (PHI), Personally identifiable information (PII), trade secrets of corporations or intellectual property. Most data breaches involve overexposed and vulnerable unstructured data - files, documents, and sensitive information.

According to the nonprofit consumer organization Privacy Rights Clearinghouse, a total of 227,052,199 individual records containing sensitive personal information were involved in security breaches in the United States between January 2005 and May 2008, excluding incidents where sensitive data was apparently not actually exposed.

Many jurisdictions have passed data breach notification laws, requiring a company that has been subject to a data breach to inform customers and take other steps to remediate possible injuries.

Definition

This may include incidents such as theft or loss of digital media such as computer tapes, hard drives, or laptop computers containing such media upon which such information is stored unencrypted, posting such information on the world wide web or on a computer otherwise accessible from the Internet without proper information security precautions, transfer of such information to a system which is not completely open but is not appropriately or formally accredited for security at the approved level, such as unencrypted e-mail, or transfer of such information to the information systems of a possibly hostile agency, such as a competing corporation or a foreign nation, where it may be exposed to more intensive decryption techniques.

ISO/IEC 27040 defines a data breach as: *compromise of security that leads to the accidental or unlawful destruction, loss, alteration, unauthorized disclosure of, or access to protected data transmitted, stored or otherwise processed.*

Trusted Environment

The notion of a trusted environment is somewhat fluid. The departure of a trusted staff member with access to sensitive information can become a data breach if the staff member retains access to the data subsequent to termination of the trust relationship. In distributed systems, this can also occur with a breakdown in a web of trust.

Data Privacy

Most such incidents publicized in the media involve private information on individuals, *i.e.* social security numbers, *etc.*. Loss of corporate information such as trade secrets, sensitive corporate information, details of contracts, *etc.* or of government information is frequently unreported, as there is no compelling reason to do so in the absence of potential damage to private citizens, and the publicity around such an event may be more damaging than the loss of the data itself.

Insider Versus External Threats

Those working inside an organization are a major cause of data breaches. Estimates of breaches caused by accidental "human factor" errors range from 37% by Ponemon Institute to 14% by the Verizon 2013 Data Breach Investigations Report. The external threat category includes hackers, cybercriminal organizations and state-sponsored actors. Professional associations for IT asset managers work aggressively with IT professionals to educate them on best risk-reduction practices for both internal and external threats to IT assets, software and information. While security prevention may deflect a high percentage of attempts, ultimately a motivated attacker will likely find a way into any given network. One of the top 10 quotes from Cisco CEO John Chambers is, "There are two types of companies: those that have been hacked, and those that don't know they have been hacked." FBI Special Agent for Cyber Special Operations Leo Taddeo warned on Bloomberg television, "The notion that you can protect your perimeter is falling by the wayside & detection is now critical."

Medical Data Breach

Some celebrities have found themselves to be the victims of inappropriate medical record access breaches, albeit more so on an individual basis, not part of a typically much larger breach. Given the series of medical data breaches and the lack of public trust, some countries have enacted laws requiring safeguards to be put in place to protect the security and confidentiality of medical information as it is shared electronically and to give patients some important rights to monitor their medical records and receive notification for loss and unauthorized acquisition of health information. The United States and the EU have imposed mandatory medical data breach notifications.

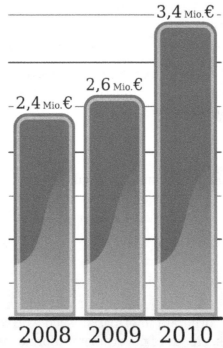

Average cost of data breaches in Germany

Consequences

Although such incidents pose the risk of identity theft or other serious consequences, in most cases there is no lasting damage; either the breach in security is remedied before the information is accessed by unscrupulous people, or the thief is only interested in the hardware stolen, not the data it contains. Nevertheless, when such incidents become publicly known, it is customary for the offending party to attempt to mitigate damages by providing to the victims subscription to a credit reporting agency, for instance, new credit cards, or other instruments. In the case of Target, the 2013 breach cost Target a significant drop in profit, which dove an estimated 40 percent in the 4th quarter of the year.

The Yahoo breach disclosed in 2016 may be one of the most expensive today. It may lower the price of its acquisition by Verizon by $1 billion. Cybercrime cost energy and utilities companies an average of $12.8 million each year in lost business and damaged equipment according to DNV GL, an international certification body and classification society based in Norway. Data breaches cost healthcare organizations $6.2 billion in the last two years (presumably 2014 and 2015), according to a Ponemon study.

Major Incidents

2016

- In March 2016, the COMELEC website of Philippines got defaced by hacktivist group, "Anonymous Philippines". A larger problem arose when a group called LulsZec Pilipinas uploaded COMELEC's entire database on Facebook the following day.

- In April 2016, news media carried information stolen from a successful network attack of the Central American law firm, Mossack Fonesca, and the resulting "Panama Papers" sent reverberations throughout the world. Perhaps a justified vindication of illegal or unethical activity, this nonetheless illustrates the impact of secrets coming to light. The Prime Minister of Iceland was forced to resign and a major reshuffling of political offices occurred in countries as far flung as Malta. Multiple investigations were immediately initiated in countries around the world, including a hard look at international or offshore banking rules in the U.S. Obviously the implications are enormous to the ability of an organization—whether a law firm or a governmental department—to keep secrets.

- In September 2016 Yahoo reported that up to 500 million accounts in 2014 had been breached in an apparent "state sponsored" data breach.

2015

- In October 2015, the British telecommunications provider TalkTalk suffered a data breach when a group of 15-year-old hackers stole information on its 4 million customers. The stock price of the company fell substantially due to the issue – around 12% – owing largely to the bad publicity surrounding the leak.

- In July 2015, adult website Ashley Madison suffered a data breach when a hacker group stole information on its 37 million users. The hackers threatened to reveal user names and specifics if Ashley Madison and a fellow site, EstablishedMen.com, did not shut down permanently.

- In February 2015, Anthem suffered a data breach of nearly 80 million records, including personal information such as names, Social Security numbers, dates of birth, and other sensitive details.

- In June 2015, The Office of Personnel Management of the U.S. government suffered a data breach in which the records of 4 million current and former federal employees of the United States were hacked and stolen.

2014

- In August 2014, nearly 200 photographs of celebrities were posted to the image board website 4chan. An investigation by Apple found that the images were obtained "by a very targeted attack on user names, passwords and security questions".

- In September 2014, Home Depot suffered a data breach of 56 million credit card numbers.

- In October 2014, Staples suffered a data breach of 1.16 million customer payment cards.

- In November 2014 and for weeks after, Sony Pictures Entertainment suffered a data breach involving personal information about Sony Pictures employees and their families, e-mails between employees, information about executive salaries at the company, copies of (previously) unreleased Sony films, and other information. The hackers involved claim to have taken over 100 terabytes of data from Sony.

2013

- In October 2013, Adobe Systems revealed that their corporate data base was hacked and some 130 million user records were stolen. According to Adobe, "For more than a year, Adobe's authentication system has cryptographically hashed customer passwords using the SHA-256 algorithm, including salting the passwords and iterating the hash more than 1,000 times. This system was not the subject of the attack we publicly disclosed on October 3, 2013. The authentication system involved in the attack was a backup system and was designated to be decommissioned. The system involved in the attack used Triple DES encryption to protect all password information stored."

- In late November to early December 2013, Target Corporation announced that data from around 70 million credit and debit cards was stolen. It is the second largest credit and debit card breach after the TJX Companies data breach where almost 46 million cards were affected.

- In 2013, Edward Snowden published a series of secret documents that revealed widespread spying by the United States National Security Agency and similar agencies in other countries.

2012

- In the Summer of 2012, Wired.com Senior Writer Mat Honan claims that "hackers destroyed my entire digital life in the span of an hour" by hacking his Apple, Twitter, and Gmail passwords in order to gain access to his Twitter handle and in the process, claims the hackers wiped out every one of his devices, deleting all of his messages and documents, including every picture he had ever taken of his 18-month-old daughter. The exploit was achieved with a combination of information provided to the hackers by Amazon's tech support through social engineering, and the password recovery system of Apple which used this information. Related to his experience, Mat Honan wrote a piece outlining why passwords cannot keep users safe.

- In October 2012, a law enforcement agency contacted the South Carolina Department of Revenue (DoR) with evidence that Personally Identifiable Information (PII) of three individuals had been stolen. It was later reported that an estimated 3.6 million Social Security numbers were compromised along with 387,000 credit card records.

2011

- In April 2011, Sony experienced a data breach within their PlayStation Network. It is estimated that the information of 77 million users was compromised.

- In March 2011, RSA suffered a breach of their SecurID token system seed-key warehouse, where the seed keys for their 2 Factor Aunthetication system were stolen, allowing the attackers to replicate the hardware tokens used for secure access in corporate and government environments.

- In June 2011, Citigroup disclosed a data breach within their credit card operation, affecting approximately 210,000 or 1% of their customers' accounts.

- Throughout the year 2010, Chelsea Manning (then known as Bradley Manning) released large volumes of secret military data to the public.

2009

- In December 2009 a RockYou! password database was breached containing 32 million user names and plaintext passwords, further compromising the use of weak passwords for any purpose.

- In May 2009 the United Kingdom parliamentary expenses scandal was revealed by The Daily Telegraph. A hard disk containing scanned receipts of UK Members of Parliament and Peers in the House of Lords was offered to various UK newspapers in late April, with The Daily Telegraph finally acquiring it. They published details in installments from 8 May onwards. Although it was intended by Parliament that the data was to be published, this was to be in redacted form, with details the individual members considered "sensitive" blanked out. The newspaper published unredacted scans which showed details of the claims, many of which appeared to be in breach of the rules and suggested widespread abuse of the generous expenses system. The resulting media storm led to the resignation of the Speaker of the House of Commons and the prosecution and imprisonment of several MPs and Lords for fraud. The expenses system was overhauled and tightened up, being put more on a par with private industry schemes. The Metropolitan Police Service continues to investigate possible frauds, and the Crown Prosecution Service is considering further prosecutions. Several MPs and Lords apologised and made whole, partial or no restitution, and retained their seats. Others who had been shamed in the media did not offer themselves for re-election at the United Kingdom general election, 2010. Although numbering less than 1,500 individuals, the affair received the largest global media coverage of any data breach (as at February 2012).

- In January 2009 Heartland Payment Systems announced that it had been "the victim of a security breach within its processing system", possibly part of a "global cyber fraud operation". The intrusion has been called the largest criminal breach of card data ever, with estimates of up to 100 million cards from more than 650 financial services companies compromised.

2008

- In January 2008, GE Money, a division of General Electric, disclosed that a magnetic tape containing 150,000 social security numbers and in-store credit card information from 650,000 retail customers is known to be missing from an Iron Mountain Incorporated storage facility. J.C. Penney is among 230 retailers affected.

- Horizon Blue Cross and Blue Shield of New Jersey, January, 300,000 members

- Lifeblood, February, 321,000 blood donors

- British National Party membership list leak

- In Early 2008, Countrywide Financial (since acquired by Bank of America) allegedly fell victim to a data breach when, according to news reports and court documents, employee Rene L. Rebollo Jr. stole and sold up to 2.5 million customers' personal information including social security numbers. According to the legal complaint: "Beginning in 2008 – coincidentally after they sold their mortgage portfolios under wrongful and fraudulent 'securitization pools,' and coincidentally after their mortgage portfolio went into massive default as a result thereof – Countrywide learned that the financial information of potentially millions of customers had been stolen by certain Countrywide agents, employees or other individuals." In July 2010, Bank of America settled more than 30 related class-action lawsuits by offering free credit monitoring, identity theft insurance and reimbursement for losses to as many as 17 million consumers impacted by the alleged data breach. The settlement was estimated at $56.5 million not including court costs.

2007

- D. A. Davidson & Co. 192,000 clients' names, customer account and social security numbers, addresses and dates of birth

- The 2007 loss of Ohio and Connecticut state data by Accenture

- TJ Maxx, data for 45 million credit and debit accounts

- 2007 UK child benefit data scandal

- CGI Group, August, 283,000 retirees from New York City

- The Gap, September, 800,000 job applicants

- Memorial Blood Center, December, 268,000 blood donors

- Davidson County Election Commission, December, 337,000 voters

2006

- AOL search data scandal (sometimes referred to as a "Data *Valdez*", due to its size)

- Department of Veterans Affairs, May, 28,600,000 veterans, reserves, and active duty military personnel,

- Ernst & Young, May, 234,000 customers of Hotels.com (after a similar loss of data on 38,000 employees of Ernst & Young clients in February)

- Boeing, December, 382,000 employees (after similar losses of data on 3,600 employees in April and 161,000 employees in November, 2005)

2005

- Ameriprise Financial, stolen laptop, December 24, 260,000 customer records

- ChoicePoint, February, 163,000 consumer records

References

- Seema Kedar (1 January 2009). Database Management Systems. Technical Publications. p. 15. ISBN 978-81-8431-584-4.

- Sandle, Paul; Baker, Liana B. (2016-09-08). "HP Enterprise strikes $8.8 billion deal with Micro Focus for software assets". Reuters. Retrieved 2016-09-13.

- "5 IT Security Lessons from the Comelec Data Breach". IT Solutions & Services Philippines - Aim.ph. Retrieved 2016-05-06.

- Freytas-tamura, Kimiko De (2016-10-30). "Iceland's Prime Minister Resigns, After Pirate Party Makes Strong Gains". The New York Times. ISSN 0362-4331. Retrieved 2016-11-10.

- Ltd, Allied Newspapers. "Watch: Will Panama scandal go away after the reshuffle?". Times of Malta. Retrieved 2016-11-10.

- "Target Confirms Unauthorized Access to Payment Card Data in U.S. Stores". Target Corporation. 19 December 2013. Retrieved 19 January 2016.

- "GE Money Backup Tape With 650,000 Records Missing At Iron Mountain". InformationWeek. Retrieved 11 May 2016.

- "TalkTalk Hacked...Again". Check&Secure. 2015-10-23. Archived from the original on 2015-12-23. Retrieved 2015-10-23.

- United States Department of Health and Human Services, Administration for Children and Families. Information Memorandum. Retrieved 2015-09-01.

- Verizon Data Breach Investigations Report | Verizon Enterprise Solutions. VerizonEnterprise.com. Retrieved 2014-06-10.

- "Apple Media Advisory: Update to Celebrity Photo Investigation". Business Wire. StreetInsider.com. September 2, 2014. Retrieved 2014-09-05.

- "Staples: Breach may have affected 1.16 million customers' cards". Fortune. December 19, 2014. Retrieved 2014-12-21.

- James Cook (December 16, 2014). "Sony Hackers Have Over 100 Terabytes Of Documents. Only Released 200 Gigabytes So Far". Business Insider. Retrieved December 18, 2014.

- Goodin, Dan. (2013-11-01) How an epic blunder by Adobe could strengthen hand of password crackers. Ars Technica. Retrieved 2014-06-10.

- Greenberg, Andy (9 June 2011). "Citibank Reveals One Percent Of Credit Card Accounts Exposed In Hacker Intrusion". Forbes. Retrieved 2014-09-05.

- Honan, Mat (2012-11-15). "Kill the Password: Why a String of Characters Can't Protect Us Anymore". Wired (magazine). Retrieved 2013-01-17.

- "Protecting the Individual from Data Breach". The National Law Review. Raymond Law Group. 2014-01-14. Retrieved 2013-01-17.

- Manning, Jeff (2010-04-13). "D.A. Davidson fined over computer security after data breach". The Oregonian. Retrieved 2013-07-26.

Database Application: An Overview

Database application is a program that is used in computers; the basic purpose of this program is to retrieve information from computerized database. Inventory management software, content management system, airline reservations system and enterprise software are other aspects elucidated in this section. This chapter discusses the application of database in a critical manner providing key analysis on the subject matter.

Database Application

A database application is a computer program whose primary purpose is entering and retrieving information from a computerized database. Early examples of database applications were accounting systems and airline reservations systems, such as SABRE, developed starting in 1957.

A characteristic of modern database applications is that they facilitate simultaneous updates and queries from multiple users. Systems in the 1970s might have accomplished this by having each user in front of a 3270 terminal to a mainframe computer. By the mid-1980s it was becoming more common to give each user a personal computer and have a program running on that PC that connected to a database server. Information would be pulled from the database, transmitted over a network, and then arranged, graphed, or otherwise formatted by the program running on the PC. Starting in the mid-1990s it became more common to build database applications with a Web interface. Rather than develop custom software to run on a user's PC, the user would use the same Web browser program for every application. A database application with a Web interface had the advantage that it could be used on devices of different sizes, with different hardware, and with different operating systems. Examples of early database applications with Web interfaces include amazon.com, which used the Oracle relational database management system, the photo.net online community, whose implementation on top of Oracle was described in the book Database-Backed Web Sites (Ziff-Davis Press; May 1997), and eBay, also running Oracle.

Electronic medical records are referred to on emrexperts.com, in December 2010, as "a software database application". A 2005 O'Reilly book uses the term in its title: Database Applications and the Web.

Some of the most complex database applications remain accounting systems, such as SAP, which may contain thousands of tables in only a single module. Many of today's most widely used computer systems are database applications, for example, Facebook, which was built on top of MySQL.

The etymology of the phrase "database application" comes from the practice of dividing computer software into systems programs, such as the operating system, compilers, the file system, and tools such as the database management system, and application programs, such as a payroll check processor. On a standard PC running Microsoft Windows, for example, the Windows operating system contains all of the systems programs while games, word processors, spreadsheet programs, photo editing programs, etc. would be application programs. As "application" is short for "application program", "database application" is short for "database application program".

Not every program that uses a database would typically be considered a "database application". For example, many physics experiments, e.g., the Large Hadron Collider, generate massive data sets that programs subsequently analyze. The data sets constitute a "database", though they are not typically managed with a standard relational database management system. The computer programs that analyze the data are primarily developed to answer hypotheses, not to put information back into the database and therefore the overall program would not be called a "database application".

Inventory Management Software

Inventory management software is a computer-based system for tracking inventory levels, orders, sales and deliveries. It can also be used in the manufacturing industry to create a work order, bill of materials and other production-related documents. Companies use inventory management software to avoid product overstock and outages. It is a tool for organizing inventory data that before was generally stored in hard-copy form or in spreadsheets.

Features

Inventory management software is made up of several key components, all working together to create a cohesive inventory for many organizations' systems. These features include:

Order Management

Should inventory reach a specific threshold, a company's inventory management system can be programmed to tell managers to reorder that product. This helps companies avoid running out of products or tying up too much capital in inventory.

Asset Tracking

When a product is in a warehouse or store, it can be tracked via its barcode and/or other tracking criteria, such as serial number, lot number or revision number. Systems. for Business, Encyclopedia of Business, 2nd ed. Nowadays, inventory management software often utilizes barcode, radio-frequency identification (RFID), and/or wireless tracking technology.

Service Management

Companies that are primarily service-oriented rather than product-oriented can use inventory management software to track the cost of the materials they use to provide services, such as cleaning supplies. This way, they can attach prices to their services that reflect the total cost of performing them.

Product Identification

Barcodes are often the means whereby data on products and orders is inputted into inventory management software. A barcode reader is used to read barcodes and look up information on the products they represent. Radio-frequency identification (RFID) tags and wireless methods of product identification are also growing in popularity.

Modern inventory software programs may use QR codes or NFC tags to identify inventory items and smartphones as scanners.This method provides an option for small businesses to track inventory using barcode scanning without a need to purchase expensive scanning hardware.

Inventory Optimization

A fully automated demand forecasting and inventory optimization system to attain key inventory optimization metrics such as:

- Reorder point: the number of units that should trigger a replenishment order

- Order quantity: the number of units that should be reordered, based on the reorder point, stock on hand and stock on order

- Lead demand: the number of units that will be sold during the lead time

- Stock cover: the number of days left before a stockout if no reorder is made

- Accuracy: the expected accuracy of the forecasts

History

The Universal Product Code (UPC) was adopted by the grocery industry in April 1973 as the standard barcode for all grocers, though it was not introduced at retailing locations until 1974. This helped drive down costs for inventory management because retailers in the United States and Canada didn't have to purchase multiple barcode readers to scan competing barcodes. There was now one primary barcode for grocers and other retailers to buy one type of reader for.

In the early 1980s, personal computers began to be popular. This further pushed down the cost of barcodes and readers. It also allowed the first versions of inventory management software to be put into place. One of the biggest hurdles in selling readers and barcodes to retailers was the fact that they didn't have a place to store the information they scanned. As computers became more common and affordable, this hurdle was overcome. Once barcodes and inventory management programs started spreading through grocery stores, inventory management by hand became less practical. Writing inventory data by hand on paper was replaced by scanning products and inputting information into a computer by hand.

Starting in the early 2000s, inventory management software progressed to the point where businesspeople no longer needed to input data by hand but could instantly update their database with barcode readers.

Also, the existence of cloud based business software and their increasing adoption by businesses mark a new era for inventory management software. Now they usually allow integrations with other business backend processes, like accounting and online sales.

Purpose

Companies often use inventory management software to reduce their carrying costs. The software is used to track products and parts as they are transported from a vendor to a warehouse, between warehouses, and finally to a retail location or directly to a customer.

Inventory management software is used for a variety of purposes, including:

- Maintaining a balance between too much and too little inventory.
- Tracking inventory as it is transported between locations.
- Receiving items into a warehouse or other location.
- Picking, packing and shipping items from a warehouse.
- Keeping track of product sales and inventory levels.
- Cutting down on product obsolescence and spoilage.
- Avoiding missing out on sales due to out-of-stock situations.

Manufacturing Uses

Manufacturers primarily use inventory management software to create work orders and bills of materials. This facilitates the manufacturing process by helping manufacturers efficiently assemble the tools and parts they need to perform specific tasks. For more complex manufacturing jobs, manufacturers can create multilevel work orders and bills of materials, which have a timeline of processes that need to happen in the proper order to build a final product. Other work orders that can be created using inventory management software include reverse work orders and auto work orders. Manufacturers also use inventory management software for tracking assets, receiving new inventory and additional tasks businesses in other industries use it for.

Advantages of ERP inventory Management Software

There are several advantages to using inventory management software in a business setting.

Cost Savings

A company's inventory represents one of its largest investments, along with its workforce and locations. Inventory management software helps companies cut expenses by minimizing the amount of unnecessary parts and products in storage. It also helps companies keep lost sales to a minimum by having enough stock on hand to meet demand.

Increased Efficiency

Inventory management software often allows for automation of many inventory-related tasks. For example, software can automatically collect data, conduct calculations, and create records. This not only results in time savings, cost savings, but also increases business efficiency.

Warehouse Organization

Inventory management software can help distributors, wholesalers, manufacturers and retailers optimize their warehouses. If certain products are often sold together or are more popular than others, those products can be grouped together or placed near the delivery area to speed up the process of picking. By 2018, 66% of warehouses "are poised to undergo a seismic shift, moving from still prevalent pen and paper processes to automated and mechanized inventory solutions. With these new automated processes, cycle counts will be performed more often and with less effort, increasing inventory visibility, and leading to more accurate fulfillment, fewer out of stock situations and fewer lost sales. More confidence in inventory accuracy will lead to a new focus on optimizing mix, expanding a selection and accelerating inventory turns."

Updated Data

Up-to-date, real-time data on inventory conditions and levels is another advantage inventory management software gives companies. Company executives can usually access the software through a mobile device, laptop or PC to check current inventory numbers. This automatic updating of inventory records allows businesses to make informed decisions.

Data Security

With the aid of restricted user rights, company managers can allow many employees to assist in inventory management. They can grant employees enough information access to receive products, make orders, transfer products and do other tasks without compromising company security. This can speed up the inventory management process and save managers' time.

Insight into Trends

Tracking where products are stocked, which suppliers they come from, and the length of time they are stored is made possible with inventory management software. By analysing such data, companies can control inventory levels and maximize the use of warehouse space. Furthermore, firms are more prepared for the demands and supplies of the market, especially during special circumstances such as a peak season on a particular month. Through the reports generated by the inventory management software, firms are also able to gather important data that may be put in a model for it to be analyzed.

Disadvantages of ERP inventory Management Software

The main disadvantages of inventory management software are its cost and complexity.

Expense

Cost can be a major disadvantage of inventory management software. Many large companies use inventory management software, but small businesses can find it difficult to afford it. Barcode readers and other hardware can compound this problem by adding even more cost to companies. The advantage of allowing multiple employees to perform inventory management tasks is tempered by the cost of additional barcode readers. Use of smartphones as QR code readers has been a way that smaller companies avoid the high expense of custom hardware for inventory management.

Complexity

Inventory management software is not necessarily simple or easy to learn. A company's management team must dedicate a certain amount of time to learning a new system, including both software and hardware, in order to put it to use. Most inventory management software includes training manuals and other information available to users. Despite its apparent complexity, inventory management software offers a degree of stability to companies. For example, if an IT employee in charge of the system leaves the company, a replacement can be comparatively inexpensive to train compared to if the company used multiple programs to store inventory data.

Benefits of Cloud Inventory Management Software

The main benefits of a cloud inventory management software include:

Real Time Tracking of Inventory

For startups and SMBs, tracking inventory in real time is very important. Not only can business owners track and collect data but also generate reports. At the same time, entrepreneurs can access cloud-based inventory data from a wide range of internet enabled devices, including: smartphones, tablets, laptops, as well as traditional desktop PCs. In addition, users do not have to be inside business premises to use web based inventory program and can access the inventory software while on the road.

Cut Down Hardware Expenses

Because the software resides in the cloud, business owners do not have to purchase and maintain expensive hardware. Instead, SMBs and startups can direct capital and profits towards expanding the business to reach a wider audience. Cloud-based solutions also eliminate the need to hire a large IT workforce. The service provider will take care of maintaining the inventory software.

Fast Deployment

Deploying web based inventory software is quite easy. All business owners have to do is sign up for a monthly or yearly subscription and start using the inventory management software via the internet. Such flexibility allows businesses to scale up relatively quickly without spending a large amount of money.

Easy Integration

Cloud inventory management software allows business owners to integrate with their existing systems with ease. For example, business owners can integrate the inventory software with their eCommerce store or cloud-based accounting software. The rise in popularity of 3rd party market-places, such as Amazon, eBay and Shopify, prompted cloud-based inventory management companies to include the integration of such sites with the rest of a business owner's retail business, allowing one to view and control stock across all channels.

Enhanced Efficiency

Cloud inventory systems increase efficiency in a number of ways. One is real-time inventory monitoring. A single change can replicate itself company-wide instantaneously. As a result, businesses can have greater confidence in the accuracy of the information in the system, and management can more easily track the flow of supplies and products – and generate reports. In addition, cloud-based solutions offer greater accessibility.

Improved Coordination

Cloud inventory programs also allow departments within a company to work together more efficiently. Department A can pull information about Department B's inventory directly from the software without needing to contact Department B's staff for the information. This inter-departmental communication also makes it easier to know when to restock and which customer orders have been shipped, etc. Operations can run more smoothly and efficiently, enhancing your customer's experience. Accurate inventory information can also have a huge impact on your company's bottom line. It allows you to see where the bottlenecks and workflow issues are – and to calculate break-even points as well as profit margins.

Disadvantages of Cloud Inventory Management Software

Security & Privacy

Using the cloud means that your data is managed by a Third Party provider and there can be a risk of your data being accessed by unauthorized users.

Dependency

Since maintenance is managed by the vendor, you are essentially fully dependant on your provider. Before signing up for an account or purchasing the software, it is essential that you research on the best providers available in the market to ensure that the vendor is reliable and the software has all the features that meets your business needs.

Decreased Flexibility

Depending on which Cloud Service Provider you decide to work with, system and software upgrades will be performed based on their schedule, hence businesses may experience some limitations in flexibility in the process.

Integration

Not all on-premises systems or service providers can be synced with the cloud software used.

Content Management System

A content management system (CMS) is a computer application that supports the creation and modification of digital content. It is often used to support multiple users working in a collaborative environment.

CMS features vary widely. Most CMSs include Web-based publishing, format management, history editing and version control, indexing, search, and retrieval. By their nature, content management systems support the separation of content and presentation.

A web content management system (WCM or WCMS) is a CMS designed to support the management of the content of Web pages. Most popular CMSs are also WCMSs. Web content includes text and embedded graphics, photos, video, audio, maps, and code (e.g., for applications) that displays content or interacts with the user.

Such a content management system (CMS) typically has two major components:

- A content management application (CMA) is the front-end user interface that allows a user, even with limited expertise, to add, modify and remove content from a Web site without the intervention of a webmaster.

- A content delivery application (CDA) compiles that information and updates the Web site.

Digital asset management systems are another type of CMS. They manage things such as documents, movies, pictures, phone numbers and scientific data. CMSs can also be used for storing, controlling, revising, and publishing documentation.

Based on marketshare statistics, the most popular content management system is WordPress, used by over 27% of websites on the internet. Other popular content management systems include Joomla and Drupal.

Common Features

Content management systems will often contain the following features:

- SEO-friendly URLs
- Integrated and online help
- Modularity and extensibility
- User and group functionality
- Templating support for changing designs
- Install and Upgrade wizards
- Integrated audit logs
- Compliancy with various accessibility frameworks and standards, such as WAI-ARIA

Advantages

- Reduced need to code from scratch

- The ability to create a website quickly

- The ability to create a unified look and feel

- Version control

- Edit permission management

Disadvantages

- Limited or no ability to create functionality not envisioned in the CMS (layouts, web apps, etc.)

- Increased need for special expertise and training for content authors

Airline Reservations System

An airline reservation system (ARS) is part of the so-called passenger service systems (PSS), which are applications supporting the direct contact with the passenger.

ARS eventually evolved into the computer reservations system (CRS). A computer reservation system is used for the reservations of a particular airline and interfaces with a global distribution system (GDS) which supports travel agencies and other distribution channels in making reservations for most major airlines in a single system.

Overview

Airline reservations systems contain airline schedules, fare tariffs, passenger reservations and ticket records. An airline's direct distribution works within their own reservation system, as well as pushing out information to the GDS. A second type of direct distribution channel are consumers who use the internet or mobile applications to make their own reservations. Travel agencies and other indirect distribution channels access the same GDS as those accessed by the airlines' reservation systems, and all messaging is transmitted by a standardized messaging system that functions on two types of messaging that transmit on SITA's HLN [high level network]. These message types are called Type A [usually EDIFACT format] for real time interactive communication and Type B [TTY] for informational and booking type of messages. Message construction standards set by IATA and ICAO, are global, and apply to more than air transportation. Since airline reservation systems are business critical applications, and they are functionally quite complex, the operation of an in-house airline reservation system is relatively expensive.

Prior to deregulation, airlines owned their own reservation systems with travel agents subscribing to them. Today, the GDS are run by independent companies with airlines and travel agencies as major subscribers.

As of February 2009, there are only four major GDS providers in the market space: Amadeus, Travelport (which operates the Apollo, Worldspan and Galileo systems), Sabre and Shares. There is one major Regional GDS, Abacus, serving the Asian marketplace and a number of regional players serving single countries, including Travelsky (China), Infini and Axess (both Japan) and Topas (South Korea). Of these, Infini is hosted within the Sabre complex, Axess is in the process of moving into a partition within the Worldspan complex, and Topas agencies will be migrating into Amadeus.

Reservation systems like Navitaire and Radixx International hosts "ticket-less" airlines and "hybrid" - (airlines that use e-ticketing in addition to ticket-less to accommodate code-shares and interlines).

Radixx International is a hybrid travel distribution and PSS designed to enable airlines to increase revenue and profitability by expanding distribution to sell through any channel whether ticketed or ticketless.

In addition to these "standardized" GDS, some airlines have proprietary versions which they use to run their flight operations. A few examples are Deltamatic's OSS system and EDS SHARES. SITA Reservations remains the largest neutral multi-host airline reservations system, with over 100 airlines currently managing inventory.

Inventory Management

An airline's inventory contains all flights with their available seats. The inventory of an airline is generally divided into service classes (e.g. first, business or economy class) and up to 26 booking classes, for which different prices and booking conditions apply. Inventory data is imported and maintained through a schedule distribution system over standardized interfaces. One of the core functions of the inventory management is the inventory control. Inventory control steers how many seats are available in the different booking classes, by opening and closing individual booking classes for sale. In combination with the fares and booking conditions stored in the Fare Quote System, the price for each sold seat is determined. In most cases, inventory control has a real time interface to an airline's Yield management system to support a permanent optimization of the offered booking classes in response to changes in demand or pricing strategies of a competitor.

Availability Display and Reservation (PNR)

Users access an airline's inventory through an availability display. It contains all offered flights for a particular city-pair with their available seats in the different booking classes. This display contains flights which are operated by the airline itself as well as code share flights which are operated in co-operation with another airline. If the city pair is not one on which the airline offers service, it may display a connection using its own flights or display the flights of other airlines. The availability of seats of other airlines is updated through standard industry interfaces. Depending on the type of co-operation, it supports access to the last seat (last seat availability) in real-time. Reservations for individual passengers or groups are stored in a so-called passenger name record (PNR). Among other data, the PNR contains personal information such as name, contact information or special services requests (SSRs) e.g. for a vegetarian meal, as well as the flights (segments) and issued tickets. Some reservation systems also allow to store customer data in profiles to avoid data re-entry each time a new reservation is made for a known passenger. In addition, most systems have interfaces to CRM systems or customer loyalty applications (aka frequent traveller systems). Before a flight departs, the so-called passenger name list (PNL) is handed over to the departure control system that is used to check-in passengers and baggage. Reservation data such as the number of booked passengers and special service requests is also transferred to flight operations systems, crew management and catering systems. Once a flight has departed, the reservation system is updated with a list of the checked-in passengers (e.g. passengers who had a reservation but did not check in (no shows) and passengers who checked in, but did not have a reservation (go shows)). Finally, data needed for revenue accounting and reporting is handed over to administrative systems.

Fare Quote and Ticketing

Fare Basis	Airline	Booking Class	Trip Type	Fare	Cabin	Effective Date	Expiration Date	Min / Max Stay	Adv Purchase Req
TA14A0BP	DL	T	One-Way	189.00(USD)	E	02/16/11			14
TA03A0SG	DL	T	One-Way	209.00(USD)	E	02/28/11			03
UA10A0UY	DL	U	One-Way	236.00(USD)	E				10
LA10A0VY	DL	L	One-Way	251.00(USD)	E				10
LA07A0NY	DL	L	One-Way	266.00(USD)	E				07
KA07A0JY	DL	K	One-Way	326.00(USD)	E				07
QA03A0NP	DL	Q	One-Way	396.00(USD)	E				03
HA00A0NY	DL	H	One-Way	466.00(USD)	E				
UC14A0NJ	DL	U	Round-Trip	462.00(USD)	E			V / 30	14
HA00A0UY	DL	H	One-Way	616.00(USD)	E				
MA00A0RY	DL	M	One-Way	694.00(USD)	E				
MA00UPNY	DL		One-Way	1576.00(USD)	B				
BA00UPRQ	DL		One-Way	1346.00(USD)	B				
YO	DL	Y	One-Way	1436.00(USD)	E				
YUP	DL		One-Way	1527.00(USD)	B				
FO	DL	F	One-Way	1626.00(USD)	F				
Y	DL	Y	One-Way	1669.00(USD)	E				
C	DL	C	One-Way	2213.00(USD)	B				
F	DL	F	One-Way	2766.00(USD)	F				

List of fares for travel on Delta Air Lines from San Francisco, CA to Boston, MA. Applicable booking classes, as well as specific restrictions such as minimum stay and advance purchase can be seen.

The Fares data store contains fare tariffs, rule sets, routing maps, class of service tables, and some tax information that construct the price – "the fare". Rules like booking conditions (e.g. minimum stay, advance purchase, etc.) are tailored differently between different city pairs or zones, and assigned a class of service corresponding to its appropriate inventory bucket. Inventory control can also be manipulated manually through the availability feeds, dynamically controlling how many seats are offered for a particular price by opening and closing particular classes.

The compiled set of fare conditions is called a fare basis code. There are two systems set up for the interchange of fares data — ATPCO and SITA, plus some system to system direct connects. This system distributes the fare tariffs and rule sets to all GDSs and other subscribers. Every airline employs staff who code air fare rules in accordance with yield management intent. There are also revenue managers who watch fares as they are filed into the public tariffs and make competitive recommendations. Inventory control is typically manipulated from here, using availability feeds to open and close classes of service.

The role of the ticketing complex is to issue and store electronic ticket records and the very small number of paper tickets that are still issued. Miscellaneous charges order (MCO) is still a paper document; IATA has working groups defining the replacement document the electronic multipurpose document (EMD) as at 2010. The electronic ticket information is stored in a database containing the data that historically was printed on a paper ticket including items such as the ticket number, the fare and tax components of the ticket price or exchange rate information. In the past, airlines issued paper tickets; since 2008, IATA has been supporting a resolution to move to 100% electronic ticketing. So far, the industry has not been able to comply due to various technological and international limitations. The industry is at 98% electronic ticket issuance today, although electronic processing for MCOs was not available in time for the IATA mandate.

Major Systems

Name	Description	Vendor
Avantik	Full PSS allowing any type of airline to manage its passenger flow from booking all the way through to boarding and aircraft weight & balance. Avantik caters for diversified distribution channels (offline, its own internet booking engine, 3rd party API, online travel agents, global distribution system, travel agents, tour operators & charters etc.).	Bravo
ACCELaero	PSS, reservations, departure control, inventory and e-commerce platform.	Information Systems Associates FZE
Radixx International	Radixx is a hybrid travel distribution and PSS designed to enable airlines to increase revenue and profitability by expanding distribution to sell through any channel whether ticketed or ticketless.	Radixx International
ameliaRES	PSS, DCS, Reservation Management, Codeshare, Interline and real-time inventory control system for airlines of all sizes and business models.	InteliSys Aviation Systems
Crane PAX	Crane PAX is a web based airline reservations and ticketing system. With inventory control, fares, pricing and ticketing, advance reservation, Internet Booking Engine, seat selection and sales distribution functions it manages the whole airline operations cycle up to the point of departure.	Hitit Computer Services
Travel Technology Interactive Solutions	Integrated Airline Management System and global distribution system (GDS).	Travel Technology Interactive
Navitaire New Skies Integrated Customer Centric Passenger Service System	Integrated reservations, departure control, inventory system and e-commerce platform.	Navitaire
SabreSonic Customer Sales & Service	Integrated reservations, departure control, inventory system and e-commerce platform.	Sabre Airline Solutions
SITA Horizon Customer Sales & Service	Integrated reservations, departure control, inventory system and e-commerce platform.	SITA
Altéa Res	Integrated Airline Reservation System and global distribution system (GDS).	Amadeus IT Group
KIU	A computer reservations system (CRS) and global distribution system (GDS).	KIU System
RESIBER	A Passenger Service System (PSS).	Iberia
Videcom VRS	Videcom Reservations System, GDS,IET,Codeshare for regional and international airlines.	Videcom international

Other Systems

- USAS (application)

History

The history of computer-based airline reservations systems began in the late 1950s when American Airlines required a system that would allow real-time access to flight details in all of its offices, and the integration and automation of its booking and ticketing processes. The earliest electronic reservations system, Magnetronic Reservisor, was introduced in 1952. Many years later, Sabre (Semi-Automated Business Research Environment) was developed and launched in 1964. Sabre's breakthrough was its ability to keep inventory correct in real time, accessible to agents around the world. Prior to this, manual systems required centralized reservation centers, groups of people in a room with the physical cards that represented inventory, in this case, seats on airplanes.

Agent set of the Magnetronic Reservisor system

The deregulation of the airline industry, in the Airline Deregulation Act, meant that airlines, which had previously operated under government-set fares ensuring airlines at least broke even, now needed to improve efficiency to compete in a free market. In this deregulated environment, the ARS and its descendants became vital to the travel industry.

Enterprise Software

Enterprise software, also known as enterprise application software (EAS), is computer software used to satisfy the needs of an organization rather than individual users. Such organizations would include businesses, schools, interest-based user groups, clubs, charities, or governments. Enterprise software is an integral part of a (computer-based) information system.

Services provided by enterprise software are typically business-oriented tools such as online shopping and online payment processing, interactive product catalogue, automated billing systems, security, enterprise content management, IT service management, customer relationship management, enterprise resource planning, business intelligence, project management, collaboration, human resource management, manufacturing, occupational health and safety, enterprise application integration, and enterprise forms automation.

As enterprises have similar departments and systems in common, enterprise software is often available as a suite of customizable programs. Generally, the complexity of these tools requires specialist capabilities and specific knowledge.

Definitions

Enterprise Software describes a collection of computer programs with common business applications, tools for modeling how the entire organization works, and development tools for building applications unique to the organization. The software is intended to solve an enterprise-wide problem, rather than a departmental problem. Enterprise level software aims to improve the enterprise's productivity and efficiency by providing business logic support functionality.

According to Martin Fowler, "Enterprise applications are about the display, manipulation, and storage of large amounts of often complex data and the support or automation of business processes with that data."

Although there is no single, widely accepted list of enterprise software characteristics, they generally include performance, scalability, and robustness. Furthermore, enterprise software typically has interfaces to other enterprise software (for example LDAP to directory services) and is centrally managed (a single admin page, for example).

Enterprise application software performs business functions such as order processing, procurement, production scheduling, customer information management, energy management, and accounting. It is typically hosted on servers and provides simultaneous services to a large number of users, typically over a computer network. This is in contrast to a single-user application that is executed on a user's personal computer and serves only one user at a time.

Types

Enterprise software can be categorized by business function. Each type of enterprise application can be considered a "system" due to the integration with a firm's business processes. Categories of enterprise software may overlap due to this systemic interpretation. For example, IBM's Business Intelligence platform (Cognos), integrates with a predictive analytics platform (SPSS) and can obtain records from its database packages (Infosphere, DB2). Blurred lines between package functions make delimitation difficult, and in many ways larger software companies define these somewhat arbitrary categories. Nevertheless, certain industry standard product categories have emerged, and these are shown below :

- Accounting software

- Billing Management

- Business intelligence

- Business process management

- Content management system (CMS)

- Customer relationship management (CRM)

- Database

  o Master data management (MDM)

- Enterprise resource planning (ERP)

- Enterprise asset management (EAM)

- Supply chain management (SCM)

- Backup software

References

- Andreas Mauthe; Peter Thomas (2004). Professional Content Management Systems: Handling Digital Media Assets. John Wiley & Sons. ISBN 978-0-470-85542-3.

- Sitaker, Kragen (2005). "'Enterprise software' is a social, not technical, phenomenon". Retrieved 12 November 2016.

- "Integrations and Apps for Online Inventory Management Software | TradeGecko". www.tradegecko.com. Retrieved 2015-11-24.

- "Magnetronic Reservisor". American Airlines C.R. Smith Museum. Retrieved 3 August 2014. The Magnetronic Reservisor, introduced in 1952, was the first electronic reservations system in the airline industry

- "What is enterprise application? - A Word Definition From the Webopedia Computer Dictionary". Webopedia.com. Retrieved 2013-06-16.

- "Integrate InfoSphere Warehouse data mining with IBM Cognos reporting, Part 1: Overview of InfoSphere Warehouse and Cognos integration architecture". Ibm.com. 2008-10-30. Retrieved 2013-06-16.

- Lockard, Robert (29 November 2010). "3 Advantages of Using Inventory Management Software". Inventory System Software Blog. Retrieved 23 November 2012.

- Piasecki, Dave. "Optimizing Economic Order Quantity – Carrying Costs". Inventoryops.com. Retrieved August 17, 2010.

Permissions

All chapters in this book are published with permission under the Creative Commons Attribution Share Alike License or equivalent. Every chapter published in this book has been scrutinized by our experts. Their significance has been extensively debated. The topics covered herein carry significant information for a comprehensive understanding. They may even be implemented as practical applications or may be referred to as a beginning point for further studies.

We would like to thank the editorial team for lending their expertise to make the book truly unique. They have played a crucial role in the development of this book. Without their invaluable contributions this book wouldn't have been possible. They have made vital efforts to compile up to date information on the varied aspects of this subject to make this book a valuable addition to the collection of many professionals and students.

This book was conceptualized with the vision of imparting up-to-date and integrated information in this field. To ensure the same, a matchless editorial board was set up. Every individual on the board went through rigorous rounds of assessment to prove their worth. After which they invested a large part of their time researching and compiling the most relevant data for our readers.

The editorial board has been involved in producing this book since its inception. They have spent rigorous hours researching and exploring the diverse topics which have resulted in the successful publishing of this book. They have passed on their knowledge of decades through this book. To expedite this challenging task, the publisher supported the team at every step. A small team of assistant editors was also appointed to further simplify the editing procedure and attain best results for the readers.

Apart from the editorial board, the designing team has also invested a significant amount of their time in understanding the subject and creating the most relevant covers. They scrutinized every image to scout for the most suitable representation of the subject and create an appropriate cover for the book.

The publishing team has been an ardent support to the editorial, designing and production team. Their endless efforts to recruit the best for this project, has resulted in the accomplishment of this book. They are a veteran in the field of academics and their pool of knowledge is as vast as their experience in printing. Their expertise and guidance has proved useful at every step. Their uncompromising quality standards have made this book an exceptional effort. Their encouragement from time to time has been an inspiration for everyone.

The publisher and the editorial board hope that this book will prove to be a valuable piece of knowledge for students, practitioners and scholars across the globe.

Index

A

Active Database, 9, 99

Advanced Validation Metadata, 172

Airline Reservations System, 281, 289-290

Application Programming Interface, 3, 16, 194

Application Programming Interfaces, 60, 136

Asset Tracking, 282

Attribute Metadata, 170, 172

B

Buffer Management, 66

C

Cloud Computing, 21, 56, 73, 180

Cloud Database, 9, 21, 23-24, 78, 111

Command-line Interfaces, 57, 60

Computer Memory, 3, 195

Computer Networks, 3

Computer Reservations System (crs), 289, 292

Content Management System, 281, 288, 294

D

Data Model, 3, 6-7, 11-12, 15-16, 18, 22-23, 26-27, 31, 43, 45, 47, 79, 113, 134, 143-144, 157-159, 166, 175-176, 179, 181, 183-184, 205, 239, 243-244, 249-250, 254, 257

Data Processing, 3, 73

Data Warehouse, 19, 21, 24-32, 64, 77-78, 96, 187

Data Warehouses, 9, 27, 31-32, 164

Database Administration, 57, 94, 115, 267

Database Management System (dbms), 1, 48, 61, 79, 136, 184, 194, 198, 268

Database Model, 1-2, 4, 12-13, 15, 48, 79-80, 130, 142-143, 147-148, 166, 182, 213, 257

Database Normalization, 30-31, 122, 148, 152, 188, 234, 247

Database Security, 8, 17, 264-269, 271, 273, 275, 277, 279

Deductive Database, 9

Distributed Database, 10, 17, 21, 32-37, 76, 124, 211

Document-oriented Database, 8, 10, 40, 43, 119, 121-123, 125-126, 251

Document-oriented Databases, 3, 10, 119, 126

E

Embedded Database System, 10, 136

End-user Databases, 10

Enterprise Application Software (eas), 293

Enterprise Database Management, 8

Enterprise Software, 8, 281, 293-295

Entity-attribute-value Model, 13, 136, 166

Entity-relationship Model, 7, 12-13, 31, 48, 157, 160, 164-165, 186, 198

Extension Model, 164

F

Federated Database System, 10, 113

Foreign Data Wrappers, 89, 98

Free And Open-source Software, 83-84

Full Text Search Service, 71

G

Global Distribution System (gds), 289

Graph Database, 10, 13, 21, 40, 42-47, 180, 251-252, 254, 261

Graph Query-programming Languages, 46

Graphical Front-ends, 128

Graphical User Interfaces, 57

H

Heterogeneous Database System, 10

Heterogeneous Ddbms, 34

Hierarchical Database Model, 13, 142-143

Hierarchical Databases, 48, 144

Homogeneous Distributed Databases Management System, 34

I

Idms (integrated Database Management System), 143

In-memory Database, 9, 45, 112-113, 134-135, 141, 195

Information Management System (ims), 5, 20, 144

Integrated Data Store (ids), 4, 143

Inventory Management Software, 281-287, 295

Inventory Optimization, 283

M

Mainframe Computer, 281

Microsoft Sql Server, 1, 3, 23, 38, 48-49, 58-59, 62-63, 65, 67-69, 71-73, 77, 81, 118, 176-177, 197, 215, 223, 226

Mobile Database, 11, 21, 37-38

Multitasking Kernel, 2

Multiversion Concurrency Control (mvcc), 74, 84, 139-140

N

Network Databases, 5, 10, 48, 142, 147

Network Model, 3, 5, 13, 43, 142-143, 146

Network Servers, 32

Non-volatile Random Access Memory, 134-135

O

Object Database, 48, 80, 129-131, 133-134, 184-185, 212, 250, 252

Object-oriented Database, 11, 79-80, 129-130, 183

Object-oriented Programming, 8, 80-81, 129-130, 185, 194, 243

Object-relational Databases, 3, 8, 80, 129

On-disk Databases, 135-136

Open-source Software, 8, 83-84, 97, 118

Operating System, 2, 16, 22, 34, 37-38, 60, 62, 69, 76-78, 138, 271, 281-282

Operational Databases, 9, 11, 27, 32

Operational Systems, 24-25, 27-28, 30-32

Oracle Database, 21-23, 45, 49, 58, 77, 81, 99-103, 105, 108-119, 183, 198-199

Oracle Relational Database Management System, 281

Order Management, 282

P

Parallel Database, 11, 21, 39

Passenger Service Systems (pss), 289

Probabilistic Databases, 11

Product Identification, 283

Programming Language, 46, 80, 89, 111, 128-129, 133, 185, 194, 198, 257, 260, 262

R

Real-time Databases, 11

Relational Database Management System, 48, 50, 61-62, 73, 79, 99, 139, 257-259, 281-282

Relational Database Management System (rdbms), 48, 50, 257-259

Relational Database Model, 15, 48, 143, 147-148, 182, 213

Relational Model, 1, 3, 5-7, 12-13, 15, 41, 48-50, 75-76, 82, 123, 142, 144-148, 150-151, 153-154, 159, 183-185, 188-189, 197-198, 213-214, 229-230, 238-240, 243, 249, 255

Relational Operations, 151

Row Modeling, 168

S

Semantic Model, 14, 63, 164

Service Management, 113, 282, 293

Software Engineering, 61, 157-158, 200

Spatial Database, 11

Storage Memory, 136

Structured Query Language (sql), 2, 76, 213, 249, 257, 260

T

Terminology-oriented Database, 11

Tree Structures, 144, 181

U

Unified Modeling Language, 12

Universal Data Model, 179

V

Virtual Machine Image, 21, 56

www.ingramcontent.com/pod-product-compliance
Lightning Source LLC
Jackson TN
JSHW052206130125
77033JS00004B/215